EXTREME
KILLERS

Other Books in the Profiles in Crime Series

PROFILES IN CRIME

EXTREME KILLERS

TALES OF THE WORLD'S
MOST PROLIFIC SERIAL KILLERS

MICHAEL NEWTON

STERLING
New York

STERLING
New York

An Imprint of Sterling Publishing Co., Inc.
122 Fifth Avenue
New York, NY 10011

STERLING and the distinctive Sterling logo are registered trademarks of Sterling Publishing Co., Inc.

ISBN 978-1-4549-3940-5
ISBN 978-1-4549-3944-3 (e-book)

Distributed in Canada by Sterling Publishing Co., Inc.
c/o Canadian Manda Group, 664 Annette Street
Toronto, Ontario M6S 2C8, Canada
Distributed in the United Kingdom by GMC Distribution Services
Castle Place, 166 High Street, Lewes, East Sussex BN7 1XU, England
Distributed in Australia by NewSouth Books
University of New South Wales, Sydney, NSW 2052, Australia

The text in this book contains graphic and disturbing depictions of murder.

For information about custom editions, special sales, and premium and corporate purchases,
please contact Sterling Special Sales at 800-805-5489 or specialsales@sterlingpublishing.com.

Manufactured in the United States

2 4 6 8 10 9 7 5 3 1

sterlingpublishing.com

Cover design by David Ter-Avanesyan
Interior design by Gavin C. Motnyk

For Dr. Katherine Ramsland

CONTENTS

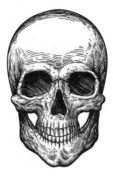

INTRODUCTION:
HUNTING HUMANS

The term "serial murderer" is relatively new, first used in print by German critic Siegfried Kracauer in 1961—and not, as is sometimes assumed, by FBI profiler Robert Ressler in the 1970s. Four years prior to Kracauer's serendipitous turn of phrase, American criminologist James Reinhardt wrote of "chain killers" who murder repeatedly and compulsively, comparing their victims to links in a chain of madness. Before that, murderers who killed in series, such as London's still unidentified "Jack the Ripper," were simply branded "mass murderers" or "homicidal maniacs."

Regardless of who takes credit for coining the term, serial killing is an act and fact as old as human history itself. In China, during the second century BCE, Prince Liu Pengli, sometimes named by scholars as history's first documented serial slayer, replaced wild game with peasants in hunts staged for recreation. His body count exceeded 100 but Liu suffered no consequences: he died peacefully from natural causes in 144 BCE, leaving his five sons an estate including 532,000 pounds of gold ($13.1 billion today) and land of equal value.

Writing in middle age, Roman historian Titus Livius (64 BCE to 12 CE) described a group of matrons who murdered ninety-odd men with poisons procured from two patrician women who described their potions as "medicinal." When forced to take their own medicine, both died, leaving 170 clients to face trial for murder, but all were apparently excused. Livius explained that "their act was regarded as a prodigy, and suggested madness rather than felonious intent."

A spiritual heiress to those early killers, Locusta of Gaul, personal poison consultant to Empress Agrippina the Younger and a favorite of Agrippina's son Nero, trained other silent killers and participated in the assassinations of Claudius (54 CE) and Britannicus (55 CE) before going rogue with personal projects. Galba, Nero's successor, had Locusta executed in 69 CE, allegedly (perhaps apocryphally) in the Colosseum; she was first raped by a specially trained giraffe, then torn apart by wild beasts.

In fifth-century Yemen, wealthy pederast Zu Shenatir lured boys to his home in Aden with promises of food and money, then stripped and sodomized an estimated 100 victims, afterward tossing them to their deaths from an upstairs window of his opulent home. His reign of terror ended when the final victim, named Zerash in one account, stabbed his attacker in the rectum with fatal results.

According to *The Newgate Calendar*, Alexander "Sawney" Bean was born in sixteenth-century East Lothian, Scotland. A laborer's son,

LOCUSTA OF GAUL (RIGHT), A POISON CONSULTANT TO EMPRESS AGRIPPINA THE YOUNGER AND A FAVORITE OF NERO (LEFT), TRAINED OTHER SILENT KILLERS AND MAY HAVE BEEN AMONG THE FIRST RECORDED EXTREME KILLERS.

ALEXANDER "SAWNEY" BEAN WAS A 16TH-CENTURY SCOTTISH LABORER. HE AND HIS FAMILY WERE REPUTED TO HAVE KILLED AND EATEN MORE THAN ONE THOUSAND PEOPLE WHO WERE TRAVELING THROUGH SCOTLAND.

Sawney soon tired of honest work and fled to a seaside cave between Girvan and Ballantrae with "Black" Agnes Duncan, a reputed harlot and self-styled witch. Living in isolation for a quarter century, the couple produced an inbred clan of forty-five children and grandchildren who fed on the flesh of more than 1,000 hapless nighttime wayfarers. Their guerrilla tactics misfired when they preyed on a newlywed couple who were traveling armed. They killed the bride but could not overtake her groom, an armed veteran soldier who returned with searchers and discovered the cannibals' lair. In custody, the tribe faced execution without formal trial: the males were emasculated, drawn, and quartered, while the women and girls were burned at the stake. Some modern scholars claim the clan was mythical, citing a dearth of formal documentation for their mass execution, but others disagree. In either case, the story survives, and inspired American film director Wes Craven's franchise of *The Hills Have Eyes* films, together with author Jack Ketchum's

"Dead River" series of novels, set in modern New England (*Off Season, Offspring,* and *The Woman*).

Another frequently forgotten monster from times past was Crown Prince Jangheon of Joeson, Korea's last and longest-ruling Confucian dynasty (1392–1897 CE). Born in 1735, Jangheon was heir apparent to his father, King Yeongjo, but suffered a mental breakdown after losing his mother and wife one month apart in 1757. Apparently deranged, he began beating palace eunuchs, decapitating one and displaying the severed head to others. He then embarked on a series of rapes and murders, exacerbated by an overwhelming phobia to wearing clothes, that decimated the royal household staff. In 1760–61, Jangheon crossed the final line of impropriety by publicly insulting his father, murdering his latest consort (one Pingae), and then attempting to kill him and his royal nephews. Finally, King Yeongjo ordered Jangheon's execution in July 1762, locking him inside a chest of rice where he died eight days later. King Yeongjo posthumously changed his late son's name to Sado, translated as "thinking of with great sadness."

Modern crime writers disagree on the identity of America's first serial killer. Candidates include racist gunman William "Wild Bill" Longley, slayer of thirty-two persons—mostly unarmed blacks and Mexicans—between 1869 and 1878, who was hanged for murdering a childhood friend; "Nebraska Fiend" Stephen Richards, slayer of at least six persons during 1878, hanged the following year; and swindler turned homicidal sadist Herman Mudgett, alias "Dr. H. H. Holmes." Credited vaguely with "hundreds" of murders, Mudgett confessed to twenty-seven before his execution in May 1896.

In fact, none of those predators was the New World's first serial killer. That dubious "honor" likely belongs to some unknown Native American or Viking explorer, but the apparent first on record was highwayman and river pirate Samuel Mason, slayer of at least twenty victims in the new United States and Spanish Louisiana between 1797 and 1803. Two of his protégés, also prolific killers, were Micajah and Wiley Harpe (née Harper), either brothers or cousins (reports differ). They impartially murdered strangers, their own common-law wives, and infant offspring (for the offense of crying), weighting their disemboweled corpses with stones for concealment in lakes and rivers.

The Harpes doubled Samuel Mason's body count along the Natchez Trace before meeting their separate fates. Vigilantes captured Micajah ("Big Harpe") in July 1799 and decapitated him along a Kentucky byway still known as Harpe's Head Road. Wiley ("Little Harpe") outran that posse but ironically ran afoul of justice in 1803, when he killed mentor Mason, presenting Mason's head to a Kentucky court and trying to collect an outstanding bounty. Locals saw through Wiley's alias of "John Sutton" and convicted him and an accomplice for murder. They hanged both in January 1804 and mounted their heads beside the Natchez Trace as a warning to future bandits.

Extreme Killers presents fifteen cases of serial murder wherein offenders were accused of and/or confessed to killing scores of victims. In all but two cases the estimated final body counts exceed 100. Of the two relative "slackers," each was convicted of 49 slayings: one has confessed to claiming seventy-one victims, while the other—Canada's most prolific serial killer to date—operated for nineteen years in rural conditions that defy a precise victim census, feeding human remains to hogs (and perhaps to neighbors).

The cases chosen were selected from a master list of fifty-two murderers who stretched the psychic envelope of recreational murder, each unique in certain ways, but hauntingly familiar when compared to one another. Time after time, authorities overlooked or turned a blind eye to clues that might have saved dozens of lives. No effort has been made to dramatize the selected accounts; no dialogue has been invented by "poetic license."

The facts are grim enough.

And by this time next year, if not before, the list will certainly be longer.

1.
"BLUEBEARD": GILLES DE RAIS

Millions worldwide know the tale of Bluebeard, penned by French author Charles Perrault in 1697. Many more have read its numerous literary imitators and seen the eight film versions released between 1923 and 2009. The story's villain, known only by his nickname, kills successive wives until his last bride bares his secret and her siblings intervene. So well-known is the story that "Bluebeard" has long served as a tag for male serial slayers of wives and lovers.

Fewer persons realize that the story's model—the first historical "Bluebeard"—was a real-life murderer whose crimes surpassed his namesake's fictional murders, or that his scores of victims were boys.

*   *   *   *   *

Gilles de Montmorency-Laval, the Baron Gilles de Rais, was born on September 10, 1404, at one of his family's several castles, the Black Tower at Champtocé-sur-Loire in western France. Maternal grandfather Jean de Craon arranged a political marriage between Guy II de Montmorency-Laval and Marie de Craon to increase his own fortune and prevent impending war between two rival clans. Gilles arrived nine months after that loveless union, followed two years later by his brother René de La Suze.

The boys lost their mother Marie to illness in January 1415. Eight months later, a wild boar fatally gored their father. Guy's will barred father-in-law Jean de Craon from raising the brothers, but Jean fought that provision in court and won in 1416, proceeding to instruct his grandsons in the duties of French noblemen pursuing fame, power, and wealthy brides.

Gilles was barely twelve when Jean arranged his marriage to four-year-old Jeanne Paynel, orphaned heiress of Lord de Hambye of Normandy, but Parliament feared that family merger and blocked the wedding until Gilles attained legal majority. Ten months later, Jean betrothed Gilles to Beatrice de Rohan, niece of the Duke of Burgundy, but that engagement failed for reasons lost to history.

In 1420, Gilles pursued another bride, Catherine de Thouars of Brittany, heiress of La Vendée and Poitou, but she rejected him. He led a raiding party to abduct her, locking her up at Champtocé, where three would-be rescuers wound up in the castle's dungeon. One died from fever, the others emerged in broken health. Catherine bowed to the inevitable and married Gilles on November 30, 1420.

Already famous at sixteen, Gilles joined the House of Montfort to liberate Brittany's Duke John VI—who had been kidnapped by Olivier de Blois, Count of Penthièvre—and received generous land grants in return, which he quickly converted to cash.

Gilles de Rais was introduced at court in 1425, welcomed as a young, courageous soldier on the rise, and elevated to command of the royal army two years later. Meanwhile, France was engulfed in a civil war that threatened the power of all native nobles.

On May 21, 1420, King Charles VI signed the Treaty of Troyes, disinheriting his son, the Dauphin Charles VII, and naming England's Henry V as legitimate successor to the French throne. That plan collapsed with Henry's death on August 31, 1422, followed closely by Charles's suicide on October 22. Charles VII claimed the throne, inheriting a kingdom riven by conflict, with much of France still occupied by English troops.

In 1427, Gilles besieged the Château of Lude on the banks of the Loir, personally slaying the English garrison's commander. In March 1429, Gilles was with Charles VII at Chinon when teenage religious zealot Joan of Arc predicted a French victory at Orléans, besieged by English forces five months earlier. Joan persuaded Charles to give her an army of 10,000 men, with Gilles appointed as her general and primary advisor. They reached Orléans on April 28 and broke the siege nine days later. By that time, Gilles had grown a beard so black that it had a blue sheen in sunlight, prompting his famous nickname *Barbe bleue*—"Bluebeard."

Charles VII's coronation was delayed until July 1429, and even then he still faced opposition from a host of rivals. The war continued, but England was reeling and forced to concede in summer 1429. Charles followed his army to Reims, where Joan stood beside him at his coronation on July 17. Charles promoted Gilles to serve as Marshal of France, a seven-star general honored with permission to add a border of the royal arms, the fleur-de-lis on an azure ground, to his family crest. Gilles was now the highest-ranking general in France—and, some say, the country's richest lord. A new father, with the birth of his daughter Maire that year, he was also one of four lords honored with assignment to convey the Holy Ampulla—a glass vial used to anoint French kings with sacred oil since 1131—from the Abbey of Saint-Remy to Notre-Dame de Reims.

Joan of Arc did not fare so well as the war with England dragged on. Georges de la Trémoille, Grand Chamberlain of France, feared that her influence over Charles might undercut his own. On May 30, 1430, Joan was captured at Compiègne, while battling Burgundian allies of England. La Trémoille saw his chance to be rid of her for good, and persuaded Pierre Cauchon, the pro-English Bishop of Beauvais, to indict her for heresy. Because that religious infraction was only punishable by death upon a repeat offense, Cauchon added a second charge of "cross-dressing" in men's armor for battle. Despite protests from Pope Martin V, Joan was condemned and burned alive at the Vieux-Marché in Rouen, on May 30, 1431.

The Hundred Years' War continued for another twenty-two years, but Gilles had no part in it. He retired to his various estates and devoted himself to a hedonistic life of debauchery and reckless spending that appalled his grandfather. At his death, on November 15, 1432, Jean showed his displeasure with Gilles by leaving his sword and breastplate to younger brother René. Finally freed from his domineering grandfather's influence, Gilles was content to seek excitement on his own, without serving the state.

Somewhere along that road, he turned to murder.

After years of battling warriors, Gilles showed a predilection for young victims who he sexually violated, both before and after death. Some sources date his first murders to 1426, but Gilles, in his later confessions, said the crimes began at Champtocé-sur-Loire in the spring of 1432. Surviving transcripts state that "at Champtocé he killed children and had them killed in large numbers, how many he is uncertain. And he committed with them the sodomitic and unnatural sin."

Later, Gilles moved his entourage to Machecoul, where the slaughter escalated.

Throughout his rampage, Gilles struggled to keep up appearances, leading a lavish lifestyle he could not afford. At Machecoul, he built a Chapel of the Holy Innocents where he presided over worship services in robes of his own personal design. He also wrote an epic play, "Le Mistère du Siège d'Orléans," with 140 speaking parts and over twenty thousand lines of dialogue, plus some five hundred extras. Players wore six hundred costumes, then discarded them after each performance, while tailors labored to recreate them for the next. Spectators enjoyed unlimited food and drink, at Gilles's expense.

Production of that spectacle proved so expensive that Gilles sold all his estates in the province of Maine, and all but his wife's property in Poitou, to fund the extravaganza's premiere in Orléans on May 8, 1435. Finally, it was too much for Gilles's family. In June 1435, relatives petitioned Pope Eugene IV to disavow the Chapel of the Holy Innocents. His refusal sent them off to King Charles, with a plea to save their family's dwindling fortune. On July 2, a royal edict branded Gilles a spendthrift and forbade sale of any further property. French subjects were banned from signing contracts with Gilles, and purchasers of the estates already sold were barred from reselling them.

Still bent on living the high life, Gilles borrowed money, using his books and manuscripts, clothing, and *objets d'art* as collateral. In August 1435 Gilles left Orléans littered with treasures used to secure loans, bound for Machecoul in Brittany. Duke Jean VI, still grateful for his rescue fifteen years earlier, rejected pleas from Gilles's family to curtail his spending. With the Duke on his side, Gilles felt secure in continuing his pedophilic rape-and-murder spree.

The first child abduction linked to Gilles de Rais was carried out by his cousin, Gilles de Sillé, in 1432. Their victim was the twelve-year-old son of Jean Jeudon, kidnapped from Machecoul. In his biography of Gilles de Rais, author Jean Benedetti describes the boy's fate.

> He was pampered and dressed in better clothes than he
> had ever known. The evening began with a large meal and

heavy drinking, particularly hippocras [wine flavored with spices], which acted as a stimulant. The boy was taken to an upper room to which only Gilles and his immediate circle was [*sic*] admitted. He was then confronted with the true nature of his situation. The shock thus produced on the boy was probably an initial source of pleasure for Gilles.

At trial, accomplice Etienne Corrillaut—commonly called "Poitou"—testified that Gilles raped the boy as he hung by his neck from a hook, then cut the child down and "comforted" him before sodomizing him again. Poitou could not recall if Gilles murdered the boy himself or had one of his servants do it. By the time he testified, there had been so many victims that he had trouble telling them apart.

Under oath, Poitou described methods of murder including slashed throats and decapitation, broken necks, and live dismemberment. Often, Poitou testified, victims were stabbed before Gilles sodomized them, taking double pleasure if they died during the rape. A necrophiliac, Gilles also enjoyed violating the small, still-warm corpses.

Gilles's own confession was even more graphic. With especially handsome boys, Gilles testified, he kissed their dead faces and "admired" their flaccid limbs. He had some victims

A DEPICTION OF GILLES DE RAIS AND SOME OF THE CHILDREN HE MURDERED.

disemboweled and "took delight" at the sight of their spilling entrails. A special pleasure for Gilles was sitting on the torsos of those gutted children, masturbating as they died beneath him.

Few victims lasted more than one night with Gilles. Once killed, accomplice Henriet Griart testified, most were cremated slowly to minimize the stench of burning flesh arising from the castles where they died. When flesh and bone had been consumed by fire, the ashes were dumped into cesspools or the castle's stagnant moat.

The slaughter of innocents under Gilles de Rais was both a family affair and a group enterprise. Cousin Gilles de Sillé delivered the first two known victims, later joined as a procurer by another cousin, Roger de Briqueville. Over time, various other men and women joined the murder crew, some providing Gilles with fresh prey, others actively participating in the torture, defilement, and murder of victims. Some of those slain were only eight or nine years old.

Orgies of pain and death provided Gilles de Rais with some relief from his sadistic psychosis, but he still had pressing monetary problems. Barred from selling off more of his land, unwilling to part with the castles where his gruesome rituals would soon become routine, he cast about for other sources of income and was struck by sudden inspiration.

Why not turn to alchemy?

Alchemy aims to mingle chemistry with magic. From antiquity, alchemists have pursued two primary goals: creating the "philosopher's stone," a legendary substance capable of turning base metals into gold or silver; and producing an "elixir of life" that confers eternal youth.

Both prospects appealed to the cash-strapped Gilles de Rais, but money was his main concern.

Outwardly, Gilles remained a pious Catholic until the moment of his death. He knew that magic of all kinds was banned by church and state alike, but that did not divert him from his quest for gold through any means available. By 1438, he was employing alchemists who promised grand results, but most were charlatans and showmen who accepted payment for their services, then delivered only simple parlor tricks.

After several false starts, Gilles welcomed a renegade priest—Father Eustache Blanchet—to his castle at Tiffauges. Blanchet supplied Gilles with books on magic rituals and demonology—peculiar reading for a Catholic priest during the age of European witch trials—and traveled the countryside in search of sorcerers who claimed extraordinary powers.

Their early attempts were ludicrous. First, Blanchet introduced Gilles to a metallurgist who claimed he could transform silver into gold. Gilles met the practitioner at a local tavern, handing him a silver florin, and left him alone to perform his ritual. Returning later, Gilles found the hoaxer dead drunk. His only skill, apparently, was turning silver into wine.

The second try was more elaborate and more expensive. Blanchet hired Jean de la Riviere, a black-magic devotee who claimed he could summon Satan. Clad in white armor and armed with a sword, Riviere led Gilles and Blanchet into the woods, leaving them in a clearing while he went off to raise the Devil in private. Soon, clanging sounds echoed through the night, as if Riviere were striking his armor with his sword. After a time, Riviere returned, claiming he had conjured Satan in a leopard's form. Delighted, Gilles and company repaired to the village of Pouzauges for a night of alcoholic revelry.

When they sobered up the next morning, Riviere announced his master plan. To raise Satan again and bind him to the will of Gilles de Rais, certain supplies would be required. The going price: twenty gold *écus à la couronne*. Gilles paid up, and Riviere promptly vanished with his loot for parts unknown.

Enraged, Gilles gave Blanchet one last chance to find a worthy sorcerer. In Italy, Blanchet met François Prelati, a twenty-two-year-old French expatriate, and persuaded him to try his luck with Gilles de Rais. The pair reached Tiffauges in May 1439, intent on raising a demon called Barron, but Prelati postponed the attempt until Midsummer's Eve—June 23—when supernatural forces are said to be most active.

Near midnight on the appointed evening, Gilles gathered his crew—Prelati, Blanchet, Poitou, Henriet Griart, and Gilles de Sillé—in the lower hall at Tiffauges. Prelati drew a large circle on the floor, filling it with cryptic signs and symbols, surrounded by guttering candles. Once the stage was set, Gilles de Rais ordered his cronies to wait in his upstairs bedroom while he and Prelati summoned Barron. Gilles clutched a note to Barron, penned by Prelati for hand delivery when the demon appeared, but two hours of chanting produced no demon.

A second attempt allegedly succeeded. Working alone in the ritual chamber, Prelati claimed to have conjured a giant serpent, retreating in fear to warn Gilles de Rais. Gilles rushed in, armed with a crucifix said to contain a splinter from the True Cross, but by the time he arrived, the snake had vanished, presumably gone back to Hell.

A third attempt reportedly raised Barron, but once again Prelati acted on his own, behind a locked door. Gilles and company, huddled in the outer hallway, heard the demon beating Prelati, leaving him battered, winded—and alone—when he finally opened the door. Blanchet, increasingly skeptical, later testified that the beating sounded like someone punching a feather bed.

Though disappointed, Gilles still trusted Prelati. When the magician suggested that success might require a human sacrifice—specifically a child's heart, eyes, and genitals—Gilles readily agreed. Since he was already raping and murdering children, why not mix business with pleasure?

Prelati's recipe was neither unique nor original. Alchemy and magic generally—sometimes spelled as "magick," to distinguish serious rituals from mere sleight of hand—often involve release of vital energy through sacrifice. Some practitioners believe orgasm is sufficient, either self-induced or through an act of copulation. Others call for blood, most commonly an animal's, as in the rites of Voodoo and Santería. Darker variations on that theme, from Stone Age Europe to the Aztecs and Incas, prefer human subjects. In the African cult of Palo Mayombe, slow and agonizing deaths allegedly release more energy, increasing a sorcerer's power over demons from the Other Side.

Why did Gilles persist in human sacrifice, when he was never privileged to meet Barron or Satan in the flesh and the wealth Prelati promised him never appeared? Some authors have suggested that he was infatuated with Prelati, an attractive man eleven years his junior, fluent in French, Italian, and Latin, charming and humorous when not engaged in bloody murder. Today, no one knows whether Prelati ever warmed Gilles's bed. He may have been too old to satisfy his benefactor sexually, but in any case, Gilles never seemed to realize that the self-styled sorcerer was cheating him.

Prelati, for his part, was no more prescient. He did not realize they were all running out of time.

The disappearance of children spread fear through Machecoul, soon giving the town a dark reputation. Andre Barbe, one of the grieving parents who later testified against the murderers, recalled meeting a stranger from Saint-Jean-d'Angély at the height of the killing spree. Upon hearing that Barbe came from Machecoul, the other man recoiled, saying the town was filled with cannibals who fed on children.

By then, Gilles had an efficient death machine in operation. Aside from his cousins, Poitou, Henriet, Blanchet, and Prelati, he had acquired a female procurer, Perrine Martin, also known as *La Meffraye* ("The Terror"). Cloaked in black, she prowled outlying villages, offering apprenticeships with "a good master" to any amenable boys.

As the toll of vanishings mounted, agitation simmered in the streets of Machecoul. On one occasion, angry parents confronted Gilles de Sillé, demanding answers. Cornered, he admitted that some of the missing boys had been kidnapped, but he blamed King Charles VI, fabricating a royal scheme to furnish England with youngsters for training as servants. It was a transparent lie, but it saved de Sillé from a lynching.

What did Gilles de Rais's family know of his ongoing crimes? Some modern historians speculate that René de La Suze had an inkling of his brother's savagery. René had supported the earlier royal edict of 1435, preventing Gilles from selling off more lands and castles. Now, late in 1439, René announced his intent to occupy and secure Castle Champtocé. Gilles rightly feared that Castle Machecoul might be next in line.

Near panic, Gilles sent Poitou and Henriet from Château de Tiffauges to Machecoul, with orders to incinerate forty-odd corpses stashed in a tower there. Whoever did the grisly job, they missed at least two skeletons, discovered by members of René's household three weeks later, when he and cousin Andre de Laval-Loheac occupied the castle.

But René did nothing.

Whether he feared scandal for his family or simply did not care about the fate of peasant children, René went through the motions of questioning Poitou and Henriet, accepting their false pleas of ignorance at face value. Thereafter, as Jean Benedetti observes, "A wall of silence was erected round the family." It would not hold indefinitely, but for the time being Gilles was safe.

Until he crossed the Church of Rome.

Gilles de Rais was desperate by spring of 1440. On May 15, he stormed a church in Saint-Étienne-de-Mer-Morte and kidnapped Father Jean le Ferron, brother of Brittany's treasurer, who had collaborated in the recent occupation of Gilles's castles by brother René. He soon released the priest, but Bishop of Nantes Jean de Malestroit took the raid as a personal insult against God and himself, launching an investigation that exposed Gilles's reign of terror.

The bishop aired his findings on July 29, citing affidavits from seven witnesses to prove that "Milord Gilles de Rais, knight, lord, and baron, our subject and under our jurisdiction, with certain accomplices, did cut the throats of, kill, and heinously massacre many young and innocent boys, that he did practice with these children unnatural lust and the vice of sodomy, often calls up or causes others to practice the dreadful invocation of demons, did sacrifice to and make pacts with the latter, and did perpetrate other enormous crimes within the limits of our jurisdiction."

Gilles de Rais initially ignored the charges, confident that his authority and noble standing placed him above the law. Cousins Gilles de Sillé and Roger de Briqueville lacked his courage and fled from Tiffauges with funds they had saved for such a contingency, both vanishing forever from the public record. Accomplices Blanchet, Henriet, Poitou, Prelati, and Perrine Martin remained at Machecoul, trusting their lord to keep them safe—though Henriet would later say that he considered suicide.

In August 1440, Arthur de Richemont, Constable of France and brother of the Duke of Brittany, seized Tiffauges while awaiting warrants to arrest Gilles de Rais and his cohorts. That order came from Bishop Malestroit on September 14, and Richemont marched on Machecoul the next day, seizing the suspects and transporting them to Nantes. There, while his accomplices languished in dungeon cells, Gilles had more comfortable private lodgings.

Pierre de l'Hôpital, chief judge of Brittany, began interrogating witnesses from Machecoul on September 18. By October 8, the tribunal—including l'Hôpital's prosecutor, friar Jean de Touscheronde, and Jean Blouyn, Vicar of the Inquisitor—had recorded testimony from seventy-five persons. One mother sketched a scene in which Poitou coerced her into giving up her ten-year-old son to serve under Gilles as a page. Poitou promised the boy an education and a comfortable life, but his mother had second thoughts the next morning, begging Gilles to relinquish the child. Bluebeard had treated her as if she were invisible, departing with the boy, who was never seen again.

On October 13, the court formally indicted Gilles on thirty-four charges of murder, sodomy, heresy, and violating the immunity of the church (for the May 15 raid). The indictment referred to 140 victims slain over fourteen years, including a son of Éonnet and Macée de Villeblanche, procured by Poitou as a page and slaughtered in August 1440. The charges also claimed that Gilles had several times expressed remorse for his crimes, once vowing to visit Jerusalem in search of absolution, but had never followed through.

When called before the court, Gilles refused to answer any of the charges lodged against him, declaring that he would rather be hanged on the spot than face interrogation by corrupt priests. On his fourth refusal, the Bishop of Nantes excommunicated Gilles and the hearing adjourned.

The shock of being exiled from his church gnawed at Gilles over the next two days. Denied communion and confession, he apparently believed that he was bound for Hell. At his next court appearance, tearful and repentant, Gilles apologized for his earlier outbursts, whereupon Jean Blouyn and the bishop absolved him, nullifying his excommunication.

Visibly relieved, Gilles confessed to murder and sodomy, but flatly denied invoking demons. He swore innocence of that charge on a Bible and volunteered for trial by fire to prove his innocence. Jean de Touscheronde was adamant, producing Henriet, Prelati, and Poitou to describe the various dark rites performed on Gilles's behalf. After hearing their testimony, Gilles told the court he had nothing to add, but urged publication of the transcript "as a warning to heretics."

Still unsatisfied, Touscheronde asked the court for permission to torture Gilles. Pierre de l'Hôpital compromised, agreeing that Gilles should be taken to the dungeon at La Tour Neuves prison for a close-up view of the Inquisition's instruments. No stranger to torture himself, Gilles amended his confession on October 21, admitting attempts to summon

Barron and Satan. Details of his confession, followed by further admissions from Poitou and Henriet on October 23, were so graphic that Pierre de l'Hôpital ordered some bits stricken from the record.

Verdicts in the case were mixed. Poitou and Henriet were condemned on October 23, followed by Gilles on the 25th. Perrine Martin and François Prelati were spared execution but sentenced to prison for life. In parting, Gilles told Prelati "Goodbye, François, my friend. Never again shall we see each other in this world. I pray that God gives you plenty of patience and understanding, and to be sure, provided you have plenty of patience and trust in God, we shall meet again in the Great Joy of Paradise."

The court's death sentence for Gilles, Henriet, and Poitou specified hanging, followed by cremation. Gilles asked to die first, setting an example for his cronies, and the court agreed. Pierre de l'Hôpital also granted Gilles's plea for a final confession and interment at the monastery of Notre-Dame des Carmes in Nantes. The ashes of his cohorts would be scattered to the winds.

At 9:00 a.m. on October 26, guards led Gilles, Henriet, and Poitou to their execution site on the Île de Nantes, at the city's center between two branches of the Loire River. Before meeting his fate, Gilles delivered a sermon to the spectators, lecturing them on "the evils of uncontrolled youth," exhorting them to raise their children in strict adherence to Catholicism. At 11 o'clock, an executioner lit Gilles's pyre and hanged him, then removed his corpse before it was seared, delivering it to "four ladies of high rank" for burial. Henriet and Poitou followed their master to the gallows and the flames.

Perrine Martin served her sentence and died in prison at Nantes, after confessing her sins to a priest. François Prelati, slippery as ever, escaped from custody, then foolishly returned to the life of an itinerant necromancer. Arrested and convicted of heresy a second time, he was hanged.

Following Gilles's execution, his widow married wealthy Jean de Vendome, an ally of the Duke of Brittany. Her daughter with Gilles,

Marie, married a French admiral but died childless in 1457. René de La Suze occupied Château de Champtocé until his death on October 30, 1473, leaving one child, a daughter, who also died childless.

Today, some historians regard Gilles de Rais's conviction and execution as a political frame-up. Advocates of his innocence note that the Duke of Brittany coveted Gilles's property, receiving title to most of it after the trial and dividing the spoils among friendly nobles. Anthropologist Margaret Murray, in her book *The Witch-Cult in Western Europe*, speculated that Gilles was not a Satanist, but rather a witch and devotee of a fertility cult revering Diana, pagan goddess of the hunt, the moon, and birthing, now the feminist deity of Dianic Wicca.

In 1992, Freemason Jean-Yves Goëau-Brissonnière, Grand Master of the Grand Lodge of France, convened a "court" comprised of former French ministers, members of Parliament, and United Nations officials to review surviving transcripts and evidence from Gilles de Rais's trial. Judge Henri Juramy, presiding, declared "The case for Gilles de Rais's innocence is very strong. No child's corpse was ever found at his castle at Tiffauges, and he appears to have confessed to escape excommunication. The accusations appear to be false charges made up by powerful rival lords to benefit from the confiscation of his lands."

That verdict had no legal effect, and Gilles's biographers generally agree that he was guilty as charged, some speculating that his final death toll may have exceeded the number cited in his indictment, perhaps rivaling the body count attributed to Hungary's Countess Erzsébet Báthory in 1610 (see Chapter 2). Defenders of the original verdict note remains found at Machecoul and stress that peasant witnesses who testified against Gilles had nothing to gain—and much to lose—by lodging false charges against the powerful Marshal of France.

2.
"THE BLOOD COUNTESS": ERZSÉBET BÁTHORY

Our next extreme killer, another European noble, is best known in modern times from four gruesome films released since 1971 and as the namesake of a Swedish "black metal" band active from 1983 to its founder's death in 2004. Unlike Gilles de Rais, this slayer was female and allegedly eclipsed Gilles's body count.

Erzsébet (Elizabeth) Báthory was born on August 7, 1560, at her family's estate at Nyírbátor, in eastern Hungary. Her parents, Baron George and Baroness Anna Báthory, ranked among the country's richest Protestants, related by blood before their marriage born of political strife. George Báthory was descended from the Ecsed branch of the clan, which had supported Archduke—later Holy Roman Emperor—Ferdinand I in his claim to the Hungarian throne, while Anna's side—the Somlyòis—had backed John Zápolya, *voivode* (military commander) of Transylvania.

Those rival kinsmen clashed at the Battle of Mohács in August 1526, resulting in division of the kingdom. Ferdinand was then recognized as king in the north and west of Hungary, while Zápolya ruled central Hungary and Transylvania until his death in July 1540. Transylvania became a semi-independent principality in 1570, but tension remained between sundered branches of the rising Báthory family, resolved—at least in theory—by the marriage of George and Anna.

Erzsébet was thus related to some of Hungary's and Eastern Europe's most prestigious figures. Her relatives included Sigismund Báthory, Prince of Transylvania; Stephen VII Báthory, Palatine (imperial court officer) of Hungary; Stephen Báthory, King of Poland; and Andrew Báthory, whose offices included those of Roman Catholic cardinal, Prince-Bishop of Warmia, and Grand Master of the Order of the Dragon, created to defend Hungarian Christianity against the Ottoman Turks. On the darker side, Erzsébet's closest kin also included brother Stephen, an alcoholic lecher; Uncle Gábor, a reputed Satan-worshipper; and Aunt Klara, a sadistic lesbian and practicing witch who introduced young Erzsébet to the pleasures of inflicting pain.

We cannot weigh the full extent of Erzsébet's childhood corruption, shrouded as her story has become in legend. Various tales suggest an early fondness for boy's clothing and sexual experimentation with serfs, allegedly resulting in Erzsébet's pregnancy at age thirteen or fourteen and the birth of a daughter, who was farmed out to peasant parents and forgotten. Perhaps significantly, that story did not surface until 1894, with publication of German author R. von Elsberg's *Die Blutgräfin* (*The Blood Countess*). Other tales, published long after the fact, claim that Erzsébet witnessed the execution of a Gypsy, bound and sewn inside a rotting horse's carcass on a charge of selling children to the Turks. In 1995, in his novel *The Blood Countess*, Alexandrei Codrescu altered that scene to depict the murder of Erzsébet's two sisters by rebellious peasants.

Habitual inbreeding among European royals left many leading families prone to a wide range of mental and physical defects, aggravated by their sense of divine entitlement and virtual immunity from prosecution in their dealings with commoners. Stories persist that Erzsébet was deranged from childhood, as evidenced by periodic "fits" and rages, diagnosed by some modern biographers as evidence of epilepsy. Contrasted with those tales are reports of her advanced education. In an age when many royals—and nearly all serfs—were illiterate, Erzsébet was fluent in Hungarian, German, Greek, and Latin. Her letters, written in adulthood and preserved in state archives, reveal a polished elegance but give no hint of any brooding madness.

What historians *can* say about Erzsébet is that in 1571—at age eleven, three years before her supposed first pregnancy—she was engaged to marry sixteen-year-old Count Ferencz Nádasdy, in a union arranged by Nádasdy's mother, Baroness Ursula Kanizsay de Kanizsa. Barely literate in Hungarian, Nádasdy spoke German and Latin well enough to negotiate battlefield treaties, but otherwise, in his own mother's estimation, he was "no scholar."

Some modern accounts say that Nádasdy learned of his fiancée's pregnancy and punished the infant's father—named as László Bende, a servant at the Báthory family's Castle Sárvár—by having him castrated and fed alive to a pack of dogs. If true, that act would not have been an aberration for Nádasdy, who was recognized in later years as a ruthless and sadistic warlord in the style of Wallachian predecessor Vlad the Impaler. By most accounts, Nádasdy's union with Erzsébet proved to be a match made in Hell.

Erzsébet and Ferencz were married on May 8, 1575, at Sárvár ("mud castle"), the Nádasdy family's seat in the western Hungarian county of Vas. Erzsébet quickly settled in as mistress of the estate, also residing at various times in other castles and villas maintained by her family and in-laws at Beckov, Bratislava, and Čachtice (all now in Slovakia), and in Vienna, Austria. Ferencz, meanwhile, immersed himself in a warrior's life, ranging far and wide to battle troops of the Ottoman Empire that had captured Belgrade in 1521 and occupied most of central and southern Hungary over the next two decades. In the process, Ferencz earned recognition as the "Black Knight of Hungary" and loaned large sums to Kings Rudolf II and Matthias II, to bankroll their endless wars against the Turks.

No definitive catalog of Nádasdy's military campaigns exists, but we know that he helped liberate a series of castles and cities held by Ottoman invaders. Those campaigns included the siege and capture of Esztergom and Visegrád in 1595, the conquest of Vác in 1597, the liberation of Székesfehérvár in 1598, and the brief occupation of Győr in 1601. Other forays probably included the Battle of Sisak in June 1593, aiding Michael the Brave in raids along the Lower Danube during 1594, participation in the Battle of Călugăreni (August 1595), the Battle of Keresztes (October 1596), and the Battle of Guruslău (August 1601).

Prince Sigismund Báthory of Transylvania also played key roles in planning those campaigns.

Nádasdy's frequent absences from home may help explain the fact that he and Erzsébet produced no children during their first decade of marriage. Daughter Anna arrived in 1585, followed in turn by Ursula (named for Nádasdy's mother), son Andrew, and daughter Katalin. The second and third Nádasdy children died young, but not before Erzsébet wrote to Ferencz in May 1596, saying, "I can write to your lordship of Anna and Ursula that they are in good health. But Kate is in misery with her mouth because that rot has appeared, and the rot is even in the bone of her jaw. The barber-surgeon went in with his iron up to the middle of her tooth and says that she will be fortunate if she does not lose some teeth. Of myself, I can say that I am better than formerly."

Katalin would survive the "rot," joined by brother Paul—another survivor—in 1598. Ferencz saw little of them, but Erzsébet apparently remained an attentive mother and spouse, signing most of her letters to Nádasdy "your loving wife" or "your servant." As befit her royal station, Erzsébet delegated many child-rearing duties to servants, chiefly her own childhood nurse, Helena Jo (often rendered as "Ilona Joo"). Other members of the household, later notorious, were Anna Darvulia of Sárvár (described in some accounts as Erzsébet's lesbian lover), and a dwarf named Janos Ujváry, nicknamed "Ficzko."

It was a motley crew, at best. Stories, spread after the fact, depict Helena Jo as a witch in the mold of Erzsébet's Aunt Klara, fond of sacrificing young children. Another member of Erzsébet's household, Dorothea "Dorka" Szentes, is also described as a witch possessed of unusual physical strength. Author Valentine Penrose, writing in 1962, claimed that Erzsébet carried a parchment made from the caul of a newborn infant, inscribed with a protection spell that read in part: "When I am in danger, send ninety-nine cats. I order you to do so because you are the supreme commander of cats. Order ninety-nine cats to come with speed and bite the heart of King Matthias. And keep Erzsébet safe from harm."

Nine years later, in his book *True Vampires of History*, Donald Glut quoted an alleged letter from Erzsébet to her husband, describing a newly learned black-magic ritual. According to Glut, she wrote, "Thurko has taught me a lovely new one. Catch a black hen and beat it to death with a white cane. Keep the blood and smear some on your enemy. If you get no chance to smear it on his body, obtain one of his garments and smear it." If true, this seems to be the only letter ever written by Erzsébet containing any reference to blood.

Glut also joined the chorus of modern authors relating Erzsébet's habit of entertaining both male and female lovers in Nádasdy's absence. Glut describes one such visitor as a pale, long-haired nobleman with a penchant for drinking blood, who supposedly taught the technique to his hostess. Penrose, curiously, disagreed on one point, suggesting that the still-unidentified guest was a woman dressed as a man.

Published accounts of Erzsébet's years at Sárvár disagree concerning Ferencz Nádasdy's participation in torture of household servants. No historian disputes his cruelty toward prisoners of war, including execution by impalement, but some claim that he only tolerated Erzsébet's sadism on the home front, while others cast him as her mentor in torment, schooling her in new techniques and even sending her black-magic spells from distant lands to try at home. One victim reportedly slain on Nádasdy's order was a sibling of Helena Jo. As described in sworn testimony at trial:

> His Lordship had the younger sister undressed until stark naked, while his Lordship looked on with his own eyes; the girl was then covered over with honey and made to stand throughout a day and a night, so that she, due to the great pain she was forced to endure, got the falling sickness. She fell to the ground. His Lordship taught the countess that in such a case one must place pieces of paper dipped in oil between the toes of the girl and set them on fire; even if she was already half dead, she would jump up.

The hotfoot technique was dubbed "kicking stars," from the sparks it produced, while biting insects were employed to torture girls smeared with honey. A variation on that theme, reserved for winter, was to douse a bound victim in water and watch her freeze to death. Over time, Erzsébet developed her own brutal repertoire, employing needles; heated keys; and coins, clubs, and whips with barbed lashes, among other tools.

Whatever Nádasdy's role in his wife's sadistic pursuits, Erzsébet would not hit her stride until after his death—another event shrouded in controversy. Most accounts agree that Ferencz died on or about January 4, 1604, but the cause of death is widely disputed, ranging from wounds suffered in battle to poisoning by his wife. One version claims Nádasdy "fell ill" in 1601 and was bedridden until his passing; another dates the onset of his sickness from December 1603. One attribution of his death to an infected wound blames the injury on a prostitute, who was enraged when Ferencz failed to pay for her services.

In any case, one day before his death, Nádasdy wrote to Lord Palatine György Thurzó, admonishing him to watch over Erzsébet and their children after Nádasdy was gone. The Black Knight of Hungary could scarcely have predicted where that stewardship would ultimately lead.

Erzsébet mourned her husband for all of four weeks, then shocked royal sensibilities by moving to Vienna, where she could enjoy the social whirl of high society. In years to come, she would drift back and forth between her castles at Beckov and Čachtice (also called Csejthe), where she had more privacy for pleasures of the flesh. Meanwhile, she grappled with the Herculean task of managing the Nádasdy estates and guarding them against rapacious neighbors.

One such was Count George Bánffy, a Transylvanian nobleman who had the temerity to usurp one of Erzsébet's smaller properties in January 1606. On February 3, Erzsébet penned the following letter from her late mother-in-law's castle at Kapuvár:

Magnifice Domine Nobis Observandissime

God give you all the best. I must write to you on the following matter: My servant János Csimber arrived home yesterday evening, and he reported to me that you have occupied my estate at Lindva. I do not understand, why have you done this thing? Just do not think, George Bánffy, that I am another Widow Bánffy! Believe me that I will not keep silent, I will let no one take my property. I wanted only to let you know this.

Ex arce nobis Kapu 3 Feb. 1606.

Elizabeta Comittissa de Báthor

P.S. I know, my good lord, that you have done this thing, have occupied my small estate because you are poor, but do not think that I shall leave you to enjoy it. You will find a man in me.

No record survives of this dispute's resolution, but Erzsébet's reference to the widow of another Bánffy, dispossessed of her property after husband Gáspar Bánffy's death in the 1580s, demonstrates her knowledge of contemporary scandals.

While defending her own estates, Erzsébet pursued King Rudolf II and successor Matthias II with demands for repayment of her husband's loans to the crown of 17,408 gulden ($11.5 million today), made to support their wars against the Turks. Both monarchs stalled interminably, pleading for more time, nursing their grudge against the widow who behaved so badly out of character for women of her era.

Erzsébet sought to strengthen her position by marrying off daughters Anna and Katalin to Counts Miklos Zrínyi and György Homonnay Drugeth, respectively, but the fate of her fortune rested on son Paul, who spent most of his time with tutor Imre Megyery (tellingly nicknamed "Imre the Red") at Sárvár. Uncle Gábor Báthory's elevation to Prince of Transylvania, in 1608, failed to benefit his niece. Erzsébet had already been forced to sell off her castle at Bratislava in 1607, followed by another at Beckov in 1609.

Those embarrassing losses fueled Erzsébet's rage toward hapless young women. She focused first on female servants, imposing sadistic penalties for the slightest real or imagined infraction. A maid who fell short of pressing the countess's clothes to perfection might have her face seared with the iron. Inadequate performance of some other simple task, such as sewing or binding straw, demanded repetition performed in the nude, with a jeering audience of male lackeys. Outdoor torture with honey and freezing water persisted, while other victims were beaten, or stabbed with hot needles. In one case, Erzsébet reportedly set a maid's pubic hair on fire with a candle. On other occasions, Erzsébet bit the girls in rabid fits of rage, leaving deep wounds.

The worst crime any servant could commit was trying to escape. The punishment for that offense was always death, with mode of execution suited to the time and place. During the winter of 1607, one girl fled while Erzsébet was attending the wedding of Count Thurzó's daughter at Bytča. When captured, the fugitive received an ice-water bath that left her frozen stiff. Another, twelve-year-old Pola, escaped from Čachtice castle and was likewise caught. Her fate involved a hanging spherical cage, too small to comfortably sit or stand in, its interior lined with sharp spikes. While Pola was suspended from the rafters, Ficzko swung the ropes and jostled her until she died from blood loss.

Over time, it seems that peasant girls recruited for domestic service were consigned directly to the dungeons of various Báthory castles, as objects of Erzsébet's sadistic amusement. Wherever the countess was staying, Erzsébet's accomplices—Anna Darvulia, Ficzko, Helena Jo, and Dorothea Szentes—roamed through the countryside and nearby villages, offering jobs to any available girls. Some victims were delivered by their parents, as when Mrs. György Szabo of Čachtice sent her two daughters to serve the countess. Other identified procurers included Mrs. Janoz Szabos of Sárvár, who gave up her own daughter, then recruited other girls; Mrs. Istvan Szabo of Vep, who brought in "a great many" victims; Mrs. Janos Barsony of Gyöngös, who also brought "many"; Mrs. Janos Liptay, who furnished "two or three" in full knowledge of their impending fate; Mrs. Janos Szilay of Köcs; Mrs. Miklos Kardos; and an unidentified Croatian woman from Sárvár.

Methods of torture varied according to Erzsébet's whim. She was known to stab servants with needles as they rode in her carriage, to sew their lips shut, burn and cut them, bite them in bestial rages, force them to eat strips of their own flesh, and starve them to the point of death. Savage beatings claimed the most lives, with Erzsébet demanding that her cronies join in when her arms grew tired or her clothing was blood-soaked. Some victims had their fingers cut or torn off with scissors and pincers, a game particularly favored by Dorothea Szentes. Early victims received Christian burials, until Pastor Janos Ponikenusz balked at their increasing numbers and refused to officiate at any future services. Thereafter, corpses were hidden under beds and floorboards, buried in fields and orchards, or dumped in rivers and canals. Inevitably, some were found, and while no law protected peasant girls from royal slayers, Erzsébet's reputation made it increasingly difficult to obtain willing recruits.

In 1609, a convergence of events laid the groundwork for Erzsébet's downfall. Anna Darvulia sickened and died, depriving Erzsébet of her most ardent accomplice and rumored lover. Her replacement in both roles, Erzsi Majorova, was the widow of a tenant farmer from Miava, who conveniently shared Erzsébet's sadistic inclinations. She also suggested a new means of obtaining victims, urging Erzsébet to open a "finishing school" at Čachtice for the daughters of lesser nobles, with the pretense of instructing them in the fine points of courtly etiquette. Some two dozen families lined up to take advantage of the service, little realizing that their daughters would, indeed, be "finished" by the ghoul squad at Čachtice.

During that same year, Erzsébet's cousin by marriage, György Thurzó, ascended to his post as Palatine of Hungary. He owed that promotion to the House of Habsburg, represented by King Matthias II of Hungary and his predecessor, Rudolf II, who had ceded the Hungarian throne but remained in overall command as Holy Roman Emperor, presiding over most of central Europe. The Habsburgs were staunch Roman Catholics, although Matthias tolerated wealthy Protestant families such as the Báthorys. Count Thurzó, despite his blood relationship to Erzsébet and their rumored sexual dalliance, was forced to walk the fine line of religious dissent between Matthias and Rudolf, always judging who could serve him best.

Inevitably, Erzsébet's charm-school students fell prey to her murderous rage. When her first boarder died, Erzsébet staged the death to resemble a suicide, but by then she was losing control. In Vienna, while residing at her home on Augustinian Street, Erzsébet heard neighbors praise the talents of young Ilona Harczy, star singer in the choir at the Church of Holy Mary. The countess summoned Harczy for a private performance; but on arrival, the girl developed stage fright. Furious, Erzsébet declared that if Harczy could not sing for her, she would sing for no one. The girl became another victim, slaughtered on the spot.

Other victims died in groups. During the summer of 1609, Erzsébet planned to visit Piešťany and enjoy the healing waters of its famous spa. In preparation for the journey, she demanded that the servants who would travel with her undertake an eight-day fast, bathing in cold water and standing nude in the Čachtice castle courtyard overnight to prevent them from sneaking food or drink. On the day she departed, Erzsébet found five of the six maids too frail to travel, whereupon she railed at Dorothea Szentes for "carrying things too far." Erzsébet and Szentes then beat five of the girls to death. The sixth survived to reach Piešťany, but died on the return journey, either from starvation or maltreatment suffered at the spa.

With younger noblewomen added to the list of dead and missing, time was running out for Erzsébet. Reports of her crimes reached the royal court by early 1610. Count Thurzó, though reluctant to involve himself, felt pressure from King Matthias II and naturally chose to place his family's broader interests above those of one demented cousin-in-law. The newly minted Palatine possessed more treasure and a larger army than King Matthias II himself, but his family remained vulnerable to any taint of scandal—and none was more deadly in that Early Modern era, marked by witch trials and religious warfare, than allegations of trafficking in the Black Arts, one of the charges lodged against his cousin.

Thurzó, an ardent Lutheran who had erected churches on his lands and issued a decree of *Cuius regio, eius religio* ("Whose realm, his religion," dictating the creed of his serfs), could scarcely ignore the allegations made against a member of his family—and, some said, his occasional lover. Before he took irrevocable steps, Thurzó knew he must investigate the claims, then learn if there was adequate support for an unprecedented move against a member of the royal family who was, for all intents and purposes, above the law. On March 5, he ordered an official inquiry into Erzsébet's alleged crimes, with testimony commencing on March 22. Over the next three months, thirty-four witnesses from the counties of Bratislava, Gyor, Nitra, Trencin, and Veszprem told their stories to chief notary Andrei de Keresztur. His final report, dated September 19, summarized the charges against Erzsébet by saying that "many young girls and virgins and other women were killed in various ways."

While that inquiry was in progress, on June 7, Báthory sons-in-law Miklos Zrínyi and György Homonnay Drugeth met privately with Count Thurzó, seeking some way to prevent the scandal from touching their families. Thurzó suggested snatching Erzsébet and depositing her in a convent, which pleased all concerned; but before that plan could be put into action, tutor Imre Megyery surprised the conspirators, filing a formal complaint against Erzsébet before Hungary's Parliament.

Historians explain Megyery's move in various ways. Some describe long-standing animosity between him and his employer (who, in turn, may have resented his seeming domination of son Paul Báthory). Others are more charitable, claiming that Megyery simply hoped to protect his student when the nightmare of Erzsébet's madness was finally revealed.

In any case, Megyery's end run forced Count Thurzó to take official notice of Erzsébet's alleged indiscretions. A court of inquiry was held before Judge Antonii Moysis Cziráky de Dienes-falva on October 27, 1610, with testimony implicating several of Erzsébet's retainers at Sárvár.

The ongoing investigation, while theoretically secret, did not escape Erzsébet's notice. On August 19, 1610, she traveled with a widowed noblewoman named Hernath to the court at Vasvár-Szombathel, to testify concerning the death of Madame Hernath's daughter while in Erzsébet's care. Despite allegations that the girl had been murdered, Erzsébet convinced the court that she had died from natural causes, and her case was excluded from Erzsébet's final list of charges.

It was a victory of sorts, but transitory. Some accounts claim that Erzsébet dictated her last will and testament on September 3, leaving all of her property and possessions to son Paul; but if so, that document has vanished, and was supplanted by a later will. In October, Erzsébet ordered her jewelry packed up and shipped from Sárvár to Čachtice, which would henceforth be her base of operations as she marshaled her defenses. On November 4, Erzsébet wrote to Prince Gábor Báthory, requesting legal documents detailing her possessions.

Erzsébet was not prepared to surrender. That winter, at Čachtice, she still felt confident enough to have the corpses of four recent victims pitched over the castle walls as food for prowling wolves. Local witnesses advised Count Thurzó of those murders. Erzsébet, meanwhile, prepared to slay her scheming enemies *en masse*.

The plan, as sketched in testimony at her subsequent trial, was bizarre. Although reputedly adept at mixing poisons in small doses, based on observations from accomplice Ficzko, Erzsébet turned to Erszi Majorova, widow of a tenant farmer from Myjava who had joined Erzsébet's inner circle following her husband's death. On command from her mistress, Majorova prepared a lethal potion for inclusion in a coffee cake. Prior to baking, Erzsébet reportedly bathed in the mixture, then discarded half the bath water and took another dip in the remainder. The cake was intended for King Matthias II and Count Thurzó, during a scheduled visit to Čachtice, but first, Erzsébet tested it on several servants. When all survived with nothing worse than bellyaches, she abandoned the plan.

As luck would have it, she had missed her final chance.

On December 27, 1610, Count Thurzó set out from Bratislava to Čachtice, accompanied by Erzsébet's sons-in-law, Imre Megyery, and a squad of soldiers. They reached Erzsébet's castle on the evening of December 29 and entered without difficulty, despite the melodramatic accounts set forth in various latter-day novels.

Outside the main door, they found the corpse of a servant called Doricza, beaten and stabbed to death for the crime of stealing a pear from Erzsébet's larder. Inside, the raiders found the bodies of two more young women. Subsequent tales of a midnight invasion with torture in progress, mass graves, and Count Thurzó cornering Erzsébet in a reeking dungeon are merely fiction. Author Raymond McNally notes that seventeenth-century Calvinist preacher Elias Laszlo, renowned for his detailed diaries, barely mentioned the raid in passing: "1610. 29 December. Elizabeth Bathory was put in the tower behind four walls, because in her rage she killed some of her female servants."

Erzsébet was not the only one arrested. Thurzó's party also apprehended Janos Ujváry, Ilona Jo, Dorothea Szentes, and a fourth suspected accomplice, Katarina Benecsky. Erszi Majorova slipped through the net but was traced and arrested soon afterward. When Count Thurzó and company left with their prisoners, Erzsébet alone remained in the castle, under guard.

But what was to be done with her?

On January 2, 1611, Thurzó convened the first trial of Erzsébet's accomplices at Bytča, before local officials Daniel Eördeögh, Kaspar Kardos, and Kaspar Nagy-Najaky. The proceedings were relatively brief and included testimony from defendants Benecsky, Jo, Szentes, and Ujváry, plus that of thirteen locals who had knowledge of young women killed or missing around Čachtice. The four accused confessed their roles in murders, corroborating each other's testimony with variations. No record has survived of any testimony gleaned from Erszi Majorova. Erzsébet was not present in court, and thus could not refute the charges blaming her for "an unbelievable number of murders." The panel condemned Jo, Szentes, and Ujváry, but found evidence insufficient to order Benecsky's execution, decreeing instead that she should be imprisoned pending further judicial action.

A second trial convened on January 7, with Supreme Court Judge Theodaz Szimma of Szülö presiding over a panel of fifteen jurists. Despite allegations of sorcery and black magic, church authorities declined to try the case or question any witnesses. King Matthias II tried repeatedly to place Erzsébet herself on trial, but Count Thurzó resisted, saying "As long as I am Lord Palatine in Hungary, this will not come to pass. The families which have won such high honors on the battlefield shall not be disgraced in the eyes of the nation by the murky shadow of this bestial female. In the interest of future generations of Nadasdys, everything is to be done in secret. For if a court were to try her, the whole of Hungary would learn of her murders, and it would seem to contravene our laws to spare her life. However, having seen her crimes with my own eyes, I have had to abandon my plan to place her in a convent for the rest of her life."

Witnesses at the second trial included Count Thurzó, Erzsébet's sons-in-law, Imre Megyery, several visitors to Castle Čachtice, and a rare survivor of Erzsébet's household staff, identified only as "the maiden Zusanna." Aside from describing tortures inflicted by defendants Jo, Szentes, and Ujváry, while begging mercy for Katarina Benecsky, Zusanna dropped a bombshell on the court, stating that Jacob Silvassy of Čachtice had found a list of victims in Erzsébet's own handwriting, numbering 650. During her four years of service to the countess, Zusanna testified, at least 80 servants had died under torture at Čachtice, to her personal knowledge.

The second court confirmed death sentences for Helena Jo, Dorothea Szentes, and Janos Ujváry, citing their "voluntary confessions" and "the ones made under torture," plus the fact that none denied the allegations made against them by other witnesses. Jo and Szentes were sentenced to have the fingers ripped from their guilty hands with red-hot pincers, then to be burned alive. Ujváry, based on his relative youth and participation in fewer slayings, would be beheaded, his corpse drained of blood before it was cremated. Zusanna's plea for mercy, coupled with a dearth of evidence, spared Katarina Benecsky from any further punishment. Erszi Majorova, belatedly captured, joined the list of those condemned and executed on January 24.

Meanwhile, King Matthias II continued pressing for Erzsébet's trial. On January 14 he ordered Thurzó to begin a new investigation of "the guilty woman responsible for the death of three hundred girls and women born into noble and peasant families." It commenced in February. After 224 new witnesses were interrogated, Thurzó delivered his report to Matthias on April 17, recommending that Erzsébet be sentenced to life under house arrest at Castle Čachtice.

Matthias countersigned that order, then felt the wrath of Hungary's Parliament, goaded by the Catholic Habsburgs to make an example of Erzsébet Báthory. Matthias sought opinions from his *curia regis* (king's court) and received that body's advice on July 26. Those learned lawyers wrote:

> It is left to Your Majesty's pleasure whether further proceedings should be instituted against the above named Lady with a view towards decapitation, or the present sentence of life imprisonment be left standing and be confirmed, the latter being recommended by the useful and faithful service of her Ladyship's deceased husband, and their daughters' service to Your Majesty, one of whom is married to Miklos Zrinyi, the other to György Homonnay, both Barons of the Realm and faithful and useful servants of Your Majesty.

Finally, after one last hearing on December 17, Matthias abandoned his efforts to execute Erzsébet and seize her property for the crown. He confirmed the life sentence, formally pronounced to Erzsébet by Count Thurzó at Čachtice, where he told her "You, Elizabeth, are like a wild animal. You are in the last months of your life. You do not deserve to breathe the air on Earth, nor to see the light of the Lord. You shall disappear from this world and shall never reappear in it again. The shadows will envelop you and you will find time to repent your bestial life. I condemn you, Lady of Čachtice, to lifelong imprisonment in your own castle."

Erzsébet was not allowed free run of the place where so many had died. In fact, she was confined within a small room in the castle's tower, its windows bricked over, its only door walled up except for a slot used for passing food trays back and forth. But captivity did not break Erzsébet Báthory's spirit. From her cell, she continued to proclaim her innocence, while greedy relatives picked over her estate. Son Paul and Imre Megyery took her castle at Sárvár, effectively blocking prosecution of their servants for complicity in any homicides committed there. Erzsébet's sons-in-law seized other Báthory lands, and even Count Thurzó's wife joined in the looting. During January 1613, Baroness Erzsébet Czobor visited Čachtice and stole items of jewelry, which she sold to finance one of her daughters' lavish weddings. That relatively petty theft inspired Hungary's highest judge, Lord Chief Justice Zsigmond Forgách, to write Thurzó on February 16, urging him to curb his wife's rapacious appetite.

On July 31, 1614, Countess Báthory summoned two priests from the Esztergom bishopric, Imre Agriensy and Andreas Kerpelich, to witness the signing of her last will and testament. They stood outside her bricked-up cell, under guard, while Erzsébet dictated that her remaining properties should be divided equally among her children, opposing further administration of her estates by son-in-law György Homonnay Drugeth. She formally signed that will during the feast of Saint Peter in Chains, on August 3.

Just under three weeks later, on August 21, a guard peered through the feeding slot in Erzsébet's door and saw her sprawled face-down on the floor. Dead at age fifty-four, Erzsébet was reportedly buried in a vault beneath the main church in Čachtice. Her body was exhumed three years later and moved to the Nádasdy family crypt at Nyírbátor. An expedition to locate her corpse found nothing in the Čachtice crypt when it was opened on July 7, 1938. Likewise, when Erzsébet's supposed grave at Nyírbátor was opened in 1995, it proved to be empty.

Erzsébet outlived her uncle Gábor, who was assassinated at Oradea on October 27, 1613 by two Balkan outlaws reportedly paid to kill him by political rival András Ghiczy. King Matthias II succeeded Rudolf as Holy Roman Emperor in July 1612, ruling until his death at Vienna in March 1619. György Thurzó survived his infamous cousin-in-law by two years and four months, dying in Bytča at age forty-nine, on Christmas Eve, 1616.

As with Gilles de Rais, some modern authors contest Erzsébet's guilt or strive to minimize her crimes. The court judgment of January 7, 1611 referred to "the satanic terror against Christian blood and horrifying cruelties unheard of among the female sex since the world began, which Erzsébet Bathory, widow of the much-esteemed and highly-considered Ferenc Nadasdy, perpetrated upon her serving maids, other women, and innocent souls, whom she extirpated from this world in almost unbelievable numbers." But how many victims, finally, died at her hands and those of her accomplices?

No trace of the murder diary listing 300, 612, or 650 victims survives today. Purported quotes from that diary—including a reference to Erzsébet's disappointment when one maid died quickly under torture, noting that "she was too small"—appear in various histories without supporting documents. In 2009, a spokesman for Hungary's National Archives denied any knowledge of the diary but averred that reports of its possession by a private collector in Nagyszombat (now Trnava, Slovakia) were merely idle gossip.

We are left, then, with the testimony of Count Thurzó and his raiding party, who discovered three fresh corpses in December 1610, and the admissions of Erzsébet's accomplices, some extracted under torture, as to how many servants were slain in their presence. At trial, Janos Ujváry claimed that "some 37" girls were killed during his sixteen years of service with the countess. Dorothea Szentes recalled the deaths of thirty-six, while Helena Jo had counted "51, perhaps more." Katarina Benecsky kept no tally but guessed that fifty girls were slain during her time in the Báthory household. Witness Zusanna, meanwhile, remembered at least eighty victims killed during her four years of service to the countess.

How are such relatively modest tallies reconciled with the much higher numbers reported by various authors? Raymond McNally, writing in 1983, suggested one possible answer.

> Did the culprits deliberately underestimate the number
> in order to soften the blow? Not at all! The reason is

simple: most previous experts assumed that Elizabeth began torturing and killing servant girls only in the year 1604 when she became a widow. This would have meant one hundred deaths per year—certainly a rather high number, even in those days of badly treated servants. But from the evidence available today it is clear that Elizabeth was torturing and killing girls from her adolescence onward, and continued unhampered until stopped by Count Thurzo, late in her life.

Conversely, some latter-day defenders of Erzsébet Báthory deny that *any* murders occurred. In that scenario, the Protestant Erzsébet was marked for a frame-up by Catholic monarchs who coveted her property and owed her a fortune in debts they would never repay once she was safely walled up at Čachtice. Even Raymond McNally, who pronounced Erzsébet guilty of slaying hundreds, suggests that the trials of 1611 were manipulated by "the secret conspiracy that had been formed among Imre Megyery at Sarvar, relatives, and Count Thurzo." The latter group, presumably, hoped to save Erzsébet's treasure for themselves, rather than see it lost to the Habsburg Empire.

From those contradictory sources, a chilling gothic legend has emerged over successive centuries. Today, Erzsébet Báthory is known primarily from tales spun long after her death, including an embellishment not raised by any witnesses at trial: according to those stories, Erzsébet despaired at growing old and sought to halt the march of time by bathing in the blood of slaughtered virgins. Some accounts, tinged with the supernatural, claim that she slashed a young maid's face one day and noticed, while wiping the blood from her hands, that it made her skin appear more youthful. From then on, the spinners of fiction maintain, Erzsébet was hell-bent on a regimen of bloodbaths to preserve her beauty.

That fable first surfaced 115 years after Erzsébet's death, in 1729, when Jesuit scholar László Turóczi examined Erzsébet's case in his *Tragica Historia*. Matthias Bel quoted Turóczi in his four-volume *Notitia Hungariae novae historico geographica* (1742), but questioned details of the priest's account. Verbatim testimony from the Hungarian trials resurfaced in 1765, published for the first time in Prague, during June and July 1817, and while those transcripts contained no mention of bloodbaths, the legend endured. British author John Paget devoted a chapter to Erzsébet's crimes in his *Hungary and Transylvania* (1839), and this was followed by a treatment in Reverend Sabine Baring-Gould's *The Book of Werewolves* (1854). Writing in an era when women were deemed incapable of killing for sadistic pleasure, those writers reduced Erzsébet's actions to a case of female vanity run amok.

One tenuous link between Countess Báthory and vampirism lies in reports of her family's association with Vlad Tepes (1431–76), the real-life model for Bram Stoker's *Dracula*. Better known to history as Vlad the Impaler, Tepes belonged to the House of Drăculeşti, which used the patronymic "Dracul" (Dragon), derived from the Order of the Dragon, founded in 1408 to battle Ottoman Turks and other enemies of Christianity. A patent of nobility granted to the House of Drăculeşti by Holy Roman Emperor Ferdinand I, in January 1535, describes the clan's ancient symbol as identical to that of the Báthory family, a sword covering three wolve's teeth.

Beyond that document, history notes that a cousin of Erzsébet's, Stephen Báthory of Ecsed (1430–1493), led 8,000 infantry and 13,000 cavalrymen in a 1476 campaign that helped Vlad Tepes capture Târgovişte, the capital of Wallachia. In November of that year, Vlad and Stephen pledged eternal loyalty to each other in their war against the Turks, but Vlad's end of that bargain fell through a month later with his death in battle outside Bucharest.

3.

AXE MEN

Modern Americans have grown accustomed since the 1980s to existing in a state of agitation over terrorism, living under government "threat warnings" that are now the background noise of daily life, like static on a poorly tuned car radio. Few realize—and no schoolbooks on history record—that there was once *another* wave of panic spanning nearly three decades across the USA.

The perpetrators, if we discount speculation and hysteria, remain unidentified today.

For a quarter century at least, persons unknown invaded private homes by night, found weapons—generally axes—on the premises, and massacred whole families, claiming more than 150 lives for reasons yet unclear. Suspects were named, some were jailed or executed when they were not lynched, but most of those attacks remain unsolved today. One theory claims that the slaughter may have run its course at last in southwestern Germany.

Axes have doubled as tools and weapons from their invention around 6000 BCE. In 970 CE, Freydís, sister of Leif Eiriksson, used one to massacre rebellious Norse settlers in Vinland (now Newfoundland, Canada).

In March 1874, five members of the German immigrant Carl Stelzenreide family were hacked to death in their home near Millstadt, Illinois. Police suspected an in-law but never charged him. Ten years later, a still unidentified "Servant Girl Annihilator" terrorized Austin, Texas, by fatally axing four young women and wounding four more plus two men.

In August 1892, authorities accused Lizzie Borden of using a hatchet to kill her father and stepmother in Fall River, Massachusetts, prompting a show trial that saw her acquitted in June 1893, after which she declared herself "the happiest woman alive." She lived until 1927, admired by some locals, disdained by others.

Twenty-one months after Borden's acquittal, a night-prowling slayer bludgeoned and shot five members of the Gus Meeks family in Linn County, Missouri, leaving one daughter alive by accident. (A pregnant victim's fetus also died in the attack.) Contrary to later legends, however, the killer's blunt instrument was a stone, not an axe. Two convicted suspects escaped from jail; one of them was never recaptured.

Fast-forward to January 7, 1898, when a home invader killed Francis Newton, his wife, and their daughter at their farm near West Brookfield, Massachusetts, 86 miles northwest of Fall River. Police grilled various

A PORTRAIT BY EDWIN H. PORTER OF ANDREW J. BORDEN'S BODY WHEN DISCOVERED AT THE BORDEN RESIDENCE IN FALL RIVER, MASSACHUSETTS, IN 1893.

suspects but missed German immigrant Paul Mueller, an ex-logger and the family's ill-tempered former hired hand. Bloodhounds tracked his scent to a nearby railroad, then lost it. If one recent theory is correct, Mueller went on to rank among America's most prolific serial killers of all time.

On November 17, 1900, someone killed Mary Van Lieu and her two-year-old son with the blunt side of an axe in Trenton Corners, New Jersey. Husband-father George, a musician, returned from a gig to find his home in smoking ruins. Police arrested Robert Hensen, a black ex-convict who allegedly had quarreled with the Van Lieus days earlier and who was found with a cut on one hand. After a five-day trial, jurors convicted him, resulting in his execution on December 27.

Which solved nothing.

On May 12, 1901, an axe-wielding slayer killed J. Wesley Allen, his wife, and their teenage daughter at their home in Shirley, Maine, then torched the house. Authorities arrested Canadian expatriate Henry Lambert on May 16, convicting and imprisoning him. An appellate court released him in May 1923, by which time dozens more victims were dead.

Residents of Cottondale, Florida, last saw the Kelly family—Henry, his wife, and their three children—alive on Halloween, 1903. Henry's mother-in-law found the house padlocked from outside on November 9 and summoned help, finding all five murdered within. The Kellys were black. Police considered suspects but jailed none.

The killer traveled 300 miles for his next strike in Statesboro, Georgia, to kill five members of the Hodges farming family on July 28, 1904. These victims were white. Authorities convicted black defendants Will Cato and Paul Reed, whereupon a lynch mob burned them alive on August 16, selling photos of the event afterward for 25 cents each.

On December 8, 1904, a prowler murdered Benjamin Hughes, wife Eva, and their two daughters at Trenton, South Carolina, setting the house afire. Some reports say fourteen-year-old Hattie Hughes was raped post-mortem; others deny it. Some accounts claim all died while asleep from axe blows, others that Ben Hughes was shot. Headlines blamed unknown African Americans, but none were jailed or lynched this time.

Still haunting Dixie, death found Virginia Linkous and her adopted son in the early hours of Christmas Day, 1904, at Radford, Virginia. Husband James and an overnight guest escaped as the house burned. Authorities accused James Linkous, convicted him, and executed him on March 17, 1905. Four weeks before Linkous's execution on February 5, Albert Boylan, his wife, and their son died from axe blows in Marion, Arkansas, 620 miles southwest of Radford by rail. That case is still officially unsolved.

On September 22, 1905, a prowler hacked Lula Wise and her four children to death in Jacksonville, Florida, burning their house afterward. Police sought Lula's ex-husband, Sam, but never found or indicted him. During the night of February 7–8, 1906, the same fate befell three members of the Christmas family in Cottonwood, Alabama. On March 17, police arrested son Will Christmas, brother-in-law Walter Holland, and his wife, as reporters said, "through the medium of a detective, his assistant, a ventriloquist, a superstitious negro, and the negro's mule." None of the suspects was convicted.

Three months later, near Milton, Florida, a home invader killed an "itinerant preacher" named Ackerman, his wife, and their seven children before torching their home on May 26, 1906. Seven weeks elapsed before the same fate befell four members of the Isaac Lyerly family, although a teenage daughter escaped from the burning house. Vigilantes captured eight black "suspects," surprisingly freed five after a kangaroo trial, then lynched Jack Dillingham, Nease Gillespie, and Gillespie's son John on August 7.

For reasons still unknown, the killer apparently refrained from further murders for nearly two years. Action resumed on March 4, 1908, with

Warren Hart and his wife slain in Frazier, Georgia. Lynchers hanged and burned black suspects John Henry and Curtry Roberts on March 6, after they allegedly confessed in custody. We may assume that they were tortured first, a common practice at the time.

On April 12, home invaders killed railroad foreman M. F. Gerrell and his wife at home in Watauga, Texas. Two of their children escaped, vaguely describing dual assailants armed with clubs and knives. Local racists blamed unidentified Mexicans but apprehended no suspects.

On July 8, a man killed Alfonse Durel with an axe and injured his wife on Bourbon Street in New Orleans, inaugurating a notorious series of murders that may or may not have been related to others reported here.

On Thanksgiving Eve that same year, November 26, 1908, six members of the Tom Edmonson family were butchered in Woodland Mills, Alabama, before their house and barn were set afire. Prosecutors indicted white sharecropper Bob Clements for killing one of the victims, Nettie Edmonson, and convicted him in February 1909. One month later, the *Atlanta Constitution* ran an odd story claiming that Tom Edmonson was still alive, living with an unnamed "negro family" on a Tennessee River island.

On September 21, 1909, six members of the George Meadows family were massacred at Hurley, Virginia, and their cabin was set afire. All died from axe blows, but father George was also shot twice. He was found outside, with his head nearly severed, half-dressed and clutching a pencil. Jurors convicted Howard Little—previously convicted of murder while serving as a U.S. Marshal in 1892, pardoned in 1896—and he was executed on February 11, 1910. Before that, on Christmas Eve, 1909, Samuel Baker (a friend of Little) murdered Henry Pennington (George Meadows's brother-in-law) and wounded his wife (George's sister). A lynch mob settled Baker's case, sans trial, on Christmas Day.

On Halloween, 1909, near Beckley, West Virginia, four members of the George Hood family died under the axe, their home incinerated. On

December 21, Luther Sherman robbed and murdered black businessman A. R. Blakey in Beckley. Subsequently convicted, Sherman "teased" police with hints of having a hand in the Hood massacre, but officers found no corroborating evidence.

In 1910, the killer's mayhem resumed on March 11 at Houston Heights, Texas. Five members of the Schultz family, "swingers" by modern standards, died gruesomely after "a sort of entertainment" at their home. Authorities found their bodies piled together, and those of Alice Schultz and her youngest daughter left nearly nude. Police grilled various suspects, jailing two who accused each other, but wound up prosecuting neither.

Three months later, on June 5, residents of Van Cleve, Iowa, found three members of James Hardy's family bludgeoned at home with a sharpened gas pipe the victims used to pry up frozen manure from their barn floor in winter. Gossips and police initially suspected surviving son Raymond, then cleared him of culpability.

An unidentified night stalker struck twice more in New Orleans the same year, first wounding August Crutti and his wife with a cleaver on August 14, then injuring grocer Joseph Rissetto and his wife in bed on September 20.

On the day of the Rissetto attacks, 1,200 miles away to the northwest, three members of the John Zoos family died from axe wounds at home near Byers, Pennsylvania, while John worked his regular shift at a graphite mine. Police developed no suspects and soon dropped the case.

Two months later precisely, on November 20, 1910, near Guilford, Missouri, a killer slaughtered Oda Hubbell, his wife, and their two children. The perpetrator shot Oda, then axed his wife and children before torching the house. Jurors convicted Oda's reputed best friend, Hezekiah Rasco, of Oda's murder. It was Rasco's second murder conviction, the first involving a woman he killed in 1896 during a quarrel over a butter churn. Released in 1905, he soon drew a two-year term for horse theft, then reportedly slaughtered the Hubbells after a contentious all-night poker game. That conviction saw him hanged on March 26, 1912.

On December 7, 1910 a postman noticed uncollected mail at the Bernhardt family farm in Johnson County, Pennsylvania. Joined by highway workers, he investigated, finding the bludgeoned corpse of Emeline Bernhardt, seventy-eight, her bachelor son George, forty-nine, and hired hands William Graves and Tom Morgan. The men had died from axe wounds, and Emeline from blows with a clock weight as she tried to hide in a closet. Despite a $500 reward, no leads developed.

The New Orleans Axeman returned on June 26, 1911, fatally wounding grocer Joseph Davi but leaving his pregnant wife Mary unscathed. Governor Jared Sanders posted a $500 reward for information that drew no takers.

Meanwhile, between January and March 1911, invaders staged late-night raids on humble homes across Louisiana and Texas. Louisiana victims in that apparent series of frenzied slaughters included three members of the Byers family in Crowley and four members of the Andrus (or "Andres") family in Lafayette. In the first Texas attack, at San Antonio, five members of the Casaway family, former New Orleans residents, were killed. In each of those cases the victims were either black or mulatto (of mixed race), or their families included at least one mixed-race child. The raids began a new and perhaps separate reign of terror that would claim 49 lives by April 1912. In the Casaway rampage, victims' corpses were moved and posed post-mortem, while the rest were found in or near their beds.

The killings shifted northward again on June 9, 1911, when a nocturnal axe murderer killed William Hill, his wife, and their two children in their beds at Ardenwald, Oklahoma. Newspapers blamed a phantom dubbed "Billy the Axman." Bloody fingerprints on the bodies and other evidence suggested that Ruth Hill and her five-year-old daughter had been sexually assaulted. Police accused neighbor Nathan Harvey on December 21, but released him six days later.

A month after the Oklahoma murders, on July 11, George and Nettie Coble died from axe wounds in bed at Rainier, Washington. Some reports claim Nettie was raped; others dispute it. Neighbor George Wilson's wife accused him, whereupon he admitted "believing" he might be guilty, then recanted. Jurors convicted him in November, despite a total lack of solid evidence.

On August 24, 1911, Richard Lee, his wife, and their teenage son were bludgeoned with a hammer in their sleep at Booneville, Indiana, their home torched afterward. Police jailed surviving son William, age 21, claiming he had murdered his kin, then locked all doors and windows before burning the house to conceal a robbery. Convicted in December 1911, William "died in his cell" at Michigan City's prison on September 13, 1914, somewhat peculiar for a twenty-four-year-old for whom there are no published references to suicide or murder.

The killer struck twice overnight on September 17, 1911, claiming three victims each from the Arthur Burnham and Henry Wayne families, next-door neighbors in Colorado Springs, Colorado. "Amateur detectives" allegedly found size six men's shoeprints at both scenes, suggesting a slayer approximately five feet four inches tall. Arthur Burnham, residing in a local sanitorium for tuberculosis patients at the time, escaped the massacre that claimed the lives of his wife and two children. Although he fell under police suspicion, hospital staffers confirmed his airtight alibi. Nonetheless, officers were still accusing him when he died from natural causes on February 5, 1912.

The axe killer(s) made a Midwestern swing after the Colorado Springs murders, striking at Monmouth, Illinois on September 30, 1911. Three members of the William Dawson family died in bed, battered with a bloody pipe left at the scene. Near their backyard fence, officers found a flashlight with the message "Colorado Springs, September 4" etched on its handle, but they could not identify its owner. In 1915, suspicion was focused on three black suspects, two of whom were serving time for burglary. Their murder motive was described as "revenge for attentions which the negroes believed Dawson had shown to their relatives," but Monmouth's police chief told reporters "I do not believe these three negroes are connected with any of the other axe murders which occurred in different parts of the country." Jurors convicted John Knight on February 2, 1918, fixing his sentence at 19 years. Alleged accomplices Tom Knight and Loving Mitchell were released for lack of evidence.

Two weeks after the Dawson murders, on October 15, neighbors found William Showman, his wife, and their three children slain with an axe in their beds at Ellsworth, Kansas. As in several other cases, police found a lamp in one room with its chimney removed, perhaps in an effort at time-delayed arson. Wife Pauline's corpse was posed in "a disgusting manner," presumably sexual. Detectives focused on suspect Charles Marzyck, Pauline's former brother-in-law and an ex-convict who'd sworn vengeance against the family and others for testifying against him at his trial for theft in 1906. Police also tried to link Marzyck with the deaths in Colorado Springs, but their theory collapsed when he was found in Canada, with an ironclad alibi for all three crimes.

By then, journalists had begun linking some of the axe murders. A *Rocky Mountain News* editorial described a single killer "traveling about the country like a millionaire or a tramp . . . obsessed with the desire to terrorize a nation." They may have been correct, but that surmise put them no closer to the murderer's identity.

At 5:30 a.m. on Halloween, 1911 Bert Jordan heard his mother cry out at their home in Mount Pleasant, Iowa. Responding, he found her sprawled across her bed downstairs, bleeding from a head wound but covered with bedding. Comatose for several days afterward, Belle Jordan survived but remembered nothing of the attack.

The "mulatto murders," as they came to be known, resumed on November 26 in Lafayette, Louisiana with the deaths of Norbert Randall, his white wife, four of their mixed-race children, and a nephew. On January 19, 1912, neighbors found Marie Warner and her three children axed to death at their cabin in nearby Crowley's "Promised Land" section, a legally sanctioned red-light district. Three days later, the killer(s) axed five members of the Walter Broussard family at Lake Charles, leaving white reporters to lament that father Walter had been "a good type of negro . . . industrious and intelligent." A note left at the Broussard scene read "When He Maketh the Inquisition for Blood, He forgetteth not the crime of the humble—Human Five." Minus the last two words, which defy explanation to this day, that proved to be a misquote of Psalm 9:12, lifted not from the Bible but from dialogue in the 1852 anti-slavery novel *Uncle Tom's Cabin*. Later that month, authorities arrested suspect Raymond Barnabet, a black sharecropper who was said to lead a twenty-member race-conscious cult called the Church of Sacrifice. New Orleans police chemist A. L. Metz found blood and brain tissue on a man's suit retrieved from teenage daughter Clementine Barnabet's closet, prompting District Attorney John Robira to file murder charges.

On February 19, home invaders killed Hattie Dove, her two children, and her sister in Beaumont, Texas, leaving their "almost nude bodies" sprawled on various beds. A note left behind repeated the cryptic message from Walter Broussard's home verbatim.

Five members of the Monroe family and a male sleepover guest were butchered in their sleep on March 26 in Glidden, Texas. The *El Paso Herald,* reporting that slaughter, also referred to a previous massacre, claiming six members of the Wexford family slain "two months ago" but providing no further specifics.

April was the worst month yet in Texas that year, with five members of the William Burton family axed in San Antonio on the night of April 11–12, and three members of an unnamed family butchered at Hempstead on the 14th, reportedly "exactly as the Burtons had been killed." Three other relatives escaped from the Burton household but could not describe their assailants.

Meanwhile, Louisiana authorities claimed they had cracked the "mulatto murders" case. At Raymond Barnabet's trial in October 1911, daughter Clementine and son Zepherin testified that their father had admitted killing "the whole damn Andrus family" in Lafayette. Jurors convicted Raymond, but an appellate court reversed that verdict on grounds that Raymond was drunk throughout his trial and no record exists of a retrial. Then, on April 5, Clementine Barnabet changed her story, claiming that *she* was responsible for multiple murders—including some committed while she was incarcerated—protected in her efforts by a magic charm and a disguise of men's clothing. She admitted to killing children to prevent them from being "left orphans in the world" after she slew their parents. She also confessed to "caressing" the bloody corpses, leading prosecutor Howard Bruner to call her a "moral pervert." Jurors concurred and recommended life imprisonment, sparing her from execution since she'd "only" slain members of her own race. Clementine failed at an attempt to flee Angola State Penitentiary on July 31, 1913, then was released by authorities on April 28, 1923, after which she disappeared from public view. As author Bill James suggests, her relatively swift release from prison, even after an escape attempt, may

A NOVEMBER 6, 1912 *DUNCAN ARIZONIAN* NEWSPAPER ITEM DETAILING THE SENTENCING OF CLEMENTINE BARNABET FOR MURDER.

Girl Killed 21 People; Gets Sentence

Negro girl must Serve Lifetime in Prison; Wholesale Murders Spread Terror; Confesses awful Crimes

Lafayettee, La., Oct. 28. — Clementine Barnabet, who murdered more than 20 persons, according to her own confession, was found guilty of murder today. The verdict calls for life imprisonment. When the jury indicate that the Bayou State's prosecutors were unconvinced of her guilt to begin with.

While white Louisianans congratulated themselves on a sloppy job well done, axe murders resumed in the Midwest. On June 5, 1912, Rollin and Anna Hudson, recent arrivals in Paola, Kansas, died in a nocturnal axe attack. A neighbor recalled Rollin claiming that Anna had cheated on him in Massillon, Ohio, where they'd married in April 1910. Police sought a "large pig-faced man" seen visiting their cottage on the night they died, after asking a neighbor where they lived, and a newspaper claimed (with no apparent evidence) that the victims "might have been chloroformed." The ugly visitor and any possible motive eluded police.

Four days later, in Villisca, Iowa, the killer (if, in fact, it was a single person) staged his second-worst crime, killing four members of the Josiah Moore family and two overnight guests—young sisters Ina and Lena Stillinger—at Moore's home. All were axed in their beds, a lamp with its chimney removed left burning in the house. A private investigator from the Burns Detective Agency targeted William "Blackie" Mansfield, whose own family would die in similar fashion in a Chicago suburb two years later, but grand jurors refused to indict him. Other suspects included "odd" Presbyterian minister George Kelly (indicted for Lena Kelly's murder in 1917 but acquitted after two trials, and later admitted to a lunatic asylum) and Iowa state senator Frank Jones (who was accused of putting out a contract on the victims but never charged, and who won a $2,225 libel judgment against the Burns detective who named him as guilty). By the year's end, another Villisca investigator, Matthew McClaughry, who served in the Bureau of Investigation (formed in 1908, and renamed the Federal Bureau of Investigation [FBI] in 1935) would name another suspect and accuse him of committing twenty-five axe murders nationwide.

Even with confessed killer Clementine Barnabet in custody, the Texas "mulatto" murders resumed briefly and haphazardly on August 16, 1912. That night, Mrs. James Dashiell woke to the pain of an axe striking her arm at her home in San Antonio. Her screams put the would-be slayer to flight and prevented the harming of her husband and their four children. Dazed, she could not describe the lone attacker to police. A story in the *Lafayette Advertiser* on August 20 referred to a prior failed assault on the Dashiell family "two months ago."

At Payson, Illinois, tragedy struck on September 27 when an unknown prowler axed Charles Pfanschmidt, his wife, their daughter, and boarder Emma Kaempen (a schoolteacher) while they slept. Authorities targeted adult son Ray Pfanschmidt as a suspect, tried him three times for murder, and, failing each time, gave up their prosecution.

An unwelcome flashback to the southern "mulatto" slayings came on November 23, 1912, when police in Neshoba County, Mississippi, found black victims William Walmsley, his wife, and their four-year-old daughter axed to death in their home near the county seat at Philadelphia. In that case, William Walmsley escaped from the house while his wife and child died, but then was cut down by the murderer while trying to scale a picket fence a hundred yards from his home. A press report claimed that the triple murder was "similar to those committed around Lake Charles, Crowley, Rayne and Lafayette, for which Clementine Barnabet has confessed." By then, of course, Clementine had been imprisoned for a month and obviously had not slipped away to Mississippi for another massacre.

An apparent break in the case arrived on December 17, when Mary Wilson and her daughter Georgia Moore were killed with an axe at their shared home in Columbia, Missouri. Suspicion focused on Henry Lee Moore—Georgia's son, Mary's grandson—who had come to visit on the morning of the slayings, contriving to "find" the bodies after asking a neighbor if anyone was home next door. Detectives learned that Moore, an ex-convict, had reached Columbia on December 16, using an alias to rent a hotel room. He denied the murders but was found with bloody clothes and a bloodstained handkerchief. Jurors convicted him in March 1913 and imposed a life sentence.

Federal agent William McClaughry then named Moore as a nomadic murderer, accusing him of twenty-three prior murders in Colorado Springs, Monmouth, Ellsworth, Paola, and Villisca. He cited similarities between the several crime scenes. Never charged with any of the other massacres, Moore served thirty-six years in prison before Governor Forrest Smith paroled him in December 1949. Released at age eighty-two, he entered a St. Louis Salvation Army Men's Center, leaving after Governor Philip Donnelly commuted his sentence in July 1956. Moore's date and place of death remain unknown. Today, while all reports confirm his guilt of double murder, Moore's involvement in the other slayings remains hotly contested.

And despite Agent McClaughry's claim that the axe murders ceased with Moore's imprisonment, nothing could be further from the truth.

On June 10, 1913, an axe-wielding home invader attacked railroad worker Arthur Kellar, his wife, and their young daughter at their home in Harrisonville, Missouri, 110 miles west of Columbia. Arthur and the child died; his wounded wife survived to stand trial and be acquitted of the slayings. Author Todd Elliott deems this crime the last "legitimate" crime of the long-running series.

Five months after the Kellar raid, however, a "hatchet fiend" terrorized Muskogee, Oklahoma, claiming at least three male victims between November 1913 and January 1914. Unlike the other cases, victims B. F. Richardson, C. S. Everret, and A. H. Orcutt were attacked at their places of business. In April 1914, police charged C. T. Hefler, a shop clerk fired by Richardson after a quarrel, with murdering his former boss. (The verdict in that case was unavailable at press time for *Extreme Killers*.)

On April 3, 1914, Mrs. Elijah Francis and two of her children died from axe wounds at their home in Arkadelphia, Arkansas. A third child escaped. Writer Todd Elliott reports this still-unsolved crime as "perhaps the first Ax-Man 'copycat' killing."

Three months later, on July 6, a killer struck again in the Chicago suburb of Blue Island, Illinois, killing four victims in their sleep. Todd Elliott describes them as members of the "Mansfield-Mislich family," meaning suspect William Mansfield from Villisca, but newspaper reports identify those slain as Jacob Neslesala and his wife, daughter, and infant grandchild. Elliott reports that immigrant Casimer Arezewski surrendered and confessed the crime to New York authorities soon afterward, but once again, no confirmation was found by press time.

The New Orleans Axeman returned to action on December 22, 1917, wounding four members of the Andollina family with no fatalities. On May 19 he fractured immigrant dairyman Vincent Miramon's skull, resulting in the victim's death five days later. On May 29, he killed grocer Joseph Girard and his young daughter. Wife Adele survived her wounds to blame Joseph's business rival Wesley Sumner, who soon was convicted and sentenced to life.

If he *was* guilty, then more than one Axeman patrolled the Crescent City.

Between the most recent assaults, on May 22, a home invader killed grocer Joseph Maggio and his wife Catherine, using an axe and Joseph's straight razor. Nearby sidewalk graffiti harked back to the May 16, 1912 *gunshot* murder of grocer Anthony Schiambra that also wounded his wife. Police suspected brother Andrew Maggio but could not crack his alibi.

Next, on June 26, 1918, an axe man wounded grocer Louis Besumer and common-law wife Harriet Lowe. Before dying on August 5, Harriet named Besumer as her attacker and a likely wartime German spy. He spent nine months in jail before jurors acquitted him of murder, deliberating for a brief nine minutes. On the night Lowe died, a prowler axed Anna Schneider, eight months pregnant, at her home. She survived to deliver a healthy daughter.

On August 10, a prowler murdered grocer Joseph Romano, leaving a bloody axe behind. Nieces Mary and Pauline glimpsed the dark-skinned, heavyset attacker fleeing but could not identify him. Other grocers reported efforts to chisel through their doors and armed themselves in self-defense as hysteria spread.

On March 10, 1919, the slayer seriously wounded grocer Charles Cortimiglia and his wife Rose, and killed their two-year-old daughter in Gretna, a New Orleans suburb south of the Mississippi River. Elderly neighbor Iorlando Jordano answered screams to discover the crime, but Rose later named Jordano as the killer, assisted by his son Frank. Charles Cortimiglia furiously denied it and divorced Rose after jurors convicted the Jordanos, sentencing Frank to hang and his father to life imprisonment.

Someone penned a letter to local newspapers from "Hell," signed "The Axeman," on March 13, 1919. It warned fearful residents that anyone not playing jazz—the killer's favorite music—at 12:15 a.m. on St. Joseph's night (March 18) would "get the axe." Police never identified the author, but one immediate beneficiary was local songwriter John Davilla, whose tune "The Mysterious Axman's Jazz (Don't Scare Me Papa)" became an instant bestseller.

On August 10, the prowler wounded grocer Steve Boca at home. Twenty-four days later, the maniac assaulted teenage housewife Sarah Laumann in bed, dropping an axe on her lawn as he fled. She recovered, with amnesia masking details of the incident. The last acknowledged attack, on October 27, 1919, killed grocer Mike Pepitone. His wife, uninjured, vaguely glimpsed a large man dashing from their home.

By then, many locals blamed Mafia "black hand" extortionists for the attacks, noting that many victims were Italian businessmen, primary targets of demands for money under threat of arson or death. Rose Cortimiglia, arrested once for prostitution since her divorce and reportedly scarred by smallpox, confessed to perjury on February 3, 1921, freeing the innocent Jordanos from prison ten months later.

But was the Axeman truly gone for good?

In December 1920, an attack identical to the Pepitone murder killed Joseph Spero and his twenty-month-old daughter Josephine, and wounded his wife Rosa in Alexandria, two hundred miles northwest of New Orleans. On January 14, 1921, a predawn attack left grocer Giovanni Orlando dead in DeRidder. In that case, police blamed "Fittified Sol," a "half-witted negro," but couldn't make charges stick. Finally, on April 12, a nocturnal attacker killed Frank Scalisi at Lake Charles, then fled when Scalisi's wife woke screaming.

The Mafia theory gained support on December 5, 1921, when Mike Pepitone's widow Esther, who had remarried in September, shot and killed Joseph Momfre in Los Angeles. Esther's new husband—another grocer, Angelo Albano—had vanished on October 27 while shopping for produce. Momfre allegedly confronted Esther on December 5, demanding money to forestall his killing her "like I did your husband." Momfre was a known racketeer and ex-convict from Louisiana, but Esther surprised him with a pistol, pumping three slugs into his back. Jurors acquitted her in April 1922, and while some authors name Momfre (or "Mumfre") as the Axeman, a definitive study of the case by Dr. Miriam Davis dismisses the L.A. events as a "false lead." Davis notes that Esther shot Momfre for killing her *second* husband, not for Mike Pepitone's murder two years earlier.

Murders similar to the American axeman murders made headlines in Europe when, on March 31, 1922, five members of the Gruber family and their maid were killed with a mattock on their farm at Hinterkaifeck, forty-three miles north of Munich, Germany. A tool for digging, the implement—a kind of pickaxe—was used to kill four adults between the ages of thirty-five and seventy-two, plus children aged two and seven. Evidence suggested that their killer occupied the farm for several days after the murders, and while that never happened in any American case, the property's isolation prevented quick discovery of the massacre. The killer was gone before a neighbor arrived on April 4.

The slaughter made regional headlines but raised no transatlantic concerns.

Six years and eight months passed before Americans confronted another notorious axe murder.

As headlines reconstruct the story, a "hatchet slayer" killed two women in Omaha, Nebraska on November 18, 1928. Then, during a November 20 home invasion, the prowler wounded Harold Stribling and his wife at home, afterward carrying Mrs. Stribling to a nearby swamp, where he presumably raped her. On November 21, a firefighter tackled black suspect Jake Bird, age twenty-six, at a local flophouse, subduing him with a hatchet Bird carried. That day, police named Bird as Omaha's stalker, alleging he had "cut five" victims and claimed "at least three" lives in recent weeks.

Bird denied the charges and on November 25 the *New York Times* reported that he had been "questioned in vain." But his arrest opened a can of worms. Mrs. Stribling repeatedly named Bird as her attacker, even remembering the belt he wore. Meanwhile, news arrived from Utah that Bird had once served Ogden's police department as an undercover operative, where he performed well until he started moonlighting as a residential burglar by night. Convicted of second-degree burglary and rape, Bird served a prison term, once assaulting a jailer during an escape attempt. He was released on January 15, 1927. His other prison time included serving two years of a twenty-year sentence for stealing three cases of whiskey in Ogden, in 1924, and five years for burglary in Michigan, where a housewife had caught him in the act.

In July 1928, while riding the rails as a hobo, Bird allegedly saw Burlington Railway special agent Conrad Barth shove Cleveland youth Gordon Grigor in front of a moving freight train at Ashland, an Omaha suburb. Grigor, dying, told police "a nigger pushed me under the wheels," but Barth was white and Bird's testimony resulted in a second-degree murder indictment against him.

Bird was waiting to testify against Barth at trial when the local hatchet attacks began. A *Baltimore Afro-American* editorial proclaimed Bird innocent, claiming that "everybody says" his prosecution was retaliation for accusing Barth and that Nebraska had refused to pay a $5,000 reward for the axe killer's capture after Bird's arrest. Bird's lawyer, who was also black, called the case a "frame-up" and mentioned hiring famed attorney Clarence Darrow, although Darrow never joined the defense team.

On January 3, 1929, grand jurors indicted Bird on two counts of assault with intent to kill. Douglas County's sheriff reported that Bird had been "chased out" of Louisiana in June, after reports of "trouble" there. At trial on January 28, Mrs. Stribling described waking, as Bird— dressed only in underwear and socks—attacked her husband with an axe, presumably dressing before he carried her off to the swamp where she clearly saw his belt. Bird denied the charges on January 31, seeming "at ease" on the witness stand, but jurors convicted him on February 1, resulting in a thirty-year sentence. Authorities dismissed Conrad Barth's murder charge while Bird's lawyer appealed his verdict, blaming an alternate suspect in Illinois. The appeal failed and Bird's defender resigned in March, claiming time spent on the case was "too great and the fee too small."

That said, Bird was released from custody in January 1933—and his tale did not end there.

On October 30, 1947, police in Tacoma, Washington caught Bird fleeing a home where Bertha Kludt and daughter Beverly lay murdered by an axe. In custody, Bird confessed to the slayings, calling it a case of burglary gone wrong. As his story unfolded, Bird described himself as a Louisiana native, "born somewhere there ain't no post office" on December 14, 1901, who had spent at least one third of his forty-five years imprisoned in Utah, Michigan, and Nebraska. When not incarcerated, he had roamed the nation, slaying as many as forty-six victims in California, Colorado, Florida, Illinois, Indiana, Iowa, Kansas, Kentucky, Michigan, Nebraska, New Jersey, Ohio, Oklahoma, South Dakota, Wisconsin, and Washington.

His first victim, Bird said, was a Los Angeles grocer slain in a holdup–murder. Next came eight-year-old Harvey Boyd, killed in East Omaha, Iowa, in June 1928. Omaha fatalities that year included J. W. Blackman, Waldo Reo, and Reo's sister Creta Brown, who were murdered before Bird's capture at the Stribling crime scene. On June 24, 1942, he killed Alta Fulkerson while burglarizing her home in Highland Park, Illinois, claiming he had committed the crime with accomplice George Howard. In September 1942, he claimed the lives of a retired watchman and his wife and teenage son in South Bend, Indiana. Five years later, Bird allegedly murdered James Winfield in Davenport, Iowa on September 7, 1947. On October 1, Bird killed eighty-one-year-old Marie Manners at her Pueblo, Colorado home. He killed his last victim before Tacoma, Lee Walker, with an axe-and-knife assault in Ogden, Utah on October 4.

Anonymous Internet blogger "Hypercallipygian" opines that Bird killed "at least five" victims, but suggests that most of his confessions were false, offered to postpone his execution in Washington. Former police chief Reed Phillips in Davenport, Iowa, told reporters in January 1948 "I don't think much of his confession" to the Winfield slaying. Phillips added "We want Bird to supply more details before we mark

Winfield's slaying off as solved." Supposed accomplice George Howard denied participating in the Fulkerson murder, while Chicago police suspected Bird of killing Mrs. Paul Gavin and her maid, Edba Sibilski, on October 22, 1942, and stealing $28,000 worth of jewelry and fur coats valued at $3,000.

Convicted at his Tacoma trial on November 26, 1947, Bird received a death sentence. On January 12, Iowa governor Robert Blue released a state police report discounting Bird's confessions to the Boyd and Winfield homicides, citing discrepancies between Bird's statements and known facts in the Boyd case, adding that Bird "didn't know anything" about Winfield's death. Three murders in Illinois, New Jersey, and Wisconsin were deemed "too painful" for survivors to discuss.

Bird's confessions bought him a thirty-day reprieve from execution, but the Washington State Supreme Court denied his retrial motion on November 30, 1948. He was hanged before 125 witnesses on July 15, 1949 and buried afterward in an unmarked grave at the Walla Walla penitentiary.

While debate over his guilt or innocence continued, five men connected to Bird's trial died from heart attacks in 1948—attributed to "The Jake Bird Hex" by reporters—while Bird awaited execution. They included Judge Edward Hodge (January 1), Undersheriff Joseph Karpach (April 5), court reporter George Harrigan (June 11), Detective Lieutenant Sherman Lyons (October 28), and defense attorney James Selden (November 26).

Echoes from America's long series of axe murders continue to the present day.

Police in Villisca received confessions to the 1912 murders as late as 1931, when a Detroit prison inmate claimed some unnamed businessman had offered him $5,000 to slaughter the Moore family nineteen years earlier. None of the false leads he provided panned out. In 1987,

Villisca made the crime a centerpiece of their "Heritage Days," striving to counteract novelist Stephen Bowman's harsh portrayal of the city in *Morning Ran Red*.

The Villisca murder axe passed from hand to hand among local residents, once traded for a box of chocolate-covered cherries, until it found a permanent home with the Villisca Historical Society. Today, the Moore murder house welcomes tourists six days weekly (closed Mondays), at a rate of $10 apiece, $5 for seniors and children under twelve. Adventurous overnight guests pay $428 for parties of one to six persons, plus $75 per additional guest thereafter.

In 2017, renowned sportswriter Bill James and daughter Rachel McCarthy James published an epic history of the axe murder series, titled *The Man from the Train*. They identify German immigrant and itinerant lumberjack Paul Mueller—five foot four, with size-six feet—as the elusive slayer, linking him to twenty-eight murders with 110 victims between 1898 and 1922, at which point Mueller returned to his homeland. The authors dissociate Mueller entirely from the New Orleans Axeman's crimes, but credit him with the Casaway "mulatto" massacre based on similarities between that crime scene and various others on their list. They attribute other slayings in that southern series to the Barnabets.

Focus on Mueller began with the discovery of his employment by the Newton family in Massachusetts, a year before their slaughter in what the Jameses call Mueller's first attack. Their book describes Mueller as a "physically repulsive man" and shabby dresser, barely able to speak English, with "poor social skills" but "a high level of intelligence." Specific trademarks of his crimes include nocturnal raids on homes near railroad tracks, the use of weapons found around the victims' homes and left there afterward, the sealing and burning of houses, the theft of small items from the homes, and evidence of sexual assault on female minors.

As previously noted, 105 years before *The Man from the Train* went to press, William McClaughry named Henry Lee Moore as the perpetrator of six massacres with twenty-five victims, based on the similarity of their circumstances. With that in mind, an introduction to McClaughry himself may prove instructive.

William's father, Illinois native Robert Wilson McClaughry (1839–1920), served as Chicago's General Superintendent of Police from 1891 to 1893, inculcating his sons with a passion for law enforcement. He died in Chicago and was buried at Monmouth, the scene of a triple murder nine years earlier. Between his time with the Chicago P.D. and his death, Robert served as warden of several major penitentiaries, including the federal lockup at Leavenworth, Kansas. Another of Robert's sons worked as warden of the Iowa State Reformatory.

Matthew launched his crime-fighting career as a records clerk at Leavenworth, hired by his father in an age when governmental nepotism was routine. He joined the U.S. Justice Department in 1907, when Attorney General Charles Bonaparte moved the DOJ's Bureau of Criminal Identification to Leavenworth, serving as America's central fingerprint repository. One year later, when Bonaparte created the tiny Bureau of Investigation under Director Stanley Finch, Matthew signed on as a special agent—all federal agents are deemed "special"—and studied the Bertillon system under its French founder, subsequently learning Scotland Yard's fingerprinting system in London.

McClaughry first heard of Henry Moore in December 1912, when police in Columbia, Missouri wrote to Leavenworth, inquiring about Moore's criminal record. McClaughry's reply confirmed Moore's prior incarceration at the Kansas Reformatory and noted six similar axe murders reported around the country after his release. McClaughry observed that an axe was used in all cases, and in five had belonged to the victims. Those killed in each case died in bed and were found covered with bedclothes at two scenes. Three attacks occurred on Sunday nights. At least four of the homes were situated within easy walking distance of railroads. Investigators found two of the six houses locked and shuttered, while three revealed evidence that the killer had lingered afterward to wash himself. At three scenes, police discovered lamps with their chimneys removed and set aside. Authorities reported evidence of robbery only in Moore's murder of his mother and grandmother. Villisca's was the only crime scene with a recognized "sexual aspect."

The Jameses, working with a much-expanded list of crimes, find more similarities in the cases they attribute to suspect Paul Mueller. More homes were locked and shuttered, some with padlocks affixed to the outside of doors. Victims were more often covered with blankets, or with pillows over their faces, sometimes buried under piles of hay if killed in barns. Bodies were often moved post-mortem, sometimes stacked atop each other, with younger females disrobed or sexually posed, including evidence of masturbation on or near their corpses. More lamps were found with chimneys removed, and others may have been responsible for homes set afire.

Massachusetts police sought Mueller in vain during 1898 but failed to locate him. No other agency suspected him of anything—or, if they did, their spokesmen kept it quiet. Even when reporters speculated on a repeat killer riding the rails in 1911–12, Mueller's name never surfaced.

And if the Jameses are correct, he got away with it, no huge surprise considering that nearly one in five *recognized* serial killers (18 percent) went unidentified and uncaptured between 1900 and 1999. Before the twentieth century dawned, Austin's "Servant Girl Annihilator" and London's "Jack the Ripper" led the way in that regard. Later, famed crimefighter Eliot Ness pursued but failed to catch Cleveland's "Mad Butcher of Kingsbury Run" in the 1930s. Eight years after that predator's last confirmed crime, police in the divided city of Texarkana fumbled their pursuit of the "Moonlight Murderer." The self-styled "Zodiac" terrorized California in the 1960s and '70s, claiming thirty-seven murders in the letters he penned to taunt authorities. The list goes on.

One explanation for the unsolved murders covered in this chapter is history itself. Police work in the era of axe men was very different in crucial ways from what we recognize today.

First, the future FBI was embryonic, its budget small, its duties chiefly limited to fraud against the U.S. government or crimes committed on federal property, including Native American reservations. Investigation of interstate crimes only began with the Mann Act of 1913, designed to stop organized prostitution (then known as "white slavery," regardless of the women's race) and did not expand further until passage of the 1919 Dyer Act, which authorized the arrest of car thieves who drove across state lines.

Meanwhile, state, county, and municipal police communicated poorly with each other, if at all, and depending on locality. They tended to "solve" cases by arresting "the usual suspects"—racial minorities, ex-convicts or fugitives, "perverts," and others deemed "crazy." When all that failed, officers focused on relatives and acquaintances of the victims, and seldom were shy about wringing confessions from them with "aggressive" questioning. Even victims themselves were not spared, as seen in New Orleans, where Rose Cortimiglia left her hospital bed for a jail cell, subjected to "third-degree" methods until she falsely accused two neighbors of slaying her child.

As for forensic science, it hardly existed in Paul Mueller's day, and that which did was poorly understood by most police. Fingerprint comparison began in the mid-nineteenth century but took decades to replace the Bertillon System—which, itself, was barely removed from the pseudoscience of phrenology, which classified criminals by measuring various body parts from head to toe.

Regarding blood, the Austrian biologist, physician, and immunologist Karl Landsteiner identified three types—A, B, and C (later changed to O)—in 1901, with type AB revealed a year later. The next discovery, blood's Rhesus (Rh) factor, did not occur until 1939. Scientists discovered deoxyribonucleic acid (DNA) in 1868 but did not recognize it as genetic material until the early 1950s, while its application to criminal cases was delayed until the mid-1980s.

Even ballistics testing was primitive in Mueller's time, and limited during most of his alleged rampage to observation of a weapon's caliber alone. There was no microscopic examination of striations left on bullets by interior gun-barrel rifling or various imperfections.

Traveling widely, with no record of his movements as he stowed away on freight trains and rarely leaving any witnesses alive, Paul Mueller—or someone else—could have avoided manhunts easily, with little risk except during the actual commission of the crimes. Since those occurred at night, primarily in tiny towns or on an isolated farm, with victims murdered in their sleep, that risk was minimized. No one who caught him in the act survived to testify.

But why would a compulsive killer stop when he (or she) had managed such a long, successful run? The short answer is *we don't know*—but certain possibilities suggest themselves.

One frequent answer is mortality itself, since homicidal maniacs eventually die, whether naturally, accidentally, by their own hands, or by the hand of someone else (as when Texas serial killer Elmer Wayne Henley shot his criminal mentor, sadist Dean Corll, in 1973). Even a killer executed for one homicide or several might leave a larger number unrecognized or unsolved in the wake of his death. Furthermore, some serial slayers might be halted by a disabling disease or injury, old age, even senility that renders them incapable of keeping up their gruesome pastime (or, in fact, of recalling it).

Another possibility is interruption of a murder series by incarceration, either in a prison or a mental institution, that takes a killer out of circulation for a period of years or permanently. Several killers profiled in this very work—Jake Bird, Henry Lucas, and Ottis Toole (see Chapter 5), Samuel Little (see Chapter 9)—spent years in custody but were released time after time to prey upon society. Lucas, indeed, served time for murdering his mother, then was freed to kill again. Some unknown slayers from the 1980s onward might be locked away right now, their worst crimes still unrecognized.

A third possibility, hotly debated, is that certain compulsive killers simply "burn out" or become sated with murder. Pakistan's Javed Iqbal (see Chapter 14) set himself a goal of 100 victims and achieved it. If he had "retired" then, without writing a confession to authorities, he might be circulating through Lahore's streets even now, a sexagenarian keeping his nose clean and living on his graphic memories. Others, like Cleveland "Mad Butcher" suspect Dr. Francis E. Sweeney, might sense manhunters closing in and will themselves to either stop killing entirely, or to move on to some new territory and technique.

As noted, Bill and Rachel James believe that Paul Mueller, their "Man from the Train," absconded to his native Germany sometime after 1915, treating himself to one last massacre at Hinterkaifeck in 1922 before he called it quits. They are not entirely certain, though, closing the first edition of their book by urging readers, "Don't indulge yourself in irrational skepticism. There's no real reason to believe that it's not him."

Or, for that matter, that it *was*.

To this day, researchers view most of the axe murders described in this chapter—including those with suspects imprisoned, executed, or lynched—as unsolved crimes.

4.
"ANGEL MAKERS"

Nagyrév is a farming village on Hungary's River Tisza, located fifty-four miles southeast of Budapest. With another nearby village, Tiszakurt, and several smaller hamlets, Nagyrév commands the "Tisza Corner," encircled by a broad loop in the river.

A hundred years ago, that region had another nickname. It was called the "murder district," for the frequency with which men suddenly dropped dead, allegedly from poisoning. The murderers, according to the rumor mill, were wives and other female relatives of those dispatched to early graves.

The plague reached Nagyrév in 1908, with the arrival of a middle-aged widow, one Madame Fazekas. Confusion still surrounds her given name. Some accounts call her Júlia; others claim she used her missing husband's first name, Julius; still others call her Marie or Zsuzsanna, the latter perhaps confusing her with the younger woman who became her leading criminal accomplice.

Fazekas was a midwife by profession and possessed more medical knowledge than anyone else in Nagyrév. Aside from delivering babies, she also performed abortions—a criminal offense in Hungary in those years, which saw her arrested ten times between 1911 and 1921. Each time, sympathetic judges dismissed the charges.

Already widowed once—or twice, by some accounts—Fazekas may have been a murderer before she first set foot in Nagyrév. If not, she soon acquired the knack, beginning with a twist on the abortion racket. Many parents in the district craved a single child, if that should be a boy.

Having produced a son and heir, they wanted no more mouths to feed, but ignorance and their religion stymied contraception. When a new, unwanted child arrived, Fazekas might be called in to appraise the situation, and another sudden crib death solved the problem.

So it was, as well, with husbands who abused or otherwise displeased their wives. Hungarian society favored arranged marriages, frequently shackling adolescent brides to much older grooms. Divorce was actively discouraged, even when the husband was a deadbeat alcoholic brute. But again, Madame Fazekas had a solution tailored to the needs of women in distress.

Her first known victim was Lewis Takacs, in 1911. His death resulted from a hefty dose of arsenic, derived from soaking lethal flypaper in water, then transferring it into the victim's favored beverage or food. Reports claim that Fazekas killed Takacs as an act of "charity" for his spouse, but she soon decided there was money to be made from setting women free. Whether a man was sadistic, senile, disabled, or simply annoying, he could be eliminated for a price. The standard rate, once Fazekas hit her stride, was 120 pengős (about $20) in advance, another 120 after the deed was accomplished, and the same again once an estate was settled.

Around the time she disposed of Lewis Takacs, Fazekas met Zsuzsanna Olah, a young widow in Nagyrév forced to marry a man she despised at age eighteen and recently liberated by the same flypaper con coction Fazekas favored. With so much in common, the two women soon joined forces, pursuing midwifery, abortion, and murder for profit with equal zeal.

And then came war.

Propelled by a political assassination, ultra-nationalism, and a web of secret alliances, the First World War began in Europe on July 28, 1914, pitting the Central Powers (Germany, Austria-Hungary, Bulgaria, and Turkey) against the opposing Triple Entente (France, the Russian empire, and the United Kingdom, joined in 1917 by the United States). Before the ceasefire in November 1918, Austria-Hungary drafted 9 million soldiers, 4 million of them from Hungary. Of those conscripted, more than 1 million Austro-Hungarian soldiers never returned to their homes. Defeat of the Central Powers shattered the empire, with Hungary losing two-thirds of its prewar territory and over half its former population to newly created nations including Czechoslovakia, Poland, and a Kingdom of Serbs, Croats, and Slovenes.

Still, things were not all bad during the "War to End All Wars." Most of the able-bodied men in Nagyrév were called away to fight, leaving their farms and families unattended. Early Austro-Hungarian victories left the winners with numerous prisoners of war in custody, and the Tisza Corner seemed an ideal holding area. Loosely guarded, and standing in for absent farmers and shopkeepers, the POWs made themselves at home, gladly accommodating any lonely women who were in the mood for romance. By late 1915, many female residents of Nagyrév and Tiszakurt had one or more foreign lovers.

Then, unhappily, their husbands started coming home, some wounded, gassed, or otherwise disabled, none of them in any mood to tolerate adultery or what might pass in Hungary as women's liberation. Midwives Fazekas and Olah—the latter known to paying clients as "Aunt Susi"—were, of course, prepared to guarantee domestic peace.

By some accounts, the first wartime victim was Peter Hegedus, in 1914. Other reports date the new wave of murders for profit from 1916. Somewhere along the way, Fazekas and Olah acquired a third partner, Christine Czordas, who joined the team after killing her husband, Balint. Those three led what police and reporters later called a "war widow cult," aided in their lethal campaign by a cousin of Fazekas who, as district clerk, filed the region's death certificates.

The "cult" had certain basic rules. First, only women could participate; a man who wanted someone killed would have to handle it himself. Further, the women must be married and entitled to relief. Spinsters and younger single women bent on slaying faithless lovers were beyond the pale. That said, the victims' list was not entirely limited to husbands. Client Marie Kardos poisoned her spouse, her lover, and her twenty-three-year-old son, the latter dying in the midst of a song she asked him to sing. Maria Varga killed her husband as a "Christmas present" to herself, then poisoned six more relatives when they annoyed her. Some practitioners remarried after slaying one spouse, then dispatched the next in turn.

As with any kind of organized crime, competitors soon tried to poach on the racket devised by Fazekas and Olah. One purported rival, another Nagyrév midwife, tried to encroach on the trade but soon was dead herself from flypaper tea. When friends of the victim blamed Fazekas, she challenged them to prove it. Witnesses proved hard to come by, after Olah and some other members of the "cult" threatened to burn their homes. The murdered rival's son tried vigilante action, but he missed his shot at Fazekas from ambush and wound up in prison.

By war's end in November 1918, murder had become a fad of sorts in Nagyrév and Tiszakurt. One client of the "Angel Makers," Madame Bukenoveski, poisoned her aged mother and dumped the woman's corpse into the Tisza, where police recovered it and logged her as an accidental drowning victim until one sharp-eyed detective noted wheelbarrow tracks leading from Bukenoveski's home to the riverbank.

Christine Balint, while helping Fazekas and Olah manage the outfit's affairs, still found time to poison her parents, two brothers, a sister-in-law, and an aunt. Her special method was to use a small preliminary dose, inducing stomach cramps, then purchase medicine for her afflicted loved ones, spiking it with arsenic to finish off the job.

Nor was arsenic simply employed to eliminate family pests. Since medieval times, poison had been known in Europe as "inheritance powder," used to clear thrones and facilitate redistribution of wealth. Once the scandal broke at last, Father Laszlo Toth, pastor of Tiszakurt, provided telling commentary on his flock:

> "The peasants hereabouts are mean and grasping," he declared, "and think only of money and comfort. All the women, who somehow seem stronger than the men, are married two or three times. Spiritually they have no existence, nor yearning for spirituality. My church is empty although I must admit that among the accused are several of my few faithful, women who have been active in all kinds of parish work."

Authorities were mindful of the high death rate within the Tisza Corner, and particularly its impact on reasonably healthy men. In each case where police investigated, though, the victims' death certificates appeared to be legitimate. A doctor raised suspicions in 1924, after one

DEFENDANTS IN THE ARSENIC POISONING CASE OF TISZAKURT, HUNGARY WALKING IN THE SZOLNOK PRISON YARD.

of his wealthier patients died from a bout of bronchitis, but police found no proof of foul play and the murders went on for another five years.

The conspiracy began unraveling in 1929, when an anonymous letter to the editor of a local newspaper accused unnamed women of slaying their husbands. Reporters were sniffing along the murder trail when another letter arrived, this one addressed to the county's attorney general at Szolnok, naming Fazekas, Olah, and Bint as killers. In that case, authorities traced the author and, finding him short of evidence, jailed him for slander.

A domestic quarrel broke the case at last, in late October 1929. The argument occurred between a female resident of Nagyrév and her hard-drinking husband, who spent sober Sunday mornings as the precentor (lead singer) at Nagyrév's church. Fed up with her husband's tippling, the lady threatened to dispose of him unless he changed his ways. Angry and more than a little frightened, the husband forced a confession of sorts from his spouse.

A neighboring widow, Ehthej Szábo, had offered to sell her poison on the Fazekas installment plan, for three payments of 120 pengős. Frau Szábo, the precentor's wife said, had freely confessed to killing her husband and brother.

The next morning, the precentor told his story to police, who arrested Szábo and transported her to Szolnok for interrogation. Facing double murder charges, she confessed and named Fazekas as the Angel Makers' ringleader. Detectives went after Fazekas then, and brought her in for questioning, pretending to accept her claims of innocence while they dispatched a flying squad to search her home in Nagyrév. There, between her attic floorboards and the ceiling of a room below, they found strips of poisonous flypaper soaking in bottles of water. Samples were drawn for testing and replaced with more water.

While the potion underwent analysis, police released Fazekas. She remained at home for two full days, under surveillance, then began to make the rounds of Nagyrév, visiting cohorts and clients, including Frau Szábo, now collaborating with prosecutors in exchange for leniency. Detectives trailed Fazekas at a discreet distance, compiling a list of suspects. Armed with names, police descended on the district's largest cemetery and began exhuming corpses. One after another yielded arsenic from hair and fingernails. Some coffins also contained small bottles of poison, buried with victims in hope they would never be found.

Arrest warrants came next, with Júlia Fazekas heading the list. She watched police approach her home, but cheated them by swallowing a bottle of her own flypaper serum as they pounded on her door. Raiders had better luck with ninety-eight other suspects, surprising them at their respective homes and carting them away to jail in Szolnok, pending trial.

Confusion shrouds the outcome of the Angel Makers' case. At least one other female suspect—Christine Balint—hanged herself in jail before trial, though some reports say three suspects besides Fazekas committed suicide.

Most accounts agree that of the original ninety-eight persons arrested, twenty-six women and two male accomplices—Joseph Madarasz and Laszlo Szabo—were tried for murder, with defense counsel Dr. J. Viragy trying to off-load their guilt onto Júlia Fazekas. Sketching life before the World War, he told jurors, "Nagyrév was Eden then. Then the war came, the peace came; poverty followed. Instead of plenty there was bareness, instead of joy, despair. No priest ever visited them, no doctor came to cure their sick. In Nagyrév, where most people could not read or write, desperation was breeding greed. And then comes into their midst the spirit of evil, reborn in Júlia Fazekas—an unlicensed village doctor, but known far and wide as the 'white Devil.' She tempted them, as perhaps no women have ever been tempted."

Jurors listened, then convicted at least twelve defendants (some reports say all twenty-eight). The court condemned Susi Olah and seven others to hang, imposed life prison terms on seven more, and sentenced the rest to serve an average of fifteen years each. In the end, only Aunt Susi and Christine Czordas were hanged, in June 1931, both reportedly in a state of unconsciousness at the time after swooning on their approach to the gallows.

An appeals court commuted the other death sentences to life imprisonment.

Few other defendants were named in newspaper reports outside of Hungary, but those identified include Julia Sijj, slayer of her father, husband, two sons, two brothers, and an uncle to inherit land; a Frau Palinka, first name unreported, who killed her husband, parents, two brothers, a sister-in-law, and an aunt for the same reason; Maria Szule, killer of her war-blinded husband "because he was no use to me," who then "married a younger man who can help me in the fields"; Maria Varga, slayer of *her* blind husband, lover Michael Ambros, and Michael's grandfather; Mrs.

THE FOUR MAIN DEFENDANTS FOR A SERIES OF MURDERS COMMITTED IN THE HUNGARIAN VILLAGE OF NAGYRÉV. A TOTAL OF FORTY WOMEN POISONED THEIR HUSBANDS, CHILDREN, AND BROTHERS SO THEY COULD MARRY THEIR LOVERS.

Louis Oser (or, Cser), who confessed to killing her father-in-law, plus two children at their births; and Marie Aszendi, who dispatched her son because he "made her look too old."

How many victims did the Angel Makers kill, all told? Again, the public record is confused and contradictory. A newspaper article from February 1930 refers to 100 murdered husbands. Another, published seven years later, describes "a slaughter of over 100 men, women and children." Some estimates place the final body count as high as 300, though only 45 slayings were proven at trial.

Recapping the case in 2004, a British reporter interviewed eighty-three-year-old Maria Gunya, who was a small child in Nagyrév when her father, a village official, joined in the 1929 investigation. Although clearly saddened by the memory, she smiled while recalling that under the threat of murder, men's behavior toward their wives in Nagyrév had "improved markedly."

That same year, archivist Dr. Geza Cseh told BBC News reporter Jim Fish, "I'm sure there are still secrets to be unearthed, here or elsewhere." He noted that while exhumations were also performed in nearby Tiszakurt, revealing further cases of murder by poison, no residents of that community were ever charged.

5.

HANDS OF DEATH: HENRY LUCAS AND OTTIS TOOLE

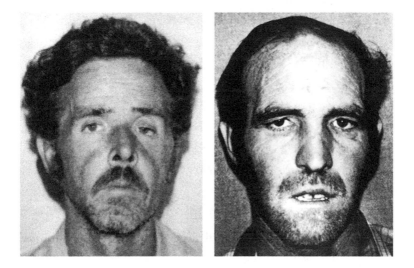

Henry Lee Lucas was never lucky in love. His second marriage—without any formal vows or license—paired him with Frieda Powell, the fifteen-year-old niece of an acquaintance commonly known as "Becky." In early 1982, when he was thrice her age, the mismatched couple roamed from Florida to California, dodging child-protection workers who sought Powell for fleeing an orphans' home. Henry, in love, staged that escape but got more than he'd bargained for.

By May, they latched on to Jack and O'Bere Smart in Hemet, California, freeloading until the Smarts proposed a plan. Henry and Becky agreed to care for O'Bere's eighty-two-year-old mother, Kate Rich, in Ringgold, Texas. They moved in with Rich on May 14, but local relatives ousted the couple four days later, after Becky cashed two forged checks on Kate's bank account.

Next, they joined the All People's House of Prayer in Stoneburg, Texas, led by Rueben Moore, but left on August 23 and hitchhiked eastward. Lucas returned the next day, telling Moore that Becky had "run off" with some anonymous trucker. Kate Rich vanished on September 16, and police feared the worst when Lucas left Stoneburg the following day. Officers found his abandoned car in Needles, California, on September 21.

Lucas drifted back to Texas, where someone torched Kate Rich's home on October 17, and deputies jailed him on a Maryland fugitive warrant, then released him when authorities there dropped a pending auto-theft charge. Lucas endured surveillance until June 4, 1983, when he told Moore that he was leaving town to "clear his name" by finding Becky and Rich. He left a pistol with Moore for safekeeping and rolled out of town in a rusty junker that died in San Juan, New Mexico. Moore brought him back, and officers were waiting on June 15 to jail Henry for possession of a firearm, banned in Texas for ex-convicts. Lucas sat in jail for four days, resisting every ploy of Montague County Sheriff Bill "Hound Dog" Conway until the night of June 18. That evening, he called jailer Joe Don Weaver, first complaining of a bright light in his cell, then muttering "Joe Don, I done some bad things."

His first confession was a scrawled note reading: "To Whom It May Concern, I, Henry Lee Lucas, to try to clear this matter up, I killed Kate Rich on September [sic] last year. I have tried to get help so long and no one will help. I have killed for the past 10 years and no one will believe it."

Elaborating for the record, he described inviting Rich to church, then killing her, raping her corpse, dissecting it and burning it in a stove at the All People's House of Prayer. Police found bone fragments inside the stove and eyeglasses from the nearby yard, identified by Rich's daughters as their mother's.

Next, Lucas briefed interrogators on Becky Powell's death. While camping on August 23, she'd quarreled with Lucas over "finding Jesus" and slapped him. Henry stabbed her, then dismembered her and scattered her remains over the desert, coming back some two weeks later to conceal the parts in several shallow graves. He led investigators to the site, and they retrieved the skeletal remains of a Caucasian female matching Powell's height and age. Since DNA profiling was unknown in U.S. courts at that time, no positive I.D. was possible, but Henry faced a second murder charge in any case.

It should have been enough to earn Lucas a seat in the electric chair at Huntsville Prison, but he wasn't finished talking yet.

As it turned out, he had done many more "bad things."

America's most controversial murderer was born August 23, 1936, at Blacksburg, Virginia. The Lucas family home was a two-room, dirt-floor cabin in the woods outside town, where Henry's alcoholic parents brewed bootleg whiskey and his mother doubled as the neighborhood prostitute. Viola Lucas ruled her family with an iron hand, while her husband Anderson Lucas—dubbed "No Legs" after a drunken railroad accident—dragged himself around the house and tried to drown his humiliation with liquor.

The brood included nine children, several dispersed to relatives, institutions, and foster homes. Henry was one of those "lucky" enough to remain with his parents, and mother Viola seems to have hated him from birth, making his life a living hell on Earth. She often beat Henry and Anderson, forcing them to witness the parade of "johns" sharing her bed. When she shot one of them, post-coitus, blood sprayed over Henry's face.

Disgusted with life, Anderson Lucas crawled outside to spend a night in the snow one evening and later succumbed to pneumonia. Henry survived his abusive upbringing, but his mother's sadism was endless. When Lucas entered school in 1943, she curled his stringy hair in ringlets, dressed him as a girl, and sent him off to class that way. Barefoot until a kindly teacher bought him shoes, Henry was beaten at home for accepting the gift. If Henry found a pet, his mother killed it, and he came to understand that life—like sex—was cheap. When Henry gashed his left eye, reportedly while "playing with a knife," Viola let him suffer until doctors had to surgically remove it, replacing it with a glass eye.

Another time, after Viola beat him with a wooden board, Henry lay semi-conscious for three days before "uncle" Bernie Dowdie—Viola's live-in lover—took him to a hospital for treatment. Dowdie also introduced the boy to bestiality, teaching Henry to kill various animals after raping and torturing them.

Henry quit school in fifth grade and never returned. At age fifteen, anxious to try sex with a human, Lucas picked up a girl near Lynchburg, strangled her when she resisted his clumsy advances, and buried her corpse near Harrisburg. This March 1951 disappearance of seventeen-year-old Laura Burnley remained unsolved for three decades, until Lucas confessed to the murder in 1983.

In 1952, police nabbed Henry and two of his half-brothers for burglary. Sentenced to the Beaumont Training School for Boys, Lucas first escaped from the lockup, then returned to serve his time. Beaumont authorities recorded his IQ as 76 ("borderline deficiency") and logged his relationship "of a sexual nature" with a black inmate, further noting erratic behavior that shifted suddenly from friendly to violent.

Released in 1953, Henry settled briefly with half-sister Nora Crawford, who later accused him of raping her twelve-year-old daughter.

In June 1954, a series of burglaries around Richmond earned Lucas a six-year prison term. He walked away from a road gang on September 14, 1957, stole a car, and drove to see half-sister Opal Jennings in Ohio, where he met a girl named Stella before police jailed him on a federal charge of driving the hot car across state lines. He served eighteen months on that count, then returned to Virginia's state pen and a series of reported homosexual affairs. A second escape attempt, in December 1957, saw Lucas recaptured the same day, but he was still discharged from prison on September 2, 1959.

Henry returned to Opal, now residing in Tecumseh, Michigan, and asked girlfriend Stella to marry him. Viola turned up on his doorstep, nagging him to end the engagement and return to Blacksburg. Both were drinking on January 11, 1960, when she hit him with a broom and Henry struck back with a knife, leaving her dead on the floor. Arrested five days later in Toledo, Ohio, Lucas confessed to the murder and boasted of raping his mother's corpse, a detail he later retracted as "something I made up." Convicted of second-degree murder in March 1960, he drew a sentence of twenty to forty years. Two months later, jailers transferred him to Ionia's state hospital for the criminally insane, where he remained on a regimen of drugs and electroshock therapy until April 1966. Paroled due to overcrowding on June 3, 1970, Lucas promised his keepers "I'll leave a present on your doorstep." He later claimed to have murdered two women mere blocks from the prison, but police deny having any such cases on file.

From prison, Henry returned to Tecumseh and moved in with kin. In December 1971, police booked him for molesting two teenage girls; at trial the charge was reduced to "simple kidnapping," and Lucas returned to the Jackson state pen. Paroled in August 1975, again over his own objections, Henry worked briefly at a Pennsylvania mushroom farm, then married Betty Crawford, a cousin's widow, in December 1975.

Three months later, the couple moved to Port Deposit, Maryland. Betty divorced him in summer 1977, claiming that Lucas molested her daughters from a previous marriage. Meanwhile, according to Henry's confessions, he had already committed a series of random murders, traveling and killing as the spirit moved him, claiming victims in Maryland and places farther afield, ranging from Delaware to Texas.

Henry's sister Almeda offered him work at her husband's wrecking yard, then accused Henry of molesting her granddaughter. Feigning contrition, Henry "borrowed" Almeda's pickup and fled Maryland, dumping the totaled truck in Jacksonville, Florida. He was moving on a swift collision course toward his partner in crime, Ottis Toole.

Once Henry started talking to Texas authorities, he continued for nearly two years, raising his confessed body count from 75 to 150, then to 360, finally adding murders committed by friends and accomplices to reach a total "way over 500." Early on, he fingered frequent traveling companion Ottis Toole as a collaborator, piquing the interest of police from coast to coast and into Canada. Detectives from around the country gathered in Monroe, Louisiana, in October 1983, comparing notes and announcing that Toole and Lucas were responsible for at least 69 murders. A second conference at Monroe, in January 1984, raised the total to 81. By March 1985, police in twenty states had "cleared" 90 murders for Lucas alone, plus another 108 committed with Toole as an accomplice.

The Texas Rangers had a tiger by the tail. In late November 1983, they moved Henry to Williamson County, the base of a "Lucas Task Force." Scores of officers lined up with files, sketches, and photographs to question Henry about far-ranging cold cases. Soon, he was also on the road.

A California tour in August 1984 reportedly "cleared" fourteen open cases. Five months later, in New Orleans, Lucas "solved" five more. In the first week of April 1985, he led a caravan across Georgia, closing the books on ten murders. In West Virginia, Lucas confessed to killing a man whose death had been ruled suicide, netting the widow a hefty life-insurance settlement. By then, Ranger critic Phil Ryan claimed Henry was "dictating orders" to his keepers, geared toward improving his living conditions. But Henry closed cases, and for all the later accusations of a massive fraud, he seemed sincere. Sporting a "Jesus Saves" T-shirt, he spoke of redemption and the need for answers sought by grieving families.

Hitchhikers were his favored prey. "Just about everyone I pick up, I kill 'em," he said. "That's the way it always turns out." From a jail in Florida, Toole chimed in: "We picked up lots of hitchhikers, you know, and Lucas killed most of the women hisself, and some of them would be shot in the head and the chest, and some of them would be choked to death, and some of them would be beat in the head with a tire tool."

Henry's motive was frequently necrophilia. "To me a live woman ain't nothing," he said. "I enjoy dead sex more than I do live sex." In some cases, as in Kennewick, Washington, corroborating evidence appeared: a match to Henry's blood found on a towel, used to wipe the hand he gashed while stabbing his victim. The more Henry talked—and the more Toole added to the grim saga of slaughter—the greater curiosity became about the deadly sidekick.

A Jacksonville native, Ottis Elwood Toole was born on March 5, 1947. His alcoholic father soon took off for parts unknown—but not before, in Toole's account, forcing five-year-old Ottis to service one of the father's male friends.

Ottis lived with a religious-fanatic mother and a sister who dressed him in girl's clothes "to play," a trauma he shared with Lucas (and at least five other notorious serial killers). Toole's grandmother, an alleged Satanist, worsened his confusion by calling him "the Devil's child" and taking him on graveyard raids that yielded human body parts for use in "magic" charms.

Toole ran away from home repeatedly but always drifted back again. He suffered from seizures and found release by torching vacant houses in his neighborhood. Questioned later about his choice of targets, Toole replied "I just hated to see them standing there." By his own admission, Toole committed his first murder at age fourteen. The victim, a traveling salesman, picked him up outside of town and drove him to the woods for sex. Afterward, Toole "got nervous" and ran the man down with his own car.

Classified as "retarded" with an IQ of 75, Toole quit school in the eighth grade and logged his first arrest, for loitering, in August 1964. Other arrests followed, building a rap sheet filled with counts of petty theft and lewd behavior. He married briefly, but his bride departed after three days' time, repulsed by Toole's overt homosexuality.

By 1974, Toole was touring the West in an old pickup truck. Acquaintances thought nothing of it, but evidence suggests he may have murdered at least four victims in a six-month period.

Police suspected Toole in the death of twenty-four-year-old Patricia Webb, shot in Lincoln, Nebraska, on April 18. Five months later, on September 19, a lone gunman invaded a Colorado Springs massage parlor, stabbing employee Yon Lee and slashing her throat before moving on to rape, shoot, and stab co-worker Sun Ok Cousin. He then set both women on fire. Lee survived to describe her assailant as clean-shaven, six feet two, and 195 pounds, driving a white pickup truck. Authorities arrested and ultimately convicted Park Estep, a mustachioed soldier who stood five feet ten, weighed a mere 150 pounds, and owned a *red* pickup.

Meanwhile, on October 10, someone snatched thirty-one-year-old Ellen Holman from Pueblo, Colorado, shot her three times in the head, and dumped her near the Oklahoma border. Detectives now believe Toole was the gunman in that crime.

No one can say with certainty when Toole first met Henry Lucas. Estimated dates for their fateful encounter range from 1975 to 1979, with some established facts weighing against the latter year. Most accounts agree that Henry met Ottis at a Jacksonville soup kitchen, sometime in 1976 or 1977, then traveled on without him, but returned to live with Toole's family in 1978.

Aside from sex with Toole, Lucas was drawn to Toole's young niece, Frieda Powell, another mentally defective child. It seems that Powell shared Lucas with Uncle Ottis, though Henry maintained that he only had sex with Toole as "a favor" and never enjoyed it. Between romantic interludes, Lucas and Toole worked together for Southeast Color Coat, a roofing company, but "came and went" as they pleased, according to the owner. Each time they made it back to Jacksonville, they were rehired. It was what they did, or claimed to do, away from Jacksonville that became the stuff of legend and enduring controversy in the early 1980s, lasting to the present day.

Toole's mother died after surgery in May 1981, prompting Ottis and Henry to hit the road with Becky and her brother, Frank Powell, Jr. The kids got homesick in Arizona, so Lucas and Toole returned them to Jacksonville, living with Toole's sister Drucilla—mother of Becky and Frank—until they stole a truck and drove the children to Delaware.

The happy travelers broke up when Ottis landed in a hospital, and Maryland police detained Henry for car theft, holding him until October 6. Two months later, Drucilla killed herself with a drug overdose, leaving Frieda and Frank at a children's shelter in Bartow, Florida. Henry sprang Becky from custody in January 1982 and they headed west again, the last time Toole would ever see his niece. He learned her fate only when Lucas finally confessed her murder to police in Texas.

The strangest tales spun by Lucas and Toole involved their mutual insistence that they frequently acted on behalf of a Florida-based satanic cult called "The Hand of Death." Both agreed that they had been recruited for the sect by "Don Meteric"—a pseudonym supplied by author Max

Call for a Jacksonville resident who directed some of their crimes, including child kidnappings and sex-slave trafficking, along with contract killings and human sacrifices incorporating cannibalism. Evidence remains elusive—but did anyone really investigate after Lucas and Toole spilled the beans?

Ex-FBI agent Kenneth Lanning, once renowned as the Bureau's child molestation "expert" and persistent debunker of "satanic panic" worldwide, heard the stories told by Henry and Ottis. Max Call claimed that FBI helicopters buzzed the Everglades, searching in vain for the cult camp described by Lucas and Toole, but Lanning's take on the matter was more revealing. "There's nothing to it," he told interviewer Sondra London in the 1990s, "so why investigate?"

Why, indeed? The story sounds absurd on its face—but there is a long historical legacy of serial killers who professed a devotion to Satanism: Charles Manson's "family"; Chicago's four-man "Ripper Crew"; "Night Stalker" Richard Ramirez; "Death Angel" Donald Harvey; "Son of Sam" David Berkowitz; the cult led by Adolfo de Jesús Constanzo and Sarah Aldrete in Matamoros, Mexico; and Russia's seven-member sect, revealed after its second set of double murders in June 2008.

The list goes on and on. Take it back in time, to Gilles de Rais (see Chapter 1) and Hungarian countess Erzsébet Báthory (see Chapter 2). Spanish witch Enriqueta Martí i Ripollés killed at least twelve children in 1912 and used parts of their bodies in "potions" for sale to gullible clients. "High Priestess of Blood" Magdalena Solís led her Mexican cult in the vampiric ritual murders of eight victims during the 1960s. Thirty years later, Indonesian sorcerer Ahmad Suradji sacrificed the first of his forty-two female victims, continuing until his arrest in 1998.

True-crime writer Sondra London corresponded with Toole for seven months before their first meeting in July 1991. Eight years after Toole's death, she wrote: "Ottis Toole's background in a generational form of 'devil-worship' that involved the ritual use of human remains and the drinking of blood has been well documented. He named the real 'Don Meteric' as a man who had known his grandmother and provided cars for Henry to drive on their journeys, as well as plenty of drugs and booze to use along the way. He identified the location of the Process Church headquarters in New Orleans [linked to Manson and company by prosecutor Vincent Bugliosi in *Helter Skelter*] and accurately described their occult philosophies. He explained how their Florida employers would sign them in and out of work to provide alibis, when they were really off doing jobs for what he called 'the cult.'

London never shared the real "Meteric's" name, perhaps because Toole's jailhouse friend, Gerard Schaefer (see Chapter 7), had begun to threaten London's daughter with a visit from The Hand of Death to further her "sex education." Against those affirmations, we have earnest statements from the FBI that no such cult ever existed, it was all part of a "hoax"—except, of course, that they made no investigation, since they showed up for the game convinced that "there was nothing to it."

Enter Hugh Aynesworth, a reporter for the *Dallas Times-Herald*. In 1963, he claimed to have been present during JFK's assassination, at Lee Harvey Oswald's arrest, and at Oswald's murder by gangster Jack Ruby, though critics dispute all three assertions. Some said Aynesworth's chief pursuit in life was debunking Kennedy conspiracy theories, discrediting alleged witnesses, and lampooning New Orleans District Attorney Jim Garrison's trial of CIA "asset" Clay Shaw on conspiracy charges in 1969. As critic Jim DiEugenio observed online, "refusing a conspiracy is his life's work."

Two decades after JFK, Aynesworth discovered Henry Lucas, first supporting Henry's confessions and then refuting them with a blizzard of sometimes inaccurate "facts." Viewed in hindsight, Aynesworth's role in the drama was nearly as strange as Henry's. In a series of *Times-Herald* stories, beginning on April 15, 1985, Aynesworth attacked Henry's "hoax" on the public, allegedly perpetrated with the connivance of police anxious to feed Lucas cold-case details and clear their books. Aynesworth claimed to have learned of the fraud from Henry's own lips, in October 1983, yet one month later he signed a contract to write Henry's biography. That deal fell through when Aynesworth learned of Henry's prior literary contract with a Waco used-car dealer, but still he pressed on, supporting the "hoax."

In September 1984, Aynesworth appeared on CBS-TV's *Nightwatch* program, raising no objection as the show aired Henry's confessions to hundreds of slayings. As late as February 1985, Aynesworth published a Lucas interview in *Penthouse* magazine, prompting Henry with leading questions, accepting each response as fact. In one passage, Aynesworth said: "According to the numbers, you started killing furiously after [1970]. What triggered this? Would you just feel like you had to kill somebody?" And later: "So after killing all over the country for four years, you met Ottis Toole in 1979 [*sic*], and for two or three years you often traveled with him."

Aynesworth's timeline of Henry's movements, spanning two full pages in the *Times-Herald*, was replete with errors. He dated Henry's "first meeting" with Toole from 1979, though Lucas had moved in with Toole's family the previous year. He cited payroll records from Southeast Color Coat to prove the killers seldom left Jacksonville, when office manager Eileen Knight confirmed that they would often "come and go." He claimed that Lucas spent "all the time" between January and March 1978 with girlfriend Rhonda Knuckles, never leaving her side, but ignored the testimony of a surviving witness, tailed by Lucas across two hundred miles of Colorado and New Mexico in February of that year. The woman recalled Henry's face and recorded his car's license number for police. At one point, Aynesworth was so anxious to clear Henry's name that he listed a victim *twice*, killed on two occasions four days apart, in July 1981.

Still, there was much to criticize in Henry's marathon confessions. Police found one alleged victim, a Virginia schoolteacher, still alive and well. Some of Henry's claims were clearly absurd, including confessions to murders in Spain and Japan, plus delivery of poison to the People's Temple cultists in Guyana. Conversely, there were problems with Henry's retraction. Soon after Aynesworth's story broke, Lucas smuggled a letter to authors Jerry Potter and Joel Norris, claiming that he had been drugged and forced to recant his original confessions. Another lie? We may never know. By the time his series finished, Lucas claimed to have killed only three victims: his mother, Kate Rich, and Becky Powell. By April 23, he had denied the Rich and Powell slayings, despite directing officers to their remains. And his mother's death, of course, had been "an accident."

Authorities reacted in various ways to Aynesworth's "exposé." Arkansas filed new murder charges against Lucas on April 23, eight days after his change of heart, and other jurisdictions remain unimpressed by his belated pleas of innocence. In Marrero, Louisiana, relatives of victim Ruth Kaiser pointed out that Lucas confessed to stealing a stereo after he killed the seventy-nine-year-old woman—a theft they never reported and that therefore could not have been "leaked" by police. As they recalled, "He described things we had forgotten about, details that never appeared in the paper and that we never put in a police report."

Investigator Jim Lawson, with Nebraska's Scotts Bluff County sheriff's office, questioned Lucas in September 1984 regarding the February 1978 murder of schoolteacher Stella McLean. "I purposely tried to trick him several times during the interview," Lawson said, "but to no avail. We even tried to 'feed' him another homicide from our area to see if he was confessing to anything and everything in an effort to build a name for himself, but he denied any participation in the crime." Those efforts failed.

Commander J. T. Duff, intelligence chief for the Georgia Bureau of Investigation, described Henry's April 1985 Peach State tour. "Lucas was not provided with any information or directions to any of the crime scenes," he said, "but gave the information to law enforcement. When a crime scene was encountered, Lucas voluntarily and freely gave details that only the perpetrator would have known."

Toole also recanted some of his confessions, though he spun no tale of trying to embarrass the authorities. Instead, he took offense primarily when lawmen branded him a liar—or when they withheld the cigarettes and coffee he demanded as an opener for any interview. A case in point was Colorado's 1974 prosecution of Park Estep. Toole confessed to those crimes in September 1984, providing details, but embarrassed prosecutors mounted a furious counterattack. After hours of hostile grilling, Toole threw in the towel. "Okay," he said, "if you say I didn't kill her, maybe I didn't." In a strange, unsatisfying compromise, Estep was later released on his first parole bid, though his name was not formally cleared. The curious display of "mercy" by Colorado's parole board convinced some observers that the state accepted Toole's guilt but refused to publicly acknowledge an error at trial.

By November 1985, police in eighteen states had reopened ninety "Lucas cases," but what of the other 108? And what of the interstate telephone conversation between Lucas and Toole, monitored by police in November 1983? At the time, Henry and Ottis had not seen or spoken to each other in at least seven months, deprived of any chance to work up a script, but their dialogue lends chilling support to the later confessions.

> *Lucas*: Ottis, I don't want you to think I'm doing this as a revenge.
> *Toole*: No. I don't want you to hold anything back about me.

Lucas: See, we got so many of them, Ottis. We got to turn up the bodies. Now, this boy and girl, I don't know anything about.

Toole: Well, maybe that's the two I killed my own self. Just like that Mexican that wasn't going to let me out of the house. I took an ax and chopped him all up. What made me—I been meaning to ask you. That time when I cooked some of those people. Why'd I do that?

Lucas: I think it was just the hands doing it. I know a lot of the things we done, in human sight, are impossible to believe.

Indeed. Beyond a doubt, the most confusing, convoluted case on record for the killer pair is that of six-year-old Adam Walsh, snatched from a Hollywood, Florida, shopping mall on July 27, 1981. His severed head surfaced in a canal near Vero Beach ten days later, but no other trace of him was ever found. Toole first confessed to Adam's murder in October 1983, startling Assistant Police Chief Leroy Hessler with claims that were "grisly beyond belief." Hessler told the media, "There are certain details only he could know. He did it. I've got details that no one else would know. He's got me convinced."

Despite that endorsement, officers reversed their stance a few weeks later, issuing statements that Toole was "no longer a suspect." Adam's father, John Walsh—later host of TV's *America's Most Wanted*—clung to his belief in Toole's guilt, buttressed in 1988 by a ghoulish letter from Toole—penned in fact by cellblock friend Gerard Schaefer (see Chapter 7)—which read:

Dear Walsh:

I'm the person who snatched, raped and murdered & cut up the little prick teaser, Adam Walsh, and dumped his smelly ass into the canal. You know the story but you don't know where his bones are. I do.

Now you are a rich fucker, money you made from the dead body of that little kid. Oh, he was a sweet piece of ass! I want to make a deal with you. Here's my deal. You pay me money and I'll tell you where the bones are so you can get them buried all decent and Christian.

I know you'll find a way to make sure I get the electric chair but at least I'll have money to spend before I burn. If you want the bones of your little cock teaser you send a private lawyer with money for me. No cops, no State Attorneys. No FDLE [Florida Department of Law Enforcement]. Just a private lawyer with a written contract. I get $5,000 as "good faith" money. Then when I show you some bones I get $45,000. You get a lawyer to make up a paper like that.

If you send the police after me before we make a deal then you don't get no bones and what's left of Adam's hot pussy can rot. I remember how the little bitch was crying for his mommy when I was ramming his asshole. I love to fuck a boy, and then I love to kill them. Now you want his bones or not? Tell the cops and you don't get shit.

Sincerely,
Ottis E. Toole

In December 2008, twelve years after Toole's death, police again reversed themselves and pronounced Toole Adam's killer, officially closing the case. By that time, of course, all DNA samples pertaining to Adam's murder had vanished from official files.

One author who disputes Toole's guilt in Adam's case is Arthur Jay Harris, who blames the slaying on Milwaukee headhunter Jeffrey Dahmer, who allegedly was vacationing in Florida in 1981. Harris goes further, claiming Adam Walsh is still alive somewhere; somehow, the head logged under his name never was photographed, autopsied, or compared to Adam's pediatric dental records. While his alleged survival joins the pantheon of American urban legends, stretching back across more than a century from Jesse James and Billy the Kid to Elvis Presley, Adam's parents remain unconvinced. Whatever one believes, this much is clear: no shortage of enigmas lingers in the wake of nomads Lucas and Toole.

The justice system took its time with Henry and Ottis, dealing first with Toole. Two houses burned in his Jacksonville neighborhood on May 23 and 31, 1983, after which teenage accomplices denounced Ottis to police on June 6. In jail, he confessed to setting forty-odd fires spanning two decades and was convicted of second-degree arson on August 5, drawing a twenty-year sentence.

Meanwhile, in Texas on June 21, prosecutors arraigned Lucas on charges of murdering Kate Rich and Becky Powell. Henry waived his right to counsel and admitted stabbing Rich, indulging in necrophilia with her corpse, then dismembering and incinerating it. "I killed Kate Rich," he told the court, "and at least a hundred more. I know it ain't normal for a person to go out and kill girls just to have sex with them." Almost plaintively, he asked the judge, "Will I still be able to go on helping find bodies?"

Overnight, Henry rocketed to international infamy, dragging Ottis along for the ride. Toole supported Henry's claims and added more, "clearing" twenty-five murders in eleven states while claiming he had assisted Lucas in at least 108 more. On August 2, 1983, authorities arraigned Lucas for the October 1979 rape–slaying of a woman initially known only as "Orange Socks," the sole piece of clothing she was wearing when found along Interstate 135 in Texas, in October 1979. (In August 2019, the California-based DNA Doe Project identified "Orange Socks" as the long-missing Debra Louise Jackson, age twenty-three at her death.)

Ten days later, while awaiting trial on that charge, Henry recanted his confession to Becky Powell's murder, then waived trial on Kate Rich's death in September, pleading guilty and accepting a seventy-five-year sentence. In November 1983, after a judge rejected pleas to rule Henry's videotaped confessions on Powell inadmissible, Lucas faced trial in that case and testified on his own behalf, weeping in remorse as he denied any memory of Becky's death. Against that claim, the state played tapes of his calm confession to stabbing Becky and raping her corpse before he scattered her truncated remains in the desert. Convicted and sentenced to life, Henry congratulated his prosecutor, saying "You did a good job."

Next, in March 1984, came Henry's trial for killing "Orange Socks." Once again, confessions weighed against him, including taped admissions that he had picked the victim up while she was hitchhiking, raped and killed her, then had sex with her again before dumping her corpse in a culvert to which he later led police. Defense counsel countered with an insanity plea, professed memory lapses during Henry's confession, and allegations that deputies "refreshed" his memory during interrogation. Convicted on April 2, Lucas received a death sentence.

Back in Florida that month, Toole faced trial for the arson–murder of sixty-four-year-old George Sonnenberg, burned to death at his Jacksonville home in January 1982. That conviction earned Toole a death sentence, followed before year's end by another for the February 1983 slaying of nineteen-year-old Ada Johnson in Tallahassee. At the same time, he confessed to the Pensacola murder of nineteen-year-old hitchhiker David Schallart, found along Interstate 10 on February 6, 1980. Both death sentences were later commuted to life on appeal.

OTTIS ELWOOD TOOLE (LEFT) IN A DUVAL, FLORIDA COURTROOM AFTER BEING SENTENCED TO DEATH FOR MURDER AND ARSON IN MAY OF 1984.

April 1985 brought exposure of the so-called "Lucas hoax," but it had little impact on Toole. In 1991, Ottis pleaded guilty to four more Florida slayings, committed during 1980 and 1981, receiving four more life sentences. Prosecutors charged Lucas in the same four cases but declined to extradite him for trial.

A sideshow to the main events occurred in October 1992, when Lucas's pen pal Phyllis Wilcox—a forty-year-old mother and grandmother from Missouri—briefly posed as Becky Powell, claiming that since she existed, Lucas was obviously innocent of her slaying. Investigators soon saw through the ruse, and Wilcox admitted to hatching the deceptive plot after eleven months of soulful correspondence with Henry, claiming that a four-hour prison visit had convinced her Lucas was "the most wonderful man that I had ever met."

As Wilcox told an Internet blogger in 2000, "After our first meeting, my feelings for Henry were stronger than ever before. I had really fallen in love with him and I had to fight to keep Texas from taking him away from me." Stranger still, her husband had instigated their correspondence and accompanied Wilcox on one prison visit, along with their youngest daughter. The strange tribe escaped prosecution and soon vanished from headlines after procuring their fifteen minutes of fame.

Meanwhile, advocates ranging from Amnesty International to Sister Helen Prejean of *Dead Man Walking* fame rallied to Henry's defense, with Amnesty citing "the belief of two former state attorneys general that Lucas was in all likelihood innocent of the crime for which he was sentenced to death." On March 31, 1998, Judge Dan Carter scheduled Henry's execution for June 30. Governor George W. Bush—a staunch advocate of capital punishment, who presided over 152 other inmate deaths during his six years in office—commuted Henry's sentence to life imprisonment on June 26, 1998, marking Lucas as the only condemned prisoner spared from death during Bush's tenure.

Addressing reporters, Bush said "Henry Lee Lucas is unquestionably guilty of other despicable crimes [for] which he has been sentenced to spend the rest of his life in prison. However, I believe there is enough doubt about this particular crime that the state of Texas should not impose its ultimate penalty by executing him." In fact, commutation left Lucas facing five life terms plus 210 additional years for nine other slayings (or eleven, based on contradictory reports).

Helen Prejean panned Bush's decision as being motivated "more by expediency than conscience," with an eye toward his presidential bid in 2000, noting that Bush

CONVICTED KILLER HENRY LEE LUCAS IN JULY, 1998.

made his decision *before* the panel's recommendation of mercy, rendered after the fact by a stacked vote of seventeen to one in the governor's favor. In short, she opined, "Bush showed where the real power lay," making a safe cosmetic move since Lucas would never leave prison alive.

Finally, as far as relatives of many "Lucas victims" were concerned, only Fate would properly adjudicate the crimes of Henry and Ottis.

Death comes to us all, and serial killers—or serial liars—are no exception. Decades of chronic intoxication caught up with Ottis Toole on September 15, 1996, when he died from cirrhosis of the liver at Florida's state prison in Raiford. (Hate-mail collaborator Gerard Schaefer had been hacked to death in his Raiford cell nine months earlier, his mother blaming Toole for the assassination, while authorities charged two-time killer Vincent Rivera.) Toole's medical records fail to support pervasive rumors that he also suffered from AIDS. John Walsh chastised police for failing to seek a deathbed confession from Toole, confirming his guilt in son Adam's murder.

Henry Lucas outlived his old partner by four and a half years. On March 13, 2001, guards found him dead in his cell at the O. B. Ellis Unit in Huntsville, Texas. They logged the official cause of death as heart failure at age sixty-four.

What should we now believe about Lucas and Toole? Amidst the contradictory confessions, recantations, and renewed admissions, along with the analyses and outright lies by fringe observers, is there any hope of finally divining "truth"?

Texas Ranger Phil Ryan, an outspoken critic of his own department's Lucas Task Force, suggested to the *Houston Chronicle* that Henry was "at most responsible for 15 murders." Dr. Eric Hickey, professor emeritus at California State University, Fresno, and dean of the California School of Forensic Studies at San Diego's Alliant International University, cites an unnamed "investigator" who interviewed Lucas multiple times as placing the final body count closer to forty. Even skeptic Sara Knox, writing from halfway around the world at Australia's University of Western Sydney, says that Lucas maintains a "reputation as one of the world's worst serial killers—even after the debunking of the majority of his confessions by the attorney general of Texas."

As for Toole, no one today disputes the six Florida murders for which he was sentenced to life in a cage. The final tally? No one living knows. But was there something in the blood or in their twisted gothic backgrounds that compelled Lucas and Toole to kill and kill again?

Perhaps we might ask Robert Joseph "Bobby Joe" Long, a distant cousin of Lucas, born at Kenova, West Virginia, seventeen years after Henry's birth. Afflicted with a surplus "X" chromosome, Long developed prominent breasts during puberty, suffering untold humiliation before surgery relieved the problem. He also sustained multiple head injuries, purportedly causing hypersexual behavior, and endured a strange relationship with his mother, sharing her bed until his teens, all the while despising her many boyfriends. Married in 1974 and divorced after siring two children, Long later became a serial rapist, claiming an estimated fifty Florida victims between 1981 and 1984. In March 1984, he graduated to murder, strangling at least ten women within eight months. His downfall came in mid-November, when victim Lisa McVey spun a tale of her own abusive childhood to Long, and he released her alive. Her description of Long and his car landed Bobby Joe in jail on November 16th.

Slapped with one death sentence, twenty-eight life prison terms, four ninety-nine-year sentences, and one paltry five-year term (for aggravated assault with a weapon, lacking intent to kill), Long was executed on May 23, 2019, after consuming a meal of roast beef, bacon, French fries, and soda. He made no final statement.

A product of nature, nurture, or an unsavory mixture of both?

It seems unfair to draw from songwriter Dave Matthews's lyrics of "Blood in the Water," but *something* reached across a generation to bind Lucas and Long, blood relatives who never met, just as coincidence or circumstance brought Lucas and Toole together in the 1970s, while Bobby Joe was enduring his ghastly formative years nearby. The final verdict, as with so many cold cases still unsolved across the continent, remains unknown.

6.

"SERIOUS MURDERS": DONALD GASKINS

Murder had become routine for Donald Gaskins by age forty-seven, in the autumn of 1980. A prolific killer, dubbed "the Redneck Charlie Manson" by some reporters, he had claimed his first life at age nineteen, in a jailhouse stabbing that earned him a nine-year sentence for manslaughter. Now, as he approached the half-century mark, he was serving nine consecutive life terms in South Carolina's state prison—one for each of the victims police had uncovered—and that paltry total was only the tip of a grisly iceberg.

Gaskins was long familiar with the varied forms of violent death. It held no mysteries for him, and only slight amusement as he aged. But the murder that he had in mind this time was different, a novelty.

He had never killed a victim on Death Row before.

The chosen target, Rudolph Tyner, was already slated for death by the state, but he wasn't dying fast enough to satisfy some people. A black man condemned for the 1978 holdup murders of white victims Bill and Myrtle Moon at their two-pump service station in Murrells Inlet—Georgetown County's "Seafood Capital of South Carolina"—Harlem native Tyner expected to spin out his life for a decade or more with stays and appeals, before keeping his final date with the electric chair. South Carolina's death penalty statutes had been twice invalidated by U.S. Supreme Court rulings since 1972, and racial aspects of the case lent weight to Tyner's appeals. Thus far, Tyner's worst problem on Death Row was feeding his narcotics habit.

Out in the free world, Tony Cimo—Myrtle Moon's son by a previous marriage—schemed to slash bureaucratic red tape and avenge his mother's death. Through prison contacts, he negotiated for a hit on Tyner, passed along from one con to the next until the buck stopped in the cell of Donald Gaskins, a maintenance trusty housed next door to Death Row. Gaskins's custodial position granted him free access to condemned inmates while he was mending broken pipes, toilets, light fixtures, virtually anything at all. Unknown to Tony Cimo, Gaskins also owned a tape recorder, which he used to capture their negotiations for posterity—a priceless blackmail instrument as good as money in the bank if he should ever manage to escape from custody.

At first, Gaskins decided poison was the way to go. Befriending Tyner on his Death Row errands, he began to slip his fellow killer junk food, marijuana, pills, and heroin. Tyner accepted all of it, unquestioning of Gaskins's generosity, and called for more. Cimo supplied a box of candy spiked with poison "strong enough to kill a horse," but Tyner merely suffered transient stomach pains. Over the next twelve months, Gaskins repeated the experiment five times, lacing his target's food and drugs with ever-stronger toxic doses, all in vain. Tyner lived on, oblivious to the "coincidence" between the arrival of his gifts from Gaskins and his trips to the infirmary.

Six strikes and out. Gaskins gave up on poison and decided he would try a bomb. Tony Cimo supplied the military grade C-4 plastic explosive, hardware, and wiring, smuggled past negligent guards in his hollowed-out boot heels. Meanwhile, Gaskins offered to connect a homemade intercom between his cell and Tyner's for conversations during lockdown, stringing wire through prison heating ducts and building a "receiver" from a plastic cup packed with C-4. Gaskins and Tyner synchronized their watches for a test run on Sunday evening, September 12, 1982.

At the appointed hour, Tyner pressed the loaded cup against his ear and spoke to Gaskins at the far end of the line. As Gaskins later told a journalist, "The last thing he heard through that speaker cup before it blew his head off was me laughing."

Gaskins always enjoyed a good killing—but this time, the last laugh belonged to his jailers. While media reports initially described Tyner's death as suicide, prison snitches started talking. Tony Cimo was interrogated, and he soon confessed the plot. A grand jury indicted Gaskins for murder, Cimo for conspiracy, and two other inmates as accessories.

The state of South Carolina had failed to execute Gaskins for nine previous murders. Now it was prepared to try again.

Few observers would agree with Donald Gaskins's claim that he was "born special and fortunate" on March 13, 1933, in rural Florence County, South Carolina. His mother, Molly Parrott, had quit school at age twelve to help her parents pick cotton and tobacco until a wealthy neighbor, Mr. Gaskins, took a shine to her and she conceived his child. Thereafter, she resided in a shack that Gaskins owned, receiving a dollar for each night he spent in her bed until their son was born, weighing a mere four pounds. Stunted from birth, he quickly earned the nickname "Pee Wee," sometimes labeled "Junior Parrott" as a facetious alternative.

From Mr. Gaskins, Molly progressed to a series of brutal "step-daddies" who paid her for sex, often performed in Pee Wee's presence, when the men would laugh at him for trying to prevent the couplings. Molly married one of them, Hinnant Hanna, in 1943, and Pee Wee acquired four half-siblings in the process. Hanna proved to be a drunk-ard who beat Pee Wee and his own children "just for practice," but Pee Wee would still insist, as an adult, that "I certainly weren't in no way what you could ever call abused."

Yet something was clearly wrong with the boy. He was "pissed off" at girls from his earliest memory, unable to explain the rage coherently. At age ten, he suffered from the onset of a lifelong "bothersomeness," which he described as feeling like "a ball of molten lead rolling around in my guts and up my spine into my head." That feeling presaged outbursts of erratic violence, sometimes assuaged by forays into petty criminal activity.

Matters went from bad to worse in school, where other children teased him mercilessly for his size and the assorted bruises that he bore from home. Teachers whipped him for failing to mesh with his class-mates, until he turned truant and finally dropped out for good at age eleven. One year later, he found work in a garage and displayed surprising skill as a mechanic. Even with his steady income added to the family pot, however, Hinnant Hanna—possibly embarrassed by his stepson's unex-pected talent—ordered him to quit and join in the backbreaking labor of a field hand, for which he earned less money.

In his spare time, Pee Wee made friends with two delinquents, Henry Marsh and Danny Smith. They called themselves the "Trouble Trio," stealing cigarettes and candy from vending machines and enjoying their booty at an abandoned shack in the woods. In 1946, caught spying on girls in a local church outhouse, Pee Wee and Henry received lashings from their parents, while Danny's ex-con father laughed it off. By 1948, the senior Marsh was coaching them through residential burglaries. They bought an old car to range farther afield, patronizing prostitutes in Columbia and Fort Jackson, sometimes teaming up to sodomize younger boys and ensure their victims' silence with threats of mayhem.

In private, The Trouble Trio obsessed over having sex with a virgin, finally settling on Henry's thirteen-year-old sister, Julie. They gang-raped her, but this time their threats failed to intimidate their prey. Julie told her mother what had happened, Mrs. Marsh informed the other parents, and familial wrath descended on the rapists in full force. Danny's father defended his boy with a shotgun, but the other two were strung up by their wrists in a barn and whipped in relays till they bled. Danny's family decamped for parts unknown, followed soon after by the Marshes, but Pee Wee stayed on, regarding Julie's rape as his life's most fulfilling moment to date.

In 1948, Pee Wee met an older man named Walt and hatched a scheme to pick up with his interrupted weekend burglaries. One Saturday, they crept into a house that both presumed empty, but found a sixteen-year-old girl at home. Instead of fleeing from the burglars, she attacked them with a hatchet, chasing both intruders out into the yard. There, Pee Wee managed to disarm her, gashing her arms and scalp with the hatchet before she collapsed, unconscious.

The girl survived and identified Gaskins, and he was soon arrested, while his partner fled the district and escaped. At trial, Pee Wee was charged with assault with a deadly weapon and intent to kill and found guilty on both counts. Junior Parrott heard his true name for the first time when the judge pronounced his sentence, sending Donald Henry Gaskins to the South Carolina Industrial School for Boys at Florence.

Gaskins later said that he received his "real education" at the state reformatory. On his first day as an inmate, a "Boss-Boy" called Poss approached him, informing Gaskins that he would be Poss's "sweetheart" at the school henceforth, or face the consequences. Pee Wee refused, and on his second day he was ambushed in the shower by a gang of twenty-some attackers, beaten down, and sodomized repeatedly. Over the next year, Gaskins spent each night in Poss's bed, unless the Boss-Boy rented him to friends for money to buy cigarettes.

During his thirteenth month in custody, Gaskins escaped with four more victims of the "school's" sexual predators. All were recaptured the next day, but Gaskins bailed out of the truck returning them to Florence and absconded to the shack where he once huddled with the Trouble Trio after robberies. Two days later, a policeman who remembered Pee Wee tracked him to the hideaway and talked him into giving up. His reward: thirty lashes with a strap and thirty days' "hard labor isolation," digging ditches in the broiling daytime heat, with whippings every night for trivial infractions.

When that sentence expired, it was back to Poss and nightly sodomy until Gaskins fled a second time, with one accomplice, remaining at large for six days before bloodhounds ran him down. This time, his punishment was fifty lashes and four months' hard labor, followed by return to his dorm, where Gaskins found "a new Boss-Boy who wasn't so easy to please." This one, Pee Wee recalled, "particularly liked to watch gang-rapes with me on the bottom."

For his third escape, Gaskins fled alone, reaching an aunt's home in Williamsburg County. She persuaded him to return after the warden promised leniency, but it was all a lie. Sentenced to further isolation with a nightly regimen of twenty lashes, Gaskins battled with a guard during his seventh beating and was clubbed unconscious, then packed off to the state mental hospital at Columbia for five weeks' observation. While there, he suffered from a burst appendix, his life saved by emergency surgery. Finally judged sane and fit for "normal" punishment, he returned to Florence in 1950, where light duty soon gave way to threats of whipping in reprisal for his prior misconduct.

Gaskins fled a fourth time, winding up in Sumter, where he joined a traveling carnival. On the road, he met and married a thirteen-year-old girl from the crew—the first of his six wives—on January 22, 1951. After one night together, for his bride's sake, he surrendered to authorities and spent the last three months of his reformatory sentence in solitary confinement.

Released on his eighteenth birthday, an unrepentant Gaskins appeared to settle on a plantation, while he teamed up with former reform school bunkmate "Slick" to loot and burn tobacco barns. They had torched six by Christmas 1956 when Pee Wee's partner fled the state. At work one day, his boss's teenage daughter teased Gaskins with rumors of his arson raids and he retaliated with a hammer, fracturing her skull. Charged with arson, attempted murder, and assault with a deadly weapon, he beat the first count at trial and struck a bargain on the other two, prosecutors promising him eighteen months in prison for a guilty plea. Unhappily for Gaskins, Judge T. B. Greniker scotched the deal, imposing a five-year sentence and adding another year for contempt after Pee Wee called him a son of a bitch.

Gaskins was bound for the Big House.

When Gaskins entered Columbia's South Carolina Penitentiary in fall 1952, it struck him as "the dreariest looking place on earth"—no great surprise, since it was built in 1867 and had been undergoing periodic renovations through the late 1920s. In place of dorms and Boss-Boys, the state pen had cellblocks and "Power Men" who took what they wanted by force, undisturbed by their guards. Gaskins went in expecting another round of gang-rapes; but instead he was ignored until the afternoon, when a hulking con approached him on the yard and told him "You belong to Arthur."

Over the next six months, while Gaskins shared his cell with a brutal rapist, he realized that the only way to save himself was to become a Power Man. To that end, knowing it meant murder, Gaskins started looking for the biggest, toughest victim he could find. He chose Hazel Brazell, a con so vicious that no one on either side of the bars dared call him by his hated given name.

To ingratiate himself with Brazell, Gaskins used the same tactic he would employ with Rudolph Tyner, almost thirty years later. He brought gifts of food from the kitchen, becoming a fixture around Brazell's cellblock, accepted as one of the crowd. On his fifth visit, Gaskins found Brazell on the toilet, only one friend stationed outside his cell. Striking swiftly, he cut Brazell's throat with a stolen paring knife and warned the lookout to flee before guards arrived. "I surprised myself at how calm I was," Gaskins later wrote in his autobiography. "I didn't really feel nothing much at all."

He admitted to killing Brazell "in a fight" and bargained a murder charge down to manslaughter, with two-thirds of the nine-year sentence running concurrent with his pre-existing term. "I figured that was a damn fair deal," Gaskins said, "considering I wouldn't never again have to be afraid of anybody in The Pen no matter how long I was there." He spent six months in solitary and emerged a Power Man in his own right, the "Pee Wee" nickname now a label of respect.

Gaskins breezed through his next two years of confinement, enjoying himself, but 1955 brought news that his wife had filed for divorce. Despondent, he hatched a plot to escape in a garbage drum, jumping from the outbound truck along the highway to Florence. After stealing a car, he drove to Florida and rejoined the carnival at Lake Wales, meeting his next wife in the process. At nineteen, Juney Alice Holden was three years younger than Gaskins. Their marriage lasted just two weeks, before he dropped her at her parents' house and hit the road. They never divorced, but that small technicality would not stop Gaskins from logging four more marriages over the next two decades.

His new love of the moment was Bettie Gates, a sideshow contortionist whose supple body proved irresistible. They left the show together, driving Pee Wee's stolen car to Cookeville, Tennessee, where Gates claimed her brother was jailed pending trial on some undisclosed charge. On arrival, Gates confessed that she was wanted in five states on counts ranging from forgery to armed assault. Gaskins agreed to deliver bail money and a carton of cigarettes, then returned from that mission to find Gates and his car missing from their motel. He was awaiting her return when police came to arrest him, breaking the news that Bettie's "brother"—in fact, her husband—had escaped from jail using a razor hidden with the smokes Pee Wee provided.

Putnam County's sheriff initially accepted Gaskins's tale of being duped, but the recovery of his stolen car and false I.D. resulted in his being jailed on a fugitive warrant from South Carolina. Before his return to the Palmetto State, he served three months in Tennessee for aiding an escape, plus six more for slashing another inmate in a brawl. Back at South Carolina's state pen, he spent a "miserable" time in solitary before FBI agents arrived to charge him with driving a stolen car across state lines. Conviction on that charge, under the Dyer Act of 1919, earned him three years at the federal lockup in Atlanta, Georgia.

Gaskins later described that sentence as his "college education" in crime. His cellmates, whom he dubbed the "Three Wise Men," were bodyguards for imprisoned New York Mafia "prime minister" Frank Costello, who was serving time for income tax evasion and casino skimming. Pee Wee's reputation preceded him, and Costello dubbed him "the little hatchet man," reportedly offering Gaskins work as contract muscle if he ever felt an urge to settle down.

The federal prison term was concurrent with Gaskins's remaining time in South Carolina, a favor from the court that left him eligible for parole in August 1961. Forgiving his escape, the state released him with a new suit, twenty dollars, and a bus ticket to Florence.

Whatever Gaskins may have learned from his prison "college education," it did not include a course on staying out of trouble. Reunited briefly with his mother and stepfather, he returned to work in the tobacco sheds, until an argument with Hinnant Hanna came to blows and Gaskins threatened the older man's life with a pitchfork. From there, he moved in with a cousin and resumed stripping stolen cars, soon reverting to his old pattern of residential burglaries and looking for cheap sex in honky-tonk bars.

Late in 1961, Gaskins had a near-miss with salvation. He went to work for circuit-riding preacher George Todd, driving the minister's van and serving as his general assistant, but the gospel had no impact on Pee Wee. Instead, he seized the opportunity to loot homes while they traveled, selling off whatever he could steal to willing buyers on the road. Along the way, in 1962, he met wife number three, seventeen-year-old Jerri Deloris, who caught his eye despite the fact that she was "old by my standards."

Remarriage, like religion, failed to civilize Gaskins. During his second year with Rev. Todd, he was jailed for statutory rape of a twelve-year-old girl in Florence County. Taken to the courthouse for arraignment, Gaskins slipped out a window, stole a county car, and fled to Greensboro, North Carolina. There, he soon met and married wife number four—a seventeen-year-old Lumbee Indian girl named Leni Oxendine—and abandoned her after three months. "It weren't that I stopped loving her," he later wrote. "It were the edginess and bothersomeness stirring around inside me. I got so edgy and mad at the world, I just had to get away." As for his many wives, Pee Wee insisted "I truly loved them all."

Briefly reunited with wife Jerri in Georgia, Gaskins was en route with her to Florida when a highway patrolman tried to stop him for speeding. Fearing arrest as a fugitive, Gaskins drove his car into a swamp and escaped on foot, leaving Jerri to the law. From there, he returned to North Carolina and wife Leni, but she blew the whistle on him and he was extradited for trial in South Carolina. Jurors in Florence County rejected Pee Wee's argument that sex with pre-teen girls was justifiable. Convicted in 1964, he got six years for statutory rape and two more for his flight from custody.

The state pen in Columbia had been renamed the Central Correctional Institute in Gaskins's absence, but nothing else had changed. He brought his reputation with him and did easy time as a Power Man. In November 1968, Warden Willis McDougald recommended parole on grounds of good behavior, granted on the condition that Gaskins stay out of Florence County for the next two years. Upon release, Pee Wee later said "I was damned determined I never was going back to prison—which didn't mean that I wasn't ever going to do anything illegal again. I just wasn't never planning on getting caught."

That meant getting rid of witnesses, and Gaskins reckoned he was equal to the task.

And in the process, he would have some fun.

Gaskins settled in Sumter, South Carolina, working construction, stripping hot cars on weekends, and cruising bars for sex. He still suffered "them aggravated and bothersome feelings," now accompanied by headaches, stomach cramps, and pain in his groin. Increasingly, he raged and brooded over women who rejected him. He drove compulsively along the Carolina coast, later recalling "It was like I was looking for something special on them coastal highways, only I didn't know what."

In September 1969 he found out.

The hitchhiker was young and blond, bound for Charleston, thumbing rides outside Myrtle Beach. Gaskins picked her up and propositioned her. When she laughed in his face, he beat her unconscious and drove to an old logging road. There, he raped and sodomized his victim, then tortured and mutilated her with a knife. She still clung to life when he weighted her body and sank her in a swamp to drown. Leaving the scene, Gaskins recalled, "I felt truly the best I ever remembered feeling in my whole life."

Gaskins later called that first impulsive homicide his "miracle, a beam of light, like a vision." From that day on, he made a habit of trolling the coastal highways on weekends, seeking victims and exploring future dump sites. By Christmas 1969, he had committed two more "coastal kills—ones where I didn't know the victims or their names or nothing about them." It was recreational murder, refined over time until he could keep his victims alive and screaming for hours on end, sometimes for days.

In 1970, Gaskins allegedly averaged one "coastal kill" every six weeks, experimenting with different torture methods, disappointed when his victims died prematurely. "I preferred for them to last as long as possible," he wrote. The next year, Pee Wee claimed eleven nameless victims, including his first kidnap–slaying of two girls at once. Ideas for tormenting his captives came to Gaskins as he browsed through hardware stores, eyeing the tools. "I never gave no thought to stopping," he admitted. "They was a clock kind of thing. When it was time, I went and killed."

His first male murder victims were acquired by accident, two long-haired boys whom Gaskins took for girls as he drove up behind them in March 1974. Gaskins drove them to a hideout near Charleston, where he sodomized and tortured both, cooking and cannibalizing their severed genitals before he granted them the mercy of death.

The only coastal victim he recalled by name was sixteen-year-old Anne Colberson, picked up near Myrtle Beach in 1971. Gaskins was not hunting at the time, but he refused to miss a golden opportunity. Over four days of rape and torture, he became "real fond of her." Finally, "because she had been so nice to me," Gaskins stunned her with a hammer and cut her throat before dropping Colberson into quicksand.

Pee Wee lost count of the victims he'd murdered for sport between September 1969 and December 1975. They were hard to recall, he explained, "because they're mostly just a jumble of faces and bodies and memories of things I did to them." In terms of numbers, he said, "The closest figure I can come up with is eighty to ninety."

Sadistic murder was addictive for Gaskins. "I finally reached the point where I wanted the bothersomeness to start," he wrote. "I looked forward to it every month, because it felt so good relieving myself of it." The coastal kills were always recreation, though. However numerous the victims, however atrocious their suffering, they meant nothing to Gaskins. The focus of his life lay inland, where murder and business mixed.

Before 1970, despite sporadic incidents of violence with family and friends, Gaskins insisted that he never gave "any real serious thought whatsoever" to killing a personal acquaintance. "The most important thing about 1970," he wrote from prison, "was that it was the year I started doing my 'serious murders'"—defined as slayings of persons he knew, whose deaths required more planning to avoid detection.

His first two "serious" victims were a fifteen-year-old niece of Pee Wee's, Janice Kirby, and her seventeen-year-old friend, Patricia Alsobrook. Gaskins had entertained thoughts of raping Kirby but saw no opportunity until one night in November 1970, when the girls were out drinking, in need of a sober ride home. Gaskins volunteered, taking them instead to an abandoned house where he ordered both to strip. The girls fought for their lives, clubbing Gaskins with a board before he drew a gun and overpowered them, beating them unconscious. After raping both, he drowned the girls and buried them in separate locations. Police grilled Pee Wee about the double disappearance, and while he admitted to talking to the girls on the last night they were seen alive, he claimed they'd left him and driven off in a car with several unknown boys. Without a corpse or other evidence, the trail went cold.

A month later, Gaskins kidnapped, raped, and murdered Margaret "Peggy" Cuttino, the thirteen-year-old daughter of a prominent family, this time leaving the body where it would be found. His alibi looked solid when police came calling, and they later focused on another suspect, William Pierce, already serving life in Georgia for a similar offense. A false confession to Cuttino's murder brought Pierce his second life sentence, a moot point since Georgia had no intention of releasing him. Years later, when Gaskins confessed to the murder, embarrassed prosecutors rejected his statement, insisting that Pee Wee was claiming the murder "for publicity."

Pee Wee interrupted the murder spree to marry his pregnant girlfriend on January 1, 1971; and while she delivered a son in June, it was only a fleeting distraction. His next "serious" murder victim—and the first African American he ever killed—was twenty-year-old Martha Dicks, a transvestite lesbian hanger-on at the garage where Gaskins worked part-time. Dicks seemed infatuated with Gaskins, boasting falsely to friends that they were lovers. Pee Wee tolerated the jokes until Dicks claimed to be carrying his child in March 1972. Inviting her to stay after work one night, he fed Dicks a fatal overdose of pills and liquor, then discarded her corpse in a roadside ditch. Rumors of sex and racism aside, Gaskins maintained, "I didn't kill her for no reason besides her lying mouth."

Soon afterward, Gaskins moved to Charleston with his wife and child, committing his next two "serious murders" there. The victims were Eddie Brown, a twenty-four-year-old gunrunner, and his wife Bertie, described by Gaskins as "the best looking black girl I ever saw." Gaskins sold guns to Brown, including stolen military weapons, but he grew nervous when Brown informed him that federal agents were sniffing around Charleston, seeking illicit arms dealers. Fearing a setup, Gaskins shot the Browns and planted them behind the barn where he'd buried Janice Kirby in 1970.

Gaskins moved to Prospect, South Carolina, in July 1973, after his Charleston home burned down. He blamed arsonists for the fire, but he never identified the supposed culprits. Before year's end, he murdered three more victims, starting with fourteen-year-old runaway Jackie Freeman. Gaskins picked her up hitchhiking, in October, and held her captive for two days of rape, torture, and cannibalism, devouring flesh from her calf while she watched. "I always thought of Jackie as special," he recalled in his memoirs, "not really a serious murder, but likewise not just another coastal kill."

The weekend after Freeman's slaying, Gaskins bought a used hearse and put a sign in the window reading "WE HAUL ANYTHING, LIVING OR DEAD." When asked about it over drinks, he explained that he had purchased the macabre vehicle "because I kill so many people, I need a hearse to haul them to my private cemetery."

His first passengers were twenty-three-year-old Doreen Dempsey and her two-year-old daughter, Robin Michelle. Gaskins knew Dempsey from his carnie days. An unwed mother pregnant with her second child in December 1973, she planned on leaving town that month and accepted Pee Wee's offer of a ride to the local bus station. Instead, he drove into the woods and there demanded sex. Doreen agreed, then balked when Gaskins started to undress her child. Gaskins killed Doreen with a hammer, then raped and sodomized Robin before strangling her to death and burying both victims together. Years later, he would recall his brutal assault on Robin Michelle as the best sex of his life.

Pee Wee's "serious murders" continued in 1974, beginning with thirty-six-year-old car thief Johnny Sellars, who owed Gaskins $1,000 for auto parts and was slow to pay. Finally, tired of excuses, Gaskins lured Sellars to the woods and shot him with a rifle. Later the same night, hoping to forestall investigation of Sellars's disappearance, Gaskins called on Johnny's girlfriend, twenty-two-year-old Jessie Ruth Judy, and stabbed her to death, hauling her corpse to the forest for burial beside her lover.

Horace Jones, another car thief and con man, made the fatal mistake of trying to romance Pee Wee's current wife in August 1974. "That pissed me off," Gaskins recalled in his memoir *Final Truth*. Not the attempt per se, "but the way he went about doing it. I mean if he had come straight to me like a man and asked to make a deal with me for my wife, I would probably have give her to him, for a night or a week, or to keep, if the offer was good enough." As it was, he shot Jones in the woods and stole $200 from the corpse before leaving it in a shallow grave.

In autumn 1974, Gaskins separated from his fifth wife, sending their son off to live with his adult daughter. By that December, Gaskins was a grandfather, and had settled into a routine that suited him and satisfied his needs. That Christmas season, he recalled, was "the happiest and peacefullest I can remember."

Pee Wee didn't know it yet, but he was running out of time.

Writing from prison in *Final Truth*, Gaskins called 1975 "my busiest year and my killingest year." His pace of random murders on the Carolina coast remained "about the same," although he started January with a threesome, including a man and two women. Gaskins described them as "hippie types" from Oregon, whose van had broken down near Georgetown. He offered a lift to the nearest garage, then detoured to a nearby swamp and handcuffed his captives at gunpoint. Before he drowned the trio, Gaskins forced the three to engage in group sex, then castrated the man. Later, he said "It was hard to say which one suffered most. I tried to make it equal."

Pee Wee turned a profit on that triple murder, refurbishing the victims' van and selling it, but he made a critical mistake when he recruited ex-con Walter Neely to help him dispose of the vehicle. Neely drove it to Pee Wee's garage, where Gaskins customized and repainted it for sale out-of-state. The drive made Neely an accessory after the fact, but Gaskins trusted his simple-minded helper to keep a secret, inviting Neely to become his roommate. Before year's end, he would regret that choice.

Pee Wee's first "serious murder" of the year involved a contract to kill wealthy Florence County farmer Silas Yates. He took $1,500 for the job from twenty-seven-year-old Suzanne Kipper, lately furious at Yates for taking back a car, two horses, and other gifts he had given her while they were lovers. Two go-betweens on the contract, John Powell and John Owens, handled negotiations between Gaskins and Kipper. Gaskins recruited Diane Neely, friend Walter's ex-wife, to lure Yates from home on the night of February 12, 1975, claiming her car had broken down near his house. Pee Wee waited in the darkness to abduct Yates at gunpoint and drive him to the woods, where Powell and Owens watched him knife Yates to death, then helped Gaskins bury the corpse. Kipper subsequently married Owens, while Pee Wee used his knowledge of the murder to blackmail her for sex on demand.

The Yates contract came back to haunt Gaskins when Diane Neely moved in with Avery Howard, a thirty-five-year-old ex-convict who Gaskins knew from state prison. She told Howard about the murder, and together, misjudging their mark, they approached Pee Wee with a demand for $5,000 hush money. Gaskins agreed to meet them in the woods outside Prospect and bring the cash. The blackmailers arrived to find an open grave and Gaskins with a pistol in his hand. Two shots, a bit of spadework, and Pee Wee reckoned his problem was solved.

And the human juggernaut rolled on.

Kim Ghelkins was the next to die, a thirteen-year-old friend of Gaskins who enraged him by rejecting his sexual overtures. Pee Wee reacted in typical style by raping, torturing, and strangling her, planting her body in the woods.

Next up: Diane Neely's brother, twenty-five-year-old Dennis Bellamy, teamed with fifteen-year-old half-brother Johnny Knight to loot Pee Wee's chop shop that summer, while he was out of state, thus earning themselves a death sentence when Gaskins returned and discovered their theft in October. Pee Wee took Walter Neely along to help bury the pair in his "private cemetery," sparing time to point out the surrounding graves of Johnny Sellars, Jessie Judy, Avery Howard, and Walter's ex-wife. Again, for reasons never clear, he trusted Neely and allowed him to survive.

By October 1975, Kim Ghelkins's parents knew enough about her movements and acquaintances to suspect Gaskins of murder. A Sumter County deputy sheriff searched Pee Wee's home and found some of Kim's clothes in his closet, afterward securing statements that she was often seen in his company. The evidence would not support a murder charge, but Gaskins was indicted for contributing to the delinquency of a minor.

He returned from another trip to Georgia on November 14, 1975 to find police staked out around his house. Gaskins dodged them and made his way to the local bus station, but officers nabbed him before he could leave. Unable to post bond, Gaskins sat in jail for three weeks before the storm broke. Walter Neely had crumbled under interrogation, telling all to the police on advice from a neighborhood minister. He led authorities to Pee Wee's graveyard, where victims Bellamy and Knight were unearthed on December 4. A day later, diggers found the bodies of Sellars, Judy, Howard, and Diane Neely. On December 10 Walter led them to the graves of Doreen Dempsey and her child. Gaskins struck a pose of injured innocence, but all in vain. Looking back on that chaotic month, he would recall "the coroner had the bodies, Jesus had Walter, and the law had me."

Following a Florence County coroner's inquest on April 27, 1976, Gaskins and Walter Neely were each charged with eight counts of first-degree murder. Police also detained James Judy, husband of the murdered Jessie, on one count of murder and an accessory charge. Prosecutor T. Kenneth Summerford arranged for Gaskins to be tried alone in the Bellamy case, since bullets from the victim's body matched a pistol Gaskins had been carrying when he was nabbed in November 1975.

At the trial, convened on May 24, 1976, Gaskins feigned innocence, naming Walter Neely as Bellamy's lone slayer. Bellamy and Johnny Knight were both alive the last time he had seen them, Gaskins testified, leaving his garage with Neely. For all he knew, Walter had stolen his pistol to murder the men, then replaced it without Pee Wee's knowledge. Jurors dismissed the fable and convicted him on May 28, whereupon Judge Dan McEachin sentenced Gaskins to die.

That verdict frightened James Judy, who was wholly innocent of his wife's murder, into angling for a plea bargain. Police thought he had hired Gaskins to kill his wife and Johnny Sellars out of jealousy; and if a jury felt likewise, he might be sent to the electric chair. Panicked, Judy pleaded guilty in return for a life sentence and went off to serve his time.

Walter Neely was next; tried on eight counts of murder, his attorneys calling him a mentally retarded dupe who bowed to Pee Wee's every whim. "In a way," Gaskins later wrote, "I reckon that was true, too. Walter surely weren't real bright, and he did pretty much anything I asked him, up until he got borned-again and forgot all about what loyalty and friendship meant." Convicted on all counts, Neely still evoked sufficient pathos to escape with a single life sentence.

Pee Wee's attorney urged him to negotiate with prosecutors to avoid another death sentence on his seven pending murder charges. Gaskins agreed, confessing to the crimes and adding details under the influence of "truth serum," but he could have saved the effort. In November 1976, the U.S. Supreme Court invalidated South Carolina's death-penalty statute and his capital sentence was commuted to life, with seven more consecutive life terms tacked on for good measure. The attendant publicity made Gaskins "downright famous" in prison, where even guards dubbed him the "boss hog."

Still unsatisfied, the law came after Gaskins next for Silas Yates's murder, indicting him with John Owens, John Powell, and Suzanne Kipper (now married to Owens). Testifying at trial in Newberry, South Carolina, on April 25, 1977, Gaskins claimed he was the decoy who lured Yates from his home in 1975, while Powell and Owens did the actual killing. All four defendants were sentenced to life. Powell and Owens were paroled in the late 1980s, prompting Gaskins to remark that "some life sentences don't last as long as others." Kipper escaped from custody in October 1990 and remained at large until February 1993, when she was recaptured in Michigan.

South Carolina passed a new death penalty statute in 1985, and prosecutor Ken Summerford filed fresh charges against Gaskins for Johnny Knight's murder, declaring his intent to put Pee Wee on Death Row. Gaskins may have been the only player in the game who didn't realize such retroactive prosecutions are forbidden. Bargaining for life imprisonment, he confessed still more murders, giving lawmen a hitchhiker's corpse in place of Janice Kirby's since he feared discovery of other victims buried near her grave site, so far undisclosed.

The last round of confessions made Gaskins South Carolina's most prolific serial killer to date. Between that reputation and his mechanical skills, it was easy to become a maintenance trustee.

And thus easy to kill Rudolph Tyner in September 1982.

After prolonged investigation, a grand jury indicted Gaskins and Tony Cimo for Tyner's murder, along with inmate go-betweens Jack Martin and Charles Lee. Charges against Lee were dismissed after another convict, James Brown, claimed he had taken the explosive cup to Tyner's cell without knowledge of its purpose. (Brown was never charged.) Prosecutor James Anders tried Gaskins separately, calling Ken Summerford as a witness to display photos of Pee Wee's other victims, and Judge Dan Laney sentenced Gaskins to die.

Cimo, more sympathetic than Gaskins in court, received a twenty-five-year prison sentence with parole eligibility after thirty months. He served the minimum and returned to Murrell's Inlet, where he died from a prescription drug overdose on June 10, 2001.

Gaskins, meanwhile, spent the first three years of his new sentence not on Death Row, but in a rat-infested isolation unit. His attorneys appealed the confinement in 1985, but lawmen cited "reliable information" that Gaskins planned to have cronies kidnap the prosecutor's child and bargain for his release. Only after his petition for rescue from solitary was rejected did police "determine the report was an empty threat."

A year later, freed from solitary after the isolation unit was condemned as unfit for human habitation, Gaskins found Death Row "a lot nicer" than his previous quarters. In 1990, Gaskins and the state's electric chair were moved again, this time to the Broad River Correctional Institution outside Columbia.

Gaskins filled his last months with an art scam, tracing cartoon characters for sale to collectors of Death Row memorabilia and dictating his memoirs on tape for author Wilton Earl (published as *Final Truth* in 1993). As his execution date approached, Pee Wee waxed philosophical. "I truly don't mind dying," he wrote. "I've lived a damned full and good life." He had a "special mind," Gaskins declared, which gave him "permission to kill."

In fact, he decided, it was even better than that. "I have walked the same path as God," Gaskins raved. "By taking lives and making others afraid, I became God's equal. Through killing others, I became my own master. Through my own power I come to my own redemption."

He was even optimistic about his date with the chair, telling Earl, "When they put me to death, I'll die remembering the freedom and pleasure of my life. I'll die knowing that there are others coming along to take my place, and that most of them won't never get caught."

There was no escape for Pee Wee, though. The U.S. Supreme Court rejected his final appeal in June 1991, clearing the way for Gaskins to be executed in September. Hours before his date with "Old Sparky," Gaskins slashed his arms from wrists to elbows with a razor blade he had swallowed days earlier, then regurgitated, in a futile effort to postpone death. Prison medics stitched up his wounds in time for Gaskins to meet his fate at 1:05 a.m. on September 6, 1991. In fact, he went to the chair with his arms stitched and bandaged. His final words: "I'll let my lawyers talk for me. I'm ready to go."

Gaskins was the fourth inmate electrocuted since South Carolina resumed executions in 1985, and the first white man put to death for

A CROWD OUTSIDE THE BROAD RIVER CORRECTIONAL INSTITUTION REACTING AFTER THE EXECUTION OF DONALD "PEE WEE" GASKINS ON SEPTEMBER 6, 1991 FOR THE MURDER OF A FELLOW INMATE.

a black victim's murder in the Palmetto State since 1880. Nationwide, no white convict had died for killing an African American since Kansas hanged Fred L. Brady on April 15, 1944, for robbing and murdering victim Joe Williams. It was a record Pee Wee likely would have disregarded, more concerned as he was with the statistics of his one-man holocaust.

7.

"DOING DOUBLES": GERARD SCHAEFER

In June 1993, I received notice that Florida prison inmate Gerard Schaefer Jr. was suing me in federal court, alleging that a brief mention of him in a book I'd published three years earlier had libeled him and harmed his prospects for parole from a life sentence on two counts of kidnapping and murdering young women. At the time, he had served twenty years, with no parole hearings in sight.

The notice came as no particular surprise. I'd corresponded with Schaefer for several months, at first through his ex-girlfriend turned publisher, then directly to and from the state prison that housed him at

Raiford, in Union County. During our exchange of letters he had denied any killings and pitched the tale of himself as an honorable lawman framed by crooked colleagues for uncovering their ties to drug cartels. Whoever killed the women he stood trial for, he claimed they had been "drug snitches." When I preferred to tell his story as revealed in legal documents, Schaefer sent warnings of costly legal action ahead, should I defy him and neglect to tell what he called his "True Story."

In fact, among his other claims to infamy, Schaefer was well known for serial litigation, harassing journalists who had the temerity to mention him in print. He sued another author in the same week that he filed on me. A second case of *Schaefer v. Newton* followed in 1994, when he learned that I had named him in one sentence from another book, published in 1992. Again, he claimed that his "civil rights" were violated, his parole delayed—a claim I easily disproved by contacting each member of the Florida Commission of Inmate Review, receiving their assurances that they had never read my books nor even heard of me at all. If that were not enough, his first theoretical parole date was in February 2017, a quarter century after he sued me for "delaying" it.

Still, it was necessary to proceed with foiling Schaefer at his game. Federal courts take inmate allegations of abuse quite seriously, as they should, and so the case dragged on for thirteen months before Judge William Elwood Steckler. Along the way, Schaefer withdrew his second case, for reasons I would only later learn, then lost the first with a decisive ruling in my favor. Another case, against a British author, saw him labeled "libel proof." But still, it seemed that he would always find a new excuse to sue again, billing taxpayers for his folly.

And then, a few months later, he was dead, hacked to death in his cell by a fellow inmate and multiple murderer serving life plus twenty years for two slayings committed in 1990. The story should have ended there. And yet, the saga of his sickness still goes on.

* * * * *

Gerard John Schaefer Jr. was born on March 25, 1946, in Neenah, Wisconsin. Neenah's best-known resident was Charles Benjamin Clark, co-founder of the Kimberly-Clark Corporation and later a nineteenth-century U.S. congressman. Coincidentally, Gerard Schaefer Sr. worked as a traveling salesman for Kimberly-Clark. With wife Doris, he called their first child "John" around the house, and two more followed by 1955, daughter Sara and son Gary. While Doris later described her first-born's childhood as "idyllic" and deemed him "just like any other kid," Gerard Jr. felt otherwise.

In the 1970s he described himself to court-appointed psychiatrists as an "illegitimate" child, the unwanted product of a "forced wedding." He claimed his parents' marriage was a sham, adding that his father "was always critical" of him, while Doris was "always on my back to do better." Childhood, in Junior's view, was "turbulent and conflictual." As Junior's sixth birthday approached, Gerard Sr. was frequently absent, beginning a long slide into alcoholism and flagrant adultery.

Worse yet was young Gerard's belief that his father favored sister Sara, viewing his elder son with disdain. That perceived slight seemed to divide Junior's psyche. At times, he wished to be a girl; at others, he contemplated suicide. "I wanted to die," he told analysts. "I couldn't please my father, so in playing games I always got killed." By adolescence, he would graduate to sadomasochism, including self-bondage. From the sixth grade onward, Schaefer said, "I'd tie myself to a tree, struggle to get free, and I'd get excited sexually and do something to hurt myself." The ritual included masturbation coupled with fantasies of "hurting other people, women in particular." At the same age, he "discovered women's underwear—panties. Sometimes I wore them." And again, "I'd want to hurt myself."

Kimberly-Clark transferred his father to Atlanta, Georgia, where his family spent the next two years. In autumn 1958, Junior enrolled at the Marist School, a Roman Catholic preparatory institution founded in 1901. In 1960, the family moved once again, this time to Fort Lauderdale, Florida, where Schaefer's parents promptly joined yachting and country clubs. Gerard Jr. enrolled as a freshman at Saint Thomas Aquinas High School, where yearbooks list him as a member of the football team during his sophomore and junior years, although no one recalls him taking the field or joining in any other group activity.

Ex-classmates recall him as a loner, "weird" and "out of it." One claimed Schaefer would "practically stand on his head to see up a girl's skirt." In class, he angered nuns by challenging religious dogma and once penned an essay scientifically refuting the virgin birth of Jesus.

Schaefer's only high school friends identified in print to date were Mike McGonigle and John "Jack" Dolan. Neither considered Gerard a close friend, though Dolan sometimes double-dated with him. Schaefer served as best man at McGonigle's 1968 wedding. Dolan joined the Navy after graduation, but he met Schaefer again in college and would briefly share a house with him in 1970 under disturbing circumstances.

Schaefer's most influential acquaintance was his first sexual partner, called "Cindy," "C. W.," or "Cass" in his letters. In later psychiatric sessions, he called Cindy "extremely intelligent," although she wears a different face in his private correspondence. In 1991, he wrote "C. W. was a sexual disaster area who literally couldn't come unless she was slapped into insensibility, her clothing actually ripped off her back and her ass; all the while hearing what a dirty little wet assed slut she was, a rotten little sex slut on her way to Hell, etc. etc. After a few years of that I knew my way around masochistic females. That's not my erotic tastes [*sic*] personally but I was interested in it academically."

During Schaefer's senior year, as a psychiatrist reported in 1973, Cindy "went off to college and left him. That day he went into the woods and tied himself with a rope to the trees and hurt himself in the masochistic way he used to do when he was younger. This was the first time in more than two years."

Decades later, controversy surrounded the date of Schaefer's first murder. In various letters and pieces of "killer fiction," he first claimed 1965, then pushed it back to 1962, at age sixteen. In one published tale, Schaefer said his first murder was "accidental," that he'd found himself surprised to have strangled a girl while "fooling around" with a garrote. Later in the same piece, he claimed seven kills before he first had "normal sex" with a girl, the high school student who succeeded Cindy.

After Schaefer's death, Detective Dave Kelly from North Miami Beach reportedly told author Sondra London, "I personally believe Schaefer was responsible for a lot more crimes than he was confined for. I believe he probably started his activities in his early teen years, probably 12 to 14, and I'm talking murder, not just his sexual activities."

In spring 1964, Schaefer attended a high school dance, where he met brunette Sandy Stewart, one year his junior at age seventeen. Stewart admits being swept off her feet by the "dazzling young stranger." At the evening's end, she declined to give him her phone number but told him her surname. The next day, Schaefer dialed each Fort Lauderdale Stewart in turn until he found the right number and asked Sandy out on a date.

He became Stewart's first lover, impressing her as sensitive and enthusiastic, eager to please. Schaefer concealed that passion around Sandy's parents, often joining them for dinner and reportedly accompanying the Stewarts on at least one holiday vacation. Other times, he took Sandy into the Everglades, where Schaefer loved to spend time hunting and fishing. When she couldn't bring herself to kill an animal for "sport," he seemed amused, but didn't press the issue.

Life seemed perfect through early summer 1964, when John graduated and began considering his higher education plans. Sandy had another year of high school ahead of her, but Fort Lauderdale and environs teemed with colleges, if Schaefer hoped to stay close with his steady girl. Yet cracks had opened, both in Schaefer's mind and in the apple-pie façade he had erected to encircle their relationship. Before long, Sandy felt the change as well.

If any doubts remained concerning Schaefer's psychosexual confusion, he put them to rest at age eighteen. Despite his ongoing affair with Sandy Stewart, he decided to become a priest, applying to Miami's Saint John Vianney College Seminary. The seminary turned him down, and while their reasons were not publicly disclosed, Schaefer summarized them nine years later, to a court-appointed psychiatrist. "They said I didn't have enough faith. I didn't think it was fair." In retaliation, he deserted Catholicism.

September 1964 found Schaefer enrolled at Broward Community College, where his first semester's grades were mediocre. His favorite class was English, taught by novelist Harry Crews, whom Schaefer in later years often cited as the inspiration for his own unique style of writing.

Otherwise, Schaefer preferred hunting in the Everglades to study. He continued dating Sandy Stewart; but for her, their relationship felt more like therapy than romance, with Schaefer pouring out his angry, often tearful revelations of an urge to kill the "evil" women who aroused him. One such was Leigh Hainline, a neighbor and sometime tennis partner two years his senior, who allegedly disrobed before her bedroom window to taunt him. Another female neighbor of Schaefer's had the temerity to sunbathe in her own front yard, "flaunting" herself to enrage him.

For the sunbather—never identified—he told Sandy of plans to club her with a baseball bat, wrap her in a blanket, and convey her to the Everglades in his father's boat, where he would shoot her and leave her for the alligators. According to Stewart, Schaefer never killed that neighbor but "actually did sexually assault her," later recording the details in a work of "fiction" titled "Gator Bait." That story describes its first-person narrator invading the neighbor's home by night, catching her asleep, and holding her at knifepoint while he masturbates onto her buttocks. He then urinates on her head and pillow, chokes her unconscious, and writes "whore" on her back with lipstick, before finally stealing money from her purse.

At last, in summer 1965, Sandy was fed up enough to dump him. Schaefer pined and stalked her, watching her on dates with other boys and sending her notes filled with third-rate doggerel. Then, as he later told Dr. Mordecai Haber, "I started to take it out on myself. I became a masochist." Specifically, he once again tied himself to trees, a rope around his waist, and masturbated while struggling to free himself. Soon, he graduated to attacks on livestock, telling Dr. Haber "I'd cut them up, cut off their heads with a machete, and have intercourse with them."

Back at BCC in autumn 1965, Schaefer's homicidal fantasies still obsessed him, and he finally confessed them to English teacher Betty Owens. She referred Schaefer to Dr. Neil Crispo, Director of Student Activities, for help. As Crispo recalled their meeting to the *Miami Herald,* Schaefer omitted mention of his urge to murder women, digressing to discuss Army enlistment. "I asked him why he wanted to join," Crispo recalled. "He said he 'would like to kill things.'"

Crispo referred Schaefer to Dr. Adolph Koch, who later had no memory of meeting Gerard, although he told Crispo that "someone from the school psychology department had contacted Schaefer's mother." Doris thought it was Koch himself who recommended treatment for her son at the Henderson Mental Health Center in Lauderdale Lakes.

After Gerard presented himself at the clinic, Doris told the *Herald,* "I asked the psychiatrist what John's problem was, but he said he couldn't tell me. He said, 'If I disclose anything to you, you'll be looking for something. You might be overly suspicious.' He said I should leave him alone and not bug him." Meanwhile, she said, "The psychiatrist told him to write down everything that went through his mind. It was supposed to help him somehow."

Decades later, Schaefer blamed Sandy Stewart for his descent into sadism and homicide. "I will tell you here and now," he wrote to her, "that plenty of young women died because you couldn't help me solve my various crises in 1965. I tried to tell you about it but you couldn't deal with it. You bolted, abandoned me; that's when it started."

Schaefer completed one semester at BCC in 1965 before he found a new preoccupation, in the form of "Moral Re-Armament," a movement founded in May 1938 as a response to Depression-era militarism in Europe. By the 1960s, MRA was best known for "Up with People," a clean-cut super-patriotic musical troupe that urged fans to quit school and join them on tour. Schaefer traveled with their "Sing Out '66" troupe between February and July, where he met Martha "Marty" Fogg, who would later become his wife.

Back at BCC again in autumn 1966, Schaefer completed that year without another interruption and sat through an eight-week 1967 summer term to graduate with an associate degree in business administration that he'd never use.

Unknown to those around him, Schaefer had crossed the line from killing livestock to pursuit of humans—and not always single victims. Long afterward, from prison, he would write "Doing doubles is far more difficult than doing singles, but on the other hand it also puts one in a position to have twice as much fun. There can be some lively discussions about which of the victims will get to be killed first. When you have a pair of teenaged bimbolinas bound hand and foot and ready for a session with the skinning knife, neither one of the little devils wants to be the one to go first. And they don't mind telling you quickly why their best friend should be the one to die."

Authorities suggest Schaefer's first "doubles" were twenty-one-year-old Nancy Leichner and twenty-year-old Pamela Ann Nater, casual acquaintances who went on a picnic with the "Aquaholics" scuba diving club at Altoona, Florida, on October 2, 1966. The petite, attractive girls—one blonde, the other brunette—were accompanied by

Leichner's fiancé and Nater's steady boyfriend, but they were last seen walking off together, unaccompanied, entering one of the site's nature trails. Behind them, on a picnic table, they'd left their street clothes and shoes, their purses, Leichner's eyeglasses, and other personal items. Searchers scoured fifteen square miles when the women failed to return, but no trace of them has been found to this day. Polygraph tests cleared their male companions of any suspicion, and, three decades later, investigators declared themselves "certain" that Schaefer abducted and murdered both women.

In January 1968, Schaefer enrolled at Florida Atlantic University in Boca Raton, seeking a teacher's certificate. Cut off from the priesthood and washed out of Moral Re-Aarmament, he saw education as the next best way to mold young minds.

Residing in a dormitory for the first time, he found Jerry Webster living down the hall and renewed their acquaintance from high school. Schaefer also submitted stories to various fiction magazines, recounting his outdoor adventures, but none was published.

The war in Vietnam had soured for America in early 1968. The draft accelerated, and by April Schaefer's lackluster grades no longer supported a student deferment. Once gung-ho to join the Army and "kill things," he'd changed his mind and dreaded being posted in harm's way. That month, when ordered to report for his induction physical, he left a suicide note in his dorm room and fled. Jerry Webster later told the *Miami Herald,* "When they called me and told me he left a suicide note, I drove out that night to where we used to practice target shooting and found John. He did it to help him get the deferment. He was already seeing a psychiatrist to help him stay out of the army."

Decades later, Schaefer and his medical records told a different story. On May 20, 1968, Dr. Raymond Killinger, FAU's resident psychiatrist, referred Schaefer to the Florida University Testing and Evaluation Center "for psychological evaluation on an emergency basis." Psychometrist R. R. McCormick sat with Schaefer for 150 minutes, reporting "excellent" rapport and test results "prolific in psycho-dynamic information." McCormick found that Schaefer "is immature, has poor ego control, is aggressive and rebellious and primarily has an intense father conflict. In addition, his personality dynamics incline him to blame others for his own difficulties. He is extremely confused in terms of self-image and is alienated from himself and others." McCormick noted "decreased ego control and impairment in reality testing that is often found among psychotics or individuals with intra-cranial pathology." At the end of their meeting, Schaefer said "I feel fine but at times I feel different—like it isn't real. Not like I black out, but things just go."

Decades later, Schaefer treated the whole episode as a humorous scam. He wrote "I got drafted. I got down to the point to be sworn in, and in my best thespian manner, asked if it was gonna be OK to be in the army if I'm queer? Fastest dismissal you ever did see. Oh, they interrogate you but the key is to be sincere. Of *course* I want to be in the army, I just wondered if there was any rule against wearing panties? Threw me right out the door."

Schaefer also claimed he supported the fraud by attending classes in nylons and a garter belt, but no classmates recall him turning up in drag. Tellingly, that version of events only surfaced in 1973, when homicide detectives found photos of a "male figure" clad in lingerie among the many items seized from Doris Schaefer's home.

Dodging Vietnam was relatively simple, but Schaefer's long war on the home front continued. Gerard Sr. lost his job and found a mistress in May 1968, bringing her home to meet Doris in July, whereupon Doris filed for divorce, charging Gerard Sr. with adultery and habitual drunkenness. Seething, Gerard Jr. quit his summer construction job and embarked on a hunting trip to Michigan, later claiming he spent August in Chicago "with a cadre from SDS"—the radically anti-war Students for a Democratic Society—protesting the Democratic National Convention.

Wherever Schaefer spent his summer, he returned to Florida accompanied by Marty Fogg, now his fiancée. Mike McGonigle opposed the wedding as "crazy," while Jerry Webster found "genius" Marty too intelligent for Schaefer. Nonetheless, they married in December 1968, with McGonigle as best man. The couple moved in with Doris while Schaefer returned to FAU in spring 1969, still pursuing a teacher's certificate.

Briefly, they presented a façade of wedded bliss, but their union was doomed.

On his first student-teaching application, Schaefer wrote "I believe that the teacher should strive to reflect and preserve the attitudes and standards of the community in which he teaches since his actions are influential to the children in his charge." It didn't wash at Plantation High, where he lasted only a few weeks before the school canned him for "trying to impose his moral and political views on his students." Principal Bill Haines termed Schaefer's behavior "totally inappropriate."

Winter tested Schaefer's marriage. He was jobless, living with Marty in their own apartment; but as Mike McGonigle's wife told reporters, "He couldn't care less. He went hunting and fishing all the time. He wasn't mature about it. He wasn't responsible."

Unknown to Marty and the McGonigles, Schaefer was killing again.

Schaefer's parents finally divorced in September 1969, as their eldest son returned to FAU. Three days after classes started, a mysterious fate overtook an ex-neighbor, once the object of Gerard's teenage lust and self-righteous fury.

Leigh Hainline married Charles Bonadies on August 21, 1969, but their union—like Schaefer's—soon dissolved into constant arguing. One bone of contention was Leigh's claim that ex-neighbor Schaefer had offered her a job with the Central Intelligence Agency, starting at

$20,000 per year. On September 8, Charles found their apartment empty, and a note from Leigh saying she'd left for Miami. She never returned, and police found her car abandoned in a Fort Lauderdale parking lot.

Leigh's family hired a private detective. Schaefer initially denied knowledge of her whereabouts, but later told her brother that she'd called him before leaving home for Cincinnati. (CIA headquarters is in Langley, Virginia.) Her name did not appear on any flight's passenger list. Charles filed for divorce on October 6, and it was granted on March 10, 1970. Another eight years passed before Leigh's bullet-punctured skull surfaced at Boca Del Mar.

Schaefer took another stab at student teaching in autumn 1969, but he'd learned nothing from the first round. Following a series of harangues in his class on "Americanism vs. Communism," supervisor Richard Goodhart removed him on November 11. This time, the verdict went beyond rejection. Goodhart says "I told him when he left that he'd better never let me hear of his trying to get a job with any authority over other people, or I'd do anything I could to see that he didn't get it." Four years later, Schaefer blamed the school, telling psychiatrists "They only wanted black people."

Schaefer withdrew from FAU again, blaming marital problems. For once, it was closer to the truth than most of his excuses. After eleven months, his marriage was failing, though another half-year would pass before Marty filed for divorce, citing Gerard for "extreme cruelty."

Schaefer claimed his next known victim in December, a month after he blew his second teaching gig. The victim was twenty-two-year-old Carmen Hallock, nicknamed "Candy," a cocktail waitress who earned enough working nights to enroll as a full-time college student. She also briefly dated Jack Dolan. Lunching with her ex-sister-in-law on December 18, Hallock mentioned a date she had that evening, with "a teacher" from BCC who allegedly visited the Bahamas most weekends, returning with "lots of money." He'd offered Hallock some kind of "undercover" work that featured an apartment in Manhattan or Washington, D.C., with all expenses paid. Hallock seemed upbeat when she left work that night, later driving home to draw a bath. After that, she vanished.

On Christmas Day, relatives found Hallock's puppy, unfed for days, and the bathtub filled with water long since cold. Her car keys and driver's license were missing, the car found later at a park near home.

In March 1970, Schaefer petitioned FAU administrators to alter his records, changing his November 1969 withdrawal to an "incomplete" and readmitting him as a full-time student. Marty filed for divorce on May 2, and Schaefer failed to contest it.

Schaefer rebounded from the break-up with a month-long summer trip to Europe and North Africa. He later bragged of victims murdered "on three continents," and while this journey might account for some, no homicides outside of the United States have been confirmed.

Back at FAU that fall, Schaefer supported himself as a night watchman, renting a house in Osceola Village off State Road 84, sharing the digs with former Saint Thomas Aquinas classmate Jack Dolan. Dolan recalled the home's decrepit state, saying "I couldn't wait to get out of there. I was completely disgusted and a little bit scared. John was just getting a little bit weird."

As an example of that "weirdness," Dolan said Schaefer had shown him snapshots from his summer abroad, then said "I've got some other pictures too" but refused to display them, adding "You don't want to see those pictures." Three years later, when detectives found them at Doris Schaefer's home, Gerard was using Dolan as a scapegoat for his crimes.

On December 29, 1970, two Pompano Beach girls—nine-year-old Peggy Rahn and eight-year-old Wendy Stevenson—met for the first time on their last known day alive. They left other friends to buy ice cream and disappeared forever.

Polygraph tests cleared friends and family. On December 30, a store clerk reported a man buying ice cream for two young girls the previous afternoon. He identified photos of Peggy and Wendy, describing their companion as white, twenty-five to thirty years old, sandy-haired, around six feet tall and weighing 190 to 200 pounds. The clerk identified the stranger's car as a metallic blue 1966 or '67 Chevrolet with a vinyl top and wire wheels, license number unknown.

In 1973, Florida prosecutors publicly accused Schaefer of snatching the girls, and while he denied it publicly, in a private letter penned sixteen years later he admitted to roasting and cannibalizing both victims.

Security work had one sweet fringe benefit: it introduced Schaefer to Teresa Dean, seven years his junior. They dated while he pursued a degree in geography, which he attained in August 1971, and they celebrated by marrying on September 11.

Alas, Schaefer's degree was useless without a teaching license. He decided, instead, to become a cop.

Law enforcement training at BCC required twenty-two weeks of eight-hour days. But there was a drawback for Schaefer: first, enrollees had to be hired and sponsored by some certified agency. Schaefer tried the Broward County Sheriff's Office but failed its psychological exam for undisclosed reasons. His next stop: Wilton Manors, twelve miles north of Fort Lauderdale, where Chief Bernard Scott and twenty-six officers policed eleven thousand residents. Scott hired Schaefer in August 1971, unaware of his failed psych exam. In September, Schaefer entered the academy's training program, emerging as a probationary officer in January 1972.

Belinda Hutchins was a twenty-two-year-old wife and mother, living with husband William in Fort Lauderdale and working as a cocktail waitress, when Schaefer earned his badge. She had an eye for easy money, and was nabbed in a November 1970 prostitution sting, paying a $252 fine. That was Belinda's sole arrest, but sources claim she flaunted extramarital affairs and that William grappled with "drug problems." On January 4, 1972, William and their two-year-old daughter watched Belinda enter a light-blue Datsun sedan and drive away out of their lives. William reported Belinda missing on January 5, but the search went nowhere. Eighteen months later, *Inside Detective* claimed Belinda "kept a diary containing the names of many men, some of which would be recognized if made public." One name—"Jerry Sheppard"—meant nothing to police or Belinda's family. Only in May 1973, when viewing Schaefer's Datsun, would William Hutchins say "That's the car."

On February 29, 1972, thirteen-year-old Debora Lowe disappeared while walking the mile from her home to school in Pompano Beach. When she failed to arrive, administrators phoned her home and a search began. Police mistakenly believed she'd run away to visit friends in West Virginia. Subsequent investigation revealed that Gerard Schaefer had once worked with Debora's father and had visited her home numerous times, while the Lowes also attended cookouts at Schaefer's place on several occasions. Debora's family believes that Schaefer snatched and murdered her.

While females vanished in South Florida, probationary officer Schaefer worked the streets of Wilton Manors, having trouble almost from the start. Chief Scott later said his new man didn't have "an ounce of common sense. He used poor judgment, did dumb things." As one example, Scott cited a day when Schaefer, assigned to work the scene of a traffic collision, deserted his post to eat a snack.

Fellow officers reportedly complained that Schaefer was "badge-heavy," though Chief Scott denied it. FBI profiler Robert Ressler went further than that, claiming Schaefer was cited for stopping female drivers and later phoning them for dates. Neither Scott nor Ressler reported a case I unearthed in 2018, where Schaefer was fired in April 1972 for hanging an alleged drunk driver upside-down from a highway bridge. The incident prompted Chief Scott to demand psych tests on all future recruits.

In fact, however, Scott relented when Schaefer tearfully sought a second chance on April 19; but one day later, other departments contacted Scott, reporting Schaefer's applications for employment. Fed up, Scott told his fellow chiefs "I would put on a uniform and walk the streets myself before I would have him back. I didn't want him around."

Schaefer cast his eyes northward to Martin County, where newly appointed Sheriff Robert Crowder, one year Gerard's senior, needed help. Schaefer forged a letter of recommendation over Chief Scott's signature, and was hired on June 30 with no background investigation.

Crowder regretted that mistake within three weeks.

Pamela Wells (blonde) and Nancy Trotter (brunette) were strangers when they met in Stuart, Florida, on July 20, pretty teens who'd hitchhiked from Texas and Illinois, respectively. On July 21, they sunbathed at Jensen Beach, then met Schaefer in uniform as they departed. He falsely told them that hitchhiking was illegal and drove them to their rented lodgings, offering a ride back to the beach the next morning.

He kept the date, arriving in civilian garb, claiming he'd been "temporarily assigned" to plainclothes duty, a light-blue Datsun replacing yesterday's squad car. En route to the beach, he offered to show them "an old Spanish fort" on Hutchinson Island. Instead, he took them to a decrepit building swarming with mosquitos and began interrogating them.

Were there drugs at their shared apartment or elsewhere in Stuart? he asked. The new arrivals pleaded ignorance, whereupon Schaefer "told us he could dig a hole and bury us, no crime without a victim." Next he switched to discussion of ransom payments or selling the girls to "his sheik" as sex slaves. Finally, he handcuffed both girls, tied ropes around their necks, and balanced them on gnarled tree roots where slipping off meant slow strangulation, then drove off to report for his daily patrol shift. In Schaefer's absence, the girls escaped and reached a highway as a sheriff's cruiser passed and ferried them to headquarters.

Schaefer returned to find his victims missing, panicked, and raced back to tell Sheriff Crowder "You're going to be mad at me. I've done something foolish." He'd "overdone" his job, he claimed, trying to "scare" two girls out of future hitchhiking "for their own good." It was a "dumb mistake" but well intentioned.

Crowder fired him on the spot, charging Schaefer with two counts of aggravated assault and two more of false imprisonment. Schaefer posted $15,000 bail pending trial in November, while Crowder faced defeat in that month's election campaign.

Impending trial meant little to Schaefer. First, he took road trips to Michigan and the Dakotas, then came home to stalk more female prey.

Susan Place and Georgia Marie Jessup were newly minted friends in September 1972. One year apart in age—Susan was blond and seventeen, Georgia (nicknamed "Crystal") was brunette and sixteen—they took remedial classes where both were struggling to make up lost high-school credits. Aside from spotty academic skills, the girls also shared a love of music, lounging on Florida's beaches and hanging out with quasi-hippie types. Both girls were open to new friendships and discussed a life of ease, out on the open road.

Georgia met Schaefer first, as homicide detectives reconstructed the event. One night he visited her home, introducing himself to her father as "Jerry Shepherd," a self-described "outdoorsman." Days later, on September 27, Georgia left home with a suitcase, first penning a note that read "I have to find my head." That same night, "Shepherd" arrived at Susan's home with Georgia. Place told her parents, "We're just going to the beach to play guitar." Vaguely suspicious, mother Lucille Place noted the license plate on "Jerry's" blue-green Datsun, unconsciously omitting one of its first two numbers. The girls never returned, but police were blasé, telling the worried parents, "They're probably just shacking up somewhere."

On October 23 two fourteen-year-olds, Mary Briscolina and Elsie Farmer, vanished from Pompano Beach. Farmer's parents reported her missing on October 24, while Briscolina's waited a week. Again, police seemed unconcerned.

In November, Schaefer pleaded guilty on one assault charge; the other counts were dismissed. Judge D. C. Smith called him "a perfect jackass and a thoughtless fool," imposing a one-year jail term with three years' probation, with incarceration deferred until January 15.

Schaefer had two full months to kill.

On January 7 or 8, 1973—accounts differ—nineteen-year-old friends Collette Goodenough and Barbara Wilcox left Mississippi, hitchhiking toward Florida. Families waited in vain for the women to come home.

Schaefer surrendered on January 15, cheered by the prospect of early release for good behavior inside, whereupon his hunting could resume, but he reckoned without rotten luck. In prison, Schaefer wrote more stories, speaking to cellmates of plans for publication.

Construction workers found Elsie Farmer's skeletal remains on January 17 and retrieved Mary Briscolina's a month later, buried two hundred yards away. Dental records identified them but their autopsies revealed no cause of death.

In March, Lucille Place realized her error in transcribing "Jerry Sheppard's" license number and advised police, who finally traced Schaefer's Datsun. Susan's family identified the car, while William Hutchins linked it to wife Belinda's disappearance in January 1972. From jail, Schaefer denied knowing the lost victims and refused to take a polygraph exam. Cellmate Gene Floyd later described Schaefer shredding his latest stories, flushing them down a toilet.

On April 3, hikers found remains of missing victims Place and Jessup near Blind Creek, on Hutchinson Island. Dental records identified both. A bullet hole marked Place's jaw. Geography prompted detectives to remember survivors Trotter and Wells, left bound eight miles from the Place–Jessup murder site.

Four days later, officers searched Doris Schaefer's home, where Gerard had stored belongings in a spare bedroom. Their haul included photos of nude women and a "male figure" wearing lingerie; a history of torture and its publisher's letter to Schaefer, claiming inability to offer more specific details of women's executions; fragmentary stories depicting women tortured and slain, including one victim named "Carmen"; newspaper articles reporting the disappearance of Leigh Bonadies and Carmen Hallock; and pieces of women's jewelry, some bearing engraved initials.

More telling were various personal items, including five pieces of I.D. for Collette Goodenough and a notebook of poems she'd written, Barbara Wilcox's birth certificate, and two gold-filled teeth identified by Carmen Hallock's dentist. Relatives linked one piece of jewelry to Mary Briscolina, and three more to Leigh Bonadies.

Schaefer had a "logical" explanation for everything. His stories, he claimed, were "therapeutic" fiction, an explanation confirmed by mother Doris. Mention of a murdered "Carmen" was coincidental. Leigh Bonadies had given him jewelry as "collateral for a loan" before she left for parts unknown. He'd "found" I.D. from Goodenough and Wilcox while patrolling as a deputy but never turned it in to headquarters.

He also named an alternative suspect.

Jack Dolan, Schaefer said, had confessed to killing Bonadies and Hallock. *He* must have stashed Carmen's teeth in Schaefer's desk, later moved into Doris's home. As to why he sat on Jack's confessions while pretending to enforce Florida's laws, Schaefer could only shrug.

No one except for Schaefer's family believed him. On May 13, prosecutors charged him with the Place–Jessup murders. Five other cases were deferred pending discovery of remains and/or medical pronouncements of homicide. An article in *Time* magazine reported him as suspected of "at least 20 murders"; the *Miami Herald* listed twenty-six dead or missing females; and the *Palm Beach Post-Times* tallied twenty-eight, some unnamed.

Florida is known for executing murderers, but the U.S. Supreme Court had invalidated capital punishment statutes nationwide in 1972. While those laws awaited amendment and federal certification, Schaefer's penalty could not exceed life imprisonment.

Public defender Elton Schwartz opposed even that, claiming that Schaefer suffered from "a serious mental disorder" precluding conviction. Four psychiatrists examined Schaefer; all agreed that he was strange,

THE AREA WHERE THE BODIES OF TWO GIRLS WERE FOUND IN MAY OF 1973. GERALD SCHAEFER, A FORMER POLICEMAN, WAS ACCUSED OF THIS AND OTHER SERIAL MURDERS.

but none deemed him legally insane. The court scheduled his double-murder trial for September 17.

Testimony from Susan Place's family, coupled with Georgia Jessup's purse (found at Doris Schaefer's home) and combined with Gerard's graphic blood-and-guts "fiction," led to Schaefer's conviction on September 27, one year to the day since Place and Jessup had vanished. On October 4, he received two concurrent life sentences and was dispatched to the state prison at Stark.

On November 17, Schaefer's wife Teresa filed for divorce, announcing plans to wed attorney Elton Schwartz. For the next twenty-three years, Schaefer would cite that fact as proof that he had been "framed" by his own lawyer, acting in concert with corrupt police to silence Schaefer's revelations of official involvement in drug trafficking.

He was a martyr, Schaefer claimed, on par with Manhattan's Frank Serpico.

Schwartz married Teresa on December 29.

On January 5, 1977, picnickers found remains of two dismembered corpses in St. Lucie County, identified later as Collette Goodenough and Barbara Wilcox. Again, decomposition barred discovery of how they died.

In April 1978, construction workers found a human skull near Boca Raton. Punctured by bullets, the skull was identified in May as a relic of Leigh Bonadies.

In prison, Schaefer had embarked on a career as an unlicensed cell-block lawyer for his fellow inmates, while pursuing a series of dead-end appeals in his own case. Some inmates appreciated him; others despised him after revelations came out of his correspondence with convicts in other prisons in which he posed as a lovesick woman, wheedling details of their crimes that prosecutors might find useful.

On the side, he sued any author who mentioned his case in print, pleading poverty while taxpayers assumed his ever-rising legal costs. Aside from yours truly, targets of frivolous harassment claims—all ultimately dismissed—included Robert Ressler, British writer Colin Wilson, and would-be biographer Patrick Kendrick, who was forced to defer marriage in the face of mounting lawyers' fees.

In 1979, Schaefer announced his third marriage, to Filipina mail-order bride "Elen." She reached America in July 1980, lived briefly with Schaefer's father and Gerard Sr.'s second wife, then obtained her coveted green card and dropped her convict husband.

Five years later, posing as underage prostitute "Dee Dee Kelly," Schaefer collaborated with Miami police and U.S. Postal Inspectors to convict international "child porn king" Mervyn Cross, supporting federal charges and thereby branding Schaefer as a jailhouse "snitch."

In August 1985, Schaefer faced charges of plotting to escape and then murder Elton and Teresa Schwartz, his prosecutor, and the judge who'd sentenced him to life. Foiled in that scheme, Schaefer befriended fellow convicted serial killers Ted Bundy, Gerald Stano, Bernard Giles, and Ottis Toole (see Chapter 5). He played Cyrano de Bergerac for semi-literate Toole, penning a ghoulish extortion letter to TV personality John Walsh that demanded $50,000 for directions to the headless corpse of his murdered son Adam.

Walsh gave the letter to police, but neither sadistic inmate was penalized. Schaefer *did* receive thirty days in solitary, allegedly "for submitting a story to a magazine." As Schaefer explained, "The editor was so upset he wrote to the prison demanding I be punished."

Florida's parole board scheduled Schaefer's first hearing for 2017, when he was seventy-one.

In February 1989, Schaefer received a letter from ex-girlfriend Sandy Stewart, reborn as successful author Sondra London. Between March and May, Schaefer sent London seven grisly stories, later published with fragments seized from his mother's home in 1973 under the title *Killer*

Fiction. London explored Schaefer's "frame-up" fantasy, but her initial credence soured as Schaefer penned boasts of narcotics trafficking, association with satanic cults, and high rank in the Dixie Mafia. He also confessed to a long series of murders, immodestly calling himself "a master criminal" and "the greatest SK [serial killer] of them all."

As London rejected Schaefer's claims of innocence, threats followed. One such passage read: "I am *not* of your society anymore. I am of the criminal underworld. My word is my bond. Your society does not understand that anymore. If you betray my trust I can, *if* I choose, have you and your kid dead at the bottom of the Chattahoochee river within 30 days. Such matters take longer when I can't get near a phone."

On paper he confessed to slaying six named victims, then elaborated in January 1991, writing: "I am the top SK and I can prove it. In 1973 I sat down and drew up a list. As I recall, my list was just over 80. I was the best."

He raised the ante one day later, writing: "I'm not claiming a huge number. I would say it runs between 80 and 110, but over eight years and three continents. One whore drowned in her own vomit while watching me disembowel her girlfriend. I'm not sure that counts as a valid kill. Did the pregnant ones count as two kills? It can get confusing."

On September 18, 1990, Schaefer sought a new trial based on "ineffective counsel," citing Schwartz's romance with Teresa.

The motion was denied.

After *Killer Fiction*'s publication, prison guards seized Schaefer's copy, calling it "pornographic filth." In May 1991, they opened Schaefer's mail, revealing his plans to write more stories, and gave him thirty days in solitary for "conspiracy to conduct a business from his cell."

In August, Schaefer severed relations with London, then reneged in November, recommending that she grant an interview to TV's *A Current Affair*, writing: "Let's quit bickering and go out and make money!"

If only it were that easy.

London told her story to reporter Steve Dunleavy, pulling no punches. Schaefer had been "normal" in high school, she said, "except for his compulsion to kill." As for missing women, he had told her "he would take a woman out into the Everglades and she'd be alligator meat by morning." Dunleavy signed off by saying "We can only pray that Gerard Schaefer can find his hell on Earth."

Schaefer finally saw the segment in April 1992 and again "fired" London, demanding return of all materials she had received from him. Beyond that, he warned, "If you so much as mention my name in connection to the printed word or anything else I'll come after you and hound you into your grave and never quit. *You'll* become my life's work. You've tapped a Black Hole of genuine rage and it's focused on *you*."

But not exclusively. If Schaefer lost his federal appeals, he added, "I'm gonna have Schwartz & Teresa crippled. Arms and legs."

Ever inconsistent, he changed his mind again in May, approving continued sales of *Killer Fiction* and inviting London to "talk over a film deal." One month later, he reverted to type, claiming London had abandoned their contract, adding: "The very next time you say or do anything that causes me problems I am going to encourage my dope addled Satanist pals in Georgia to go pick up your slut daughter and teach her some sex education. My offer is simple: You don't fuck with me; I won't fuck with your kid."

Schaefer ultimately sued London three times (all dismissed) and sought her arrest for stealing his literary works "valued in excess of $110,000" (likewise dismissed). In December 1993, he foolishly wrote to her British publisher, raging: "My closest associate in this slimepit is an Anointed Fourth Prince of the Hand of Death who was a contract killer for the Mafia. This man has gunned down mobsters from Miami to New York. All I need to do is ask the gentleman to have Sondra and her kid murdered and it would be done. They are alive at this moment because I choose to allow it."

Schaefer's time ran out on December 3, 1995, when he was stabbed forty-two times in his cell, his throat slashed for good measure. On February 1, 1996, authorities charged inmate Vincent Rivera—serving life plus twenty years for prior murders—with that slaying.

Rivera denies killing Schaefer, while prosecutors claim Gerard angered him by taking the last hot water from a cellblock dispenser. Others suspect his death was a prison contract, punishment for doubling as a stool pigeon. Convicted on June 8, 1999, Rivera drew an additional term of fifty-three years and ten months.

Doris Schaefer blamed Ottis Toole for her son's murder, claiming Toole revealed Adam Walsh's gravesite to Gerard, who then negotiated terms for a prison transfer with Florida detectives and Adam's parents, aborted by his murder.

In July 2007, the *Tampa Bay Times* named Schaefer as the slayer of Nancy Leichner and Pam Nater in October 1966, based upon "a witness account and the recent discovery of long-mishandled confessions of the killer." Witness Brent Hoover, eleven years old when the girls disappeared in 1966, allegedly saw Schaefer following the victims around an Ocala park but waited forty-one years to speak up.

The "mishandled confession" was a statement from ex-convict Charles Sizelove, claiming Schaefer had described how he "took Leichner and Nater by gun and knifepoint and killed them." Authorities had recorded Sizelove's statement years earlier but then done nothing with it, even when prosecutors requested copies for an unrelated 1985 missing-person case.

As for the fabled book and film touted by Schaefer in his final interviews, destined to prove his innocence and set him free, neither has yet appeared. There is no reason to believe they ever will.

8.
"MONSTER OF THE ANDES": PEDRO LÓPEZ

On March 6, 1980, a flash flood near Ambato, capital of Ecuador's Tungurahua Province, unearthed the corpses of four young girls reported missing during recent weeks. All had been raped and strangled, three with such force that their eyeballs extruded from their sockets. Local police, who had dismissed the girls as runaways, belatedly reopened other missing-person files, but the case would solve itself before they had a chance to intervene.

Three days after the flood, Carvina Ramon Poveda was shopping in a local marketplace when she saw a stranger walking away with her twelve-year-old daughter Marie, clutching the girl by one hand. Poveda's screams brought market workers racing to Marie's rescue, holding her would-be kidnapper while police were summoned. In custody, the man raved incoherently, initially convincing the arresting officers that they had nabbed a lunatic.

The truth, as they would soon discover, was much worse.

In jail, the prisoner—Pedro Alonso López—stopped his babbling and refused to speak with investigators. Frustrated, they persuaded a local priest, Father Cordoba Gudino, to dress in prison garb and share López's cell. "For 27 days I hardly slept," Gudino later said, "afraid I'd be strangled in my bed. I kept a towel wrapped around my throat. But I tricked López into confessing by pretending I was a rapist too. He boasted to me of murder after murder in Ecuador, Colombia, and Peru. It was beyond my wildest nightmares. He told me everything."

The grisly tale began in childhood. López was born in Santa Isabel, Colombia, on October 8, 1948, at the onset of a ten-year civil war remembered in his homeland as *La Violencia* ("The Violence"), which claimed at least 200,000 lives by 1958.

His father, a member of the right-wing Colombian Conservative Party named Midardo Reyes, quarreled with his wife on December 28, 1947, seeking solace with prostitute Benilda López De Casteneda and impregnating her. Three months later, on April 4, 1948, Reyes was shot dead while defending a grocery store from rioters.

Pedro was the seventh of Benilda's thirteen children by various fathers, and shared a bed with his brood of siblings while their mother serviced clients in the next room, separated only by a curtain. He suffered random maternal beatings until he was forced to leave home. In hindsight, Benilda recalled Pedro as a polite child who hoped to become a teacher, but the truth was starkly different.

"My mother threw me out when I was eight," López told police, "after she caught me touching my sister's breasts. She took me to the edge of town, but I found my way home again. Next day she took me on a bus and left me off more than two hundred miles from home. There I was found by a man who took me into an abandoned building and raped me over and over again. I decided then to do the same to as many young girls as possible."

López had more to suffer, though, before he realized that violent fantasy. After his brutal rape, he drifted to Bogotá and lived by begging on the streets, sleeping in alleys and abandoned buildings, and scavenging castoff food from trash cans. A sympathetic American couple took him in, enrolling López at a school for orphans, but he fled that institution at age twelve, allegedly after a teacher molested him. Thievery supplemented his income from begging, and soon he was stealing cars and selling them to Bogotá chop shops.

Arrested for auto theft at eighteen, López was sentenced to prison where he was gang-raped by four older inmates. Seething with rage, he stalked and killed three of the rapists, slashing their throats with a crude homemade knife. Prison authorities treated those slayings as a belated form of self-defense, adding a mere two years to Pedro's sentence for the homicides.

Released in 1978, López began his odyssey of rape and murder, traveling widely throughout Colombia, Ecuador, and Peru, preying on young girls who possessed "a certain look of innocence" wherever he might find them. Some he snatched from Indian tribes, others from towns and villages where López found them unattended by their parents. When blasé authorities bothered to notice the increasing reports of lost children, they assumed that the missing girls had fallen prey to sex traffickers or to human sacrifice, still practiced to the present day in parts of South America by wealthy businessmen and drug lords.

One abduction nearly cost López his life, when Indians caught him trying to kidnap a nine-year-old girl outside Ayacucho, in northern Peru's Huamanga Province. "They had me tied up and buried in sand to my neck when they found what I had been doing to their daughters," López told his Colombian jailers. "They had placed syrup on me and were going to let me be eaten by ants. But an American missionary lady came by in her jeep and promised them she would turn me over to the police. They left me tied up in the back of her jeep and she drove away. But she released me at the border of Colombia and let me go. I didn't hurt her because she was too old to attract me."

And the slaughter of children continued.

To Father Gudino, then later to police, López admitted killing 100 girls in Colombia, 110 in Ecuador, and "many more than 100" in Peru. "I like the girls in Ecuador," he explained. "They are more gentle and trusting, more innocent. They are not as suspicious of strangers as Colombian girls." He repaid that trust with rape and slow strangulation, after luring his prey with false promises of gifts, relishing the terror in their eyes. "They never scream," he said. "They expect nothing. They are innocent." Sometimes, López staged gruesome "tea parties," propping up the corpses of his "little friends" and chatting with them, convinced that they enjoyed his company.

Confession was one thing, but the skeptical police still had to corroborate López's claims. Pedro obliged in July 1980, leading officers to graves in the provinces, Chimborazo, Cotopaxi, Pinchincha, Imbatura, and Tungurahua, where they discovered fifty-three more corpses. Prosecutors charged López with fifty-seven counts of murder, while police told reporters that that total was only the tip of a gruesome iceberg. As headlines dubbed López the "Monster of the Andes," Victor Lascaño, Ecuador's director of prison affairs, declared: "If someone confesses to 53 you find, and hundreds more you don't, you tend to believe what he says. I think his estimate of 300 is very low."

López eventually pleaded guilty to 110 counts of murder in Ecuador, receiving a life prison term on January 25, 1981. Foreign journalists and parents of his victims were amazed to learn that under the prevailing law, "life" meant a maximum of sixteen years in custody, with consecutive sentences for multiple crimes forbidden. That fixed his penalty at fifty-three days in prison for each of 110 slayings, or sixteen days per victim if police estimates of 350 murders were accurate. Extradition to Columbia or Peru (where López might have been executed) was ruled out as too expensive and time-consuming.

López had no fear of being raped in prison this time, as his homicidal reputation had preceded him. Placed in solitary confinement, he boasted of plans to write a book detailing his life and crimes, but he was barely literate and found no author willing to collaborate with him. Instead, he waited until 1994 before granting his sole prison interview, to photojournalist Ron Laytner, who served as a correspondent for the U.S. supermarket tabloid *National Examiner*.

Laytner described approaching López with some trepidation, mindful of rumors that grieving parents had offered a $25,000 reward to any prison guard or inmate who would kill him. Entering the Monster's cell, he found yellowed newspaper clippings pinned to the walls "like sick trophies to his reign of terror." Accompanied by the prison's warden, several armed guards, and the warden's daughter (serving as interpreter), Layton heard López's grisly tale.

Pedro began by declaring "I am the man of the century. No one will ever forget me." To ensure it, he sketched a vivid portrait of his modus operandi. "I walked among the markets," he explained, "searching for a girl with a certain look on her face of innocence and beauty. She would be a good girl, always working with her mother. I followed them, sometimes for two or three days, waiting for the moment she was left alone. Once, I even spent two days following a tourist family. I was told they came from England or Scotland. I really wanted to take their beautiful blond daughter, but I never got the chance. Her parents were too watchful."

Once a victim fell into his clutches, she was doomed. If kidnapped near dusk, the girl endured a night with López, waiting for dawn. "At the first sign of light I would get excited," he told Laytner. "I forced the girl into sex and put my hands against her throat. When the sun rose, I would strangle her. It was only good if I could see her eyes. I never killed anyone at night. It would have been wasted in the dark. I had to watch them by daylight. There is a wonderful moment, a divine moment, when I have my hands around a young girl's throat. Her fingers flutter briefly. The moment of death is enthralling and exciting. Only those who actually kill know what I mean. I look into her eyes and see a certain light, a spark, suddenly go out. It took them between five and fifteen minutes to die. Sometimes I had to kill them all over again."

Disposal was no problem, López said. "I would take her to a secret hideaway where prepared graves waited. Sometimes there were bodies of earlier victims there. My little friends liked to have company. I often put three or four into one hole. But after a while I got bored because they couldn't move, so I looked for more girls."

Despite his prison sentence and rumors of the contract on his life, López looked forward to more slayings in his future. "Someday, when I am released," he said, "I will feel that moment again. I will be happy to kill again. It is my mission." Questioned on that point by Laytner, López said "I will soon be a free man again. They are releasing me on good behavior."

And he was right. Late at night on August 31, 1998, guards removed López from his prison cell in Quito, Ecuador, hustled him aboard a prison van, and drove him to the Colombian border, leaving their ex-prisoner with a bottle of water, some food, and a handful of Colombian pesos. López resurfaced in Ecuador a week later, was arrested again, and was treated to another border crossing with stern warnings never to return.

Colombian police took notice of his presence then, jailing López on a twenty-year-old murder charge. He had little to fear, since Colombia had abolished capital punishment in 1910, but no one expected the trial's outcome, when jurors acquitted him on grounds of insanity. The court dispatched López to a psychiatric hospital in Bogotá, where he spent the next two years in treatment. Finally diagnosed as "cured" by state psychologists, Pedro was freed on $50 bail, with orders to see a magistrate once every month.

Instead, he vanished and has not been heard from since. A TV biography of López, broadcast on the A&E network in June 2009, claimed that Colombian authorities had issued a new arrest warrant on López, charging him with a "fresh" murder from 2002 and seeking information on his whereabouts through Interpol. If true, the warrant must have been rescinded, since no record of it remained with Interpol when I checked in August 2014.

Is the Monster of the Andes still alive and hunting little girls at age seventy-one?

Ron Laytner broke the story of López's deportation from Ecuador on December 6, 1998, prompting Carvina Poveda—whose screams led to his 1980 capture at Ambato—to tell reporters: "It will be a kindness to the world for someone to murder this fiend. The Monster of the Andes won't last long on the outside. Maybe that is why we haven't heard of more missing girls. Perhaps someone, even the police in Colombia or Ecuador, have already killed him. If they have, I hope they made him suffer."

Jose Rivas, commander of police in Ecuador's Carchi Province, claimed that López had been spotted in the Andes Mountains between Ecuador and Colombia, but circulation of his photograph proved fruitless. Prison director Victor Lascaño told journalists, "God save the children! He is unreformed and totally remorseless. This whole nightmare may start again."

So far, no evidence supports that grim prediction.

9.

"MAD DADDY": SAMUEL LITTLE

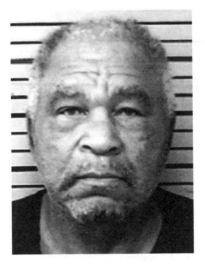

The FBI is normally conservative, politically and otherwise, but in October 2019 a spokesman took a leap of faith, naming a wheelchair-bound septuagenarian as America's most prolific serial killer of all time. The black seventy-nine-year-old, already convicted of eight murders committed between 1987 and 1994, now claims to have killed ninety-three girls and women in nineteen states nationwide from 1980 to 2005. The FBI confirms his involvement in "more than 50," while other agencies link him to a minimum of sixty-one.

*   *   *   *   *

Samuel Little was born in Reynolds, Georgia, on June 7, 1940. He describes his mother as "a lady of the night" who served multiple jail terms, and some authorities speculate that his birth occurred during her last incarceration.

Sometime afterward, she dropped him on the verge of a dirt road, leaving his care to a grandmother in Lorain, Ohio. At age sixteen, he stole a bicycle and was committed to juvenile detention at the Boys' Industrial School in Lancaster, the last gasp of his formal education. Five years later, now an adult, he drew a three-year sentence for burglarizing a Lorain furniture store. He was released in 1964.

Back in the free world, Little adopted a nomadic lifestyle, rightly calculating that local police and courts would fail to track his crimes across the country. By 1975, he'd logged twenty-six arrests in eleven states, on charges including theft, fraud, shoplifting, drunk driving, solicitation, fighting with police, armed robbery, assault with serious bodily harm, and rape, for which he'd served an aggregate sentence of ten years behind bars. When not confined, by his account, Little worked as a cemetery laborer and ambulance attendant, sometimes using the alias "Samuel McDowell," or he survived by shoplifting.

Both in and out of prison, Little honed his skills at boxing, becoming a skilled prizefighter whose powerful, rapid-fire punches earned him the nicknames "Mad Daddy," "Mad Machine," and "Machine Gun." A Los Angeles detective who jailed him in 2012 recalls him as "a big guy, about five-eleven, and I believe 235 was the weight that we used when we booked him."

Outside the boxing ring, his speed and strength served Little well in subduing smaller, weaker female victims.

Little's rootless life confounded law-enforcement efforts to control him. Christina Palazzolo, an analyst with the FBI's Violent Criminal Apprehension Program (VICAP), described Little's life on the road as a series of pit stops, driving from coast to coast in a matter of days, sleeping in his car, stealing money while en route to pay for gas, liquor, and drugs. Most of his run-ins with police, in Palazzolo's words, left him at large because negligent officers "often just wanted to shoo him out of town."

He also benefited from a phenomenon called "linkage blindness," a term coined by criminal-justice professor Dr. Steven Egger in 1984 to describe the failure of local police departments to communicate across jurisdictional lines and track serial felons at large.

In 1982, Little *was* arrested for murder in Pascagoula, Mississippi, charged with killing streetwalker Melinda Lapree, a 22-year-old woman reported missing that September.

He was also charged with raping and attempting to kill a second prostitute in December. Grand jurors declined to indict him for those crimes, but the reports drew the attention of Florida detectives.

On August 16, 1982, twenty-year-old Rosie Hill was found strangled or suffocated in woodland near a hog pen off County Road 326, near Ocala, Florida. Witnesses described "Samuel McDowell" leaving a bar with Hill shortly before her murder, and driving off in a car resembling Little's. Sheriff's deputies visited Pascagoula, Mississippi, but Little "lawyered up" after denying he'd ever met Hill.

That left the September 1982 Alachua County rape-murder of twenty-year-old Patricia Mount, found at Mt. Dora, Florida. Little pleaded not guilty, and while another witness linked him to Mount, jurors disbelieved her testimony and acquitted him in January 1984.

From Florida, Little drove across country to San Diego, California. There, in October 1984, police jailed him for kidnapping, beating, and half-strangling twenty-two-year-old survivor Lauri Barros. One month later, while he awaited trial on that charge, officers found him in the back seat of his car with another unconscious woman, also choked and beaten. Those assaults sent Little to prison for thirty months. He was released in February 1987.

Free again, he traveled 120 miles north to Los Angeles, where he committed more than ten additional murders. The LAPD dubbed him the "Choke-and-Stroke Killer," based on evidence that he strangled victims with one hand while masturbating over them with the other.

As elsewhere, Little targeted vulnerable and marginalized women, commonly strippers or sex workers. In his rush for satisfaction, he left several victims breathing, and one identified him to detectives, earning Little a brief three months in jail for rape and aggravated assault.

His choice of prey paid off, prompting him to later tell one interviewer "I never killed no senators or governors or fancy New York journalists, nothing like that. [If] I killed you, it'd be all over the news the next day. I stayed in the ghettos." Little's victims, often drug addicts and streetwalkers, drew scant attention from police. In fact, according to an FBI profile, "The one-time competitive boxer usually stunned or knocked out his victims with powerful punches and then strangled them. With no stab marks or bullet wounds, many of these deaths were not classified as homicides but attributed to drug overdoses, accidents, or natural causes."

Police apprehended Little for the last time at a Louisville, Kentucky homeless shelter on September 5, 2012. Tardy DNA analysis had linked him to three Los Angeles murders, including those of Carol Elford on July 13, 1987; Guadalupe Apodaca on September 3 of that year; and Audrey Nelson on August 14, 1989. All three had been raped and slain in typical style, discarded in a dumpster, an alley, and a garage respectively.

Extradited to L.A., Little was formally charged on January 7, 2013, still claiming innocence, while other local women described surviving Mad Daddy's assaults. Police and FBI agents reexamined dozens of cold cases nationwide. One of those reopened was the Mississippi murder of Linda Lapree.

At trial in September 2014, pathologist Dr. Eugene Carter described Audrey Nelson's injuries as demonstrating "considerable force"—in fact, "the greatest that I have seen in a twenty-seven-year practice in a county which has its share of strangulation cases." Jurors convicted Little of three murder counts on September 25, 2014, resulting in a life sentence without parole.

From Quantico, VICAP's Christina Palazzolo noted similarities between Little's technique and the January 1994 murder of twenty-two-year-old Denise Brothers in Odessa, Texas. The FBI contacted the Texas Rangers and passed that information on, while discovering an "alarming pattern" and "compelling links" to still more deaths.

Little maintained his pose of injured innocence until May 2018, when he confessed to Denise's slaying. To attract her, he said, "I told her I was an artist. She was a spicy one. I told her I could draw her so pretty, like Van Gogh. I told her she was beautiful. I said 'I love you.'" Charged on November 13, he pleaded guilty on December 13 and received another life sentence.

And once the floodgate of confessions opened, there was no shutting him up.

MULTIPLE MUGSHOTS OF SERIAL KILLER SAMUEL LITTLE.

The next confirmed murders came from Mad Daddy's old Ohio stomping ground. Victims included Anna Stewart, killed in October 1981; Mary Peyton in July 1984; Rose Evans in August 1991; and a "Jane Doe" so badly decomposed, her date of death could only be estimated as occurring between 1980 and 1989. Little pleaded guilty on August 23, 2019, and received four superfluous life sentences.

Still, that was not the end. Agent Palazzolo and Texas Ranger James Holland recorded more confessions and contacted authorities across America. Little assisted with sketches of his victims, some of whom he never knew by name. Drawing, as he explained, was one of his only three talents. The others were boxing and murder.

In media interviews, he called the slain women "his babies."

Between November 15 and 27, Little confessed to the following homicides: Brenda Alexander in Phenix City, Alabama, in 1979; a "Jane Doe" and teenager Fredonia Smith in Macon, Georgia, in 1977 and 1982, respectively; Dorothy Richards and Daisy McGuire, in 1982 and 1996 respectively, in Houma, Louisiana; Julia Critchfield, strangled and tossed off a Gulfport, Mississippi cliff in 1978, and Tupelo resident Nancy Stevens, slain in 2005; Evelyn Weston, found near Fort Jackson, South Carolina in 1978; Martha Cunningham and Linda Boards of Warren County, Kentucky, killed in 1975 and 1981; and, at long last, Floridian Rosie Hill. FBI agents confirmed Little's guilt in thirty-four murders and counting.

Geographically, Little had confessed to the following murders by October 2019, when the FBI sought public assistance with many "unmatched" revelations. Garbled media reports of various confessions complicate tabulation.

Arizona (2): A Hispanic woman killed in 1988 or 1996 and a white victim called "Ann" in 1997, both in or near Phoenix.

Arkansas (4): An unmatched confession from 1992 or '93; "Ruth" in North Little Rock; a black "Jane Doe" in Little Rock, from April 1994, where a shoplifting arrest confirms Little's presence in town; Jolanda Jones at Pine Bluff, 1994; and Tennessee hitchhiker Zena Jones (no relation to Jolanda), slain at West Memphis in 1997.

California (19): An unmatched San Bernardino confession from 1984; "Granny" and six other Los Angeles women in 1987; "Alice" and six more Los Angeles "Jane Does" between 1991 and '93; "Sheila," "T-Money," and two "Jane Does" in L.A., all from 1996.

Florida (11): A "Jane Doe" in Homestead, 1970–71; "Sarah" or "Donna" at Kendall, in 1971; "Linda," transgender female "Mary Ann," a "Jane Doe," and an unmatched confession in Miami, spanning 1971 and '72; an unnamed woman at Kendall in 1973; "Emily" and a Miami "Jane Doe" in the mid-1970s; a black woman at Plant City in 1977 or '78; plus "Jane Does" at Fort Myers and Tampa in 1984.

Georgia (9): An unnamed Savannah victim in 1974; a Macon "Jane Doe," in 1977; another at Charleston in 1977 or 1982; a Dade County victim in 1980 or '81; four Atlanta "Jane Does," during 1981–1984; and an unmatched Savannah confession from 1984.

Illinois (1): "Jo," a Missouri hitchhiker killed in Granite City sometime between 1976 and 1979.

Kentucky (1): A "hippie type" Ohio hitchhiker, killed at Covington in 1984.

Louisiana (3): Two New Orleans "Jane Does" in 1973 and 1982; another slain at Monroe sometime between 1987 and the early 1990s.

Maryland (1): A white woman, "possibly from Massachusetts," murdered in Prince George's County in 1972.

Mississippi (3): A "Jane Doe" killed at Pascagoula in 1977; another at Gulfport between 1982 and '84; and an unmatched confession dating from 1993, with no location specified.

Nevada (1): A Las Vegas streetwalker dumped near Searchlight in 1993.

Ohio (4): Aside from his four convictions, a Cincinnati "Jane Doe" dumped near Columbus in 1974; another in Cleveland during 1977 or

'78; a Willoughby Hills victim "around 1982"; and an Akron woman slain in 1991.

South Carolina (1): A black woman killed at Charleston between 1977 and 1982.

Tennessee (1): An unmatched confession from Knoxville in 1975.

Texas (2): A black "Jane Doe" at Wichita Falls in 1976 or '77; and an unmatched confession to a Houston murder committed "during 1976–77 or in 1993."

However many homicides are finally confirmed, Mad Daddy is beyond killing now, incarcerated for eight lifetimes and suffering from diabetes and heart disease. Updates on his case continue, with no abatement of public interest.

On February 12, 2019, nine formerly unmatched cases were closed without further indictments, while Little added sixteen victim portraits to his growing portfolio. By April 1, he had modified one of those sixteen and completed ten more. October 1 brought word that five more unmatched cases had been "cleared," with two more additional confessions and eight new portraits added to the list.

There seems no doubt that Little will continue "singing" and sketching until he finally meets the Grim Reaper he faithfully served for so many years.

A SKETCH OF A VICTIM OF SAMUEL LITTLE WHO WAS MURDERED IN 1971 OR 1972.

10.

"DOCTOR DEATH": HAROLD SHIPMAN

Britain's premier serial killer never used a gun, garrote, or knife. He was a licensed physician who was addicted to murdering patients, though his final body count and motives remain controversial topics sixteen years beyond his death in custody.

Harold Frederick Shipman Jr., commonly called "Fred," was born on June 14, 1946 in Nottingham, the middle child of a truck driver and a homemaker who were both devout Methodists. His domineering mother Vera favored Fred over his siblings, instilling him with an arrogant sense of entitlement that soured childhood interactions with his peers and tainted his adult relationships. Outside of the home, Vera chose his friends, booked play dates, and forced Fred to wear neckties at school.

In class, he was a mediocre student and socially aloof. A former schoolmate said "It was as if he tolerated us. If someone told a joke he would smile patiently, but Fred never wanted to join in." Still, he passed from primary to grammar school in 1957, emerging as a talented athlete. In 1961, he received a "most improved student" award for rugby, then switched to distance running in high school, serving as team vice-captain in his final year.

Sports aside, he was a social dud. As for romance, an ex-teacher recalled "I don't think he ever had a girlfriend. In fact, he took his older sister to school dances. They made a strange couple. But then, he *was* a bit strange—a pretentious lad."

Personal tragedy struck in January 1962 when his mother was diagnosed with lung cancer. Fred managed her care and watched her die slowly, comatose from morphine injections by the time she passed on June 21, 1963. That night, family members say he ran for twenty miles through pouring rain.

That same year, at age seventeen, some of his cross-country teammates suspected Fred's addiction to sniffing Sloan's Liniment, sold since 1871 as "good for man and beast," with capsicum (a nightshade derivative) the primary ingredient.

Influenced by his mother's fate and the kindly doctor who treated her, Shipman entered Leeds University Medical School in 1965, on his second attempt to pass entrance exams. He made adequate grades, but professors barely recalled him later, prompting journalists to dub him an "invisible student."

That changed when he met Primrose Oxtoby, three years his junior. A whirlwind romance ensued, and Primrose was five months pregnant at their wedding on November 5, 1966. Daughter Sarah arrived on

St. Valentine's Day. Shipman graduated in 1970, receiving provisional registration with the General Medical Council and becoming a pre-registration house officer—the equivalent of an American intern—at Yorkshire's Pontefract General Infirmary.

Shipman lost five patients between August 15 and September 28, 1970, all later deemed natural deaths. In October, he passed final exams and graduated from Leeds with his MBchB (Bachelor of Medicine, Bachelor of Surgery). He presided at the death of sixty-five-year-old Thomas Redfearn that same month, and at six more deaths by December 31. Subsequent investigation deemed five of those deaths natural, while Redfearn's case and Ruth Burley's revealed "insufficient evidence for conclusion."

In 1971, Shipman began his residency as House Officer in Surgery. Coincidentally or otherwise, he lost his next patient on New Year's Day, with two more deaths in January and another twelve by April 17. Ages of the dead ranged from ten to eighty-four years, and while eight of the fifteen were later ruled natural, seven prompted official doubts. Investigators found "cause for suspicion" with Wilfred Sanderson (sixty-two) and Ethel Follon (sixty) in March. Five more cases had insufficient evidence for conclusions.

Two weeks after the fifteenth Pontefract death, on April 21, Fred and Primrose welcomed son Christopher into their growing family. Twelve more patients died on Shipman's watch before his September promotion to Senior House Officer in Pediatrics, with nine later confirmed as natural deaths. Of those, inquiry records note that forty-six-year-old Charles Bailey did not die in the hospital, and Shipman did not certify a cause of death for seventy-six-year-old Fred Hartley. Investigators found "cause for suspicion" in the May death of Edith Swift (forty-nine), with insufficient evidence for conclusion on two others.

While mainly treating children between September 1971 and January 1972, Shipman lost five more patients. Four were infants, ranging from one stillbirth to two months of age. They, and sixty-two-year-old Tom Goodliffe on January 27, were all later confirmed as natural deaths.

Shipman advanced to Senior House Officer in Medicine, with seventy-three patients dying under his care before his next promotion in August 1972. Ages ranged from twenty-four to eighty-nine, including thirty-three men and forty women. Investigators deemed twenty-five of those deaths natural, including one at Mill Garth House nursing home, another at the patient's residence, and two in which Shipman did not sign death certificates. Another thirty presented insufficient evidence for conclusions.

The other eighteen deaths concerned later investigators. A twenty-first-century inquiry deemed three deaths "unlawful" without pursuing prosecution: Thomas Cullumbine (fifty-four) and John Brewster (eighty-four) in April 1972, and James Rhodes (seventy-one) in May. Government investigators also found "cause for some suspicion" in the case of Margaret Thompson (seventy-two), who died in Shipman's presence on March 2 while recuperating from a stroke.

Of the remaining sixteen cases, investigators found "significant suspicion" in the cases of Elizabeth Thwaites (seventy-four) and Louis Bastow (seventy-two), who died on April 11 and May 22 respectively. "Some suspicion" was expressed for the remaining fourteen, lost between February 29 and June 1: Cissie Macfarlane (fifty-seven), Mary Price (seventy-three), Butterfield Hammill (eighty-six), Ada Wandless (fifty-five), Agnes Davidson (seventy-four), Alice Smith (eighty), George Fisher (sixty-eight), Joseph Green (forty-seven), Walter Spence (seventy-five), John Harrison (seventy), Annie Nash (seventy), Norman Deyes (seventy-one), and Phyllis Cooling (fifty-eight). All but one died at PGI; Hammill passed at Ackton Hospital, three miles west of Pontefract.

Shipman advanced to Registrar in Pediatrics at Pontefract in August 1972, and three-month-old Ruth Harrison died in his care on the twenty-first of that month, her death later judged natural. In September, Fred received his DCH (Diploma in Child Health), after passing a Foundation of Practice exam and a DCH clinical exam. His next patient death—four-year-old Susan Garfitt, on October 11—was ultimately tagged with "cause for significant suspicion." Some confusion surrounds this case, as a January 2005 BBC News report on Shipman claimed that "on the evidence available, the death was almost certainly natural."

Or *was* it?

Young Susan suffered from cerebral palsy and entered PGI with severe pneumonia on her last day alive. Her mother recalled Shipman predicting Susan's imminent death "in a soothing voice," adding that "medicating her any further would only prolong her suffering." Ann Garfitt asked Shipman to "be kind," stepping out for a cup of tea and returning to find her child dead. In retrospect, she wondered if Shipman had interpreted her parting words as "unspoken consent" for euthanasia.

Shipman lost two more patients in December 1972: Christopher Smith (five months) and Violet Dunning (sixty-seven), at a local nursing home. Both deaths are regarded as natural.

Still primarily working pediatrics at PGI in 1973, Shipman lost six more patients between February 2 and August 18. Five deaths occurred at the hospital, all children ranging from one hour to one month old. The sole adult, Hannah Rider (eighty-eight), died at a local nursing home. All six are listed today as natural deaths.

In 1974, Shipman left PGI to join the Abraham Ormerod Medical Centre at Todmorden ("death-murder," in German), West Yorkshire. Other members of the practice appreciated his youth and apparent ambition, while staffers found him rude, combative, and anxious to make them feel foolish, often calling them "stupid." Author Ted Ottley dubs him a "control freak." Shipman soon began to keep a coded journal in which he labeled some patients WOW ("whining old woman") and FTPBI ("failed to put brain in").

But worse lay in store. Investigators later found that from 1974 onward, Shipman "regularly obtained controlled drugs by illicit means," becoming addicted to the synthetic opioid pethidine, frequently prescribing it to patients who never received it while taking it himself.

Between May 10, 1974 and September 27, 1975, thirty patients died under Shipman's care, with eighteen cases settled as natural deaths. Another five revealed insufficient evidence for conclusions, leaving eight that belatedly troubled authorities.

His first intended victim in Todmorden may have been Frances Oswald, a twenty-five-year-old executive officer for the Department of Health and Social Security in Rochdale who attended Abraham Ormerod Medical Centre as a patient. On August 21, 1974, Shipman gave her an injection leading to respiratory arrest and putting her life in danger. She survived and moved to the United States with her family in 1975, obtaining a doctorate and serving as a college English professor in Tennessee. Reading of Shipman's arrest and trial years later, Oswald was suspicious and signed a police report in April 2001. No prosecution resulted, but the Shipman Inquiry's final report states as fact that Fred "unlawfully administered an opiate, probably pethidine" to Oswald, nearly killing her.

The official tabulation for this period lists one unlawful killing, of Eva Lyons (seventy), at home on March 17, 1975, the day before her seventy-first birthday. A terminal cancer patient, she is listed today as Shipman's first "official" victim, with no prosecution resulting. Six other cases raised suspicion of homicide between January and August 1975, with three occurring on January 21. Victims include Lily Crossley (seventy-three), Robert Lingard (sixty-two), Elizabeth Pearce (eighty-four), Jane Rowland (eighty), Edith Roberts (sixty-seven), and Albert Williams (seventy-five).

Shipman's career at Todmorden came to an end with the onset of repeated blackouts, which Fred explained with a false diagnosis of epilepsy to cover his opioid addiction. While his partners commiserated, one of the staffers he'd insulted—receptionist Marjorie Walker—discovered irregularities in a druggist's ledger. Aside from large, frequent pethidine prescriptions for patients who never received it, Shipman had also ordered stockpiles for the practice that were missing. Called to account by his partners, Fred first sought a second chance—which was refused—then became enraged, dashing his medical bag to the floor and storming out with a threat to resign. Abraham Ormerod's doctors were still discussing the outburst when Primrose Shipman appeared, insisting that Fred would never resign, adding "You'll have to force him out!"

A unanimous partners' vote expelled Shipman, prompting his self-admission to a rehab center in York. While there, in November, police charged him with three counts of obtaining a controlled drug by deception, three of possession, and two of forging declarations of exemption. At his February trial, convicted on all charges, Fred was fined £600—about $1,000—and placed on probation with a threat of jail time for future offenses. He would not abandon forgery for good, but did stand down from medical practice for one year and 264 days, effective from December 1976.

No deaths at Shipman's hand occurred during that time.

Against the odds, Shipman returned to medicine late in 1977, accepted as a clinical officer at Donneybrook Medical Center in Hyde, Greater Manchester, where his duties were initially restricted to examining infants and furnishing advice on their development. He confessed his past offenses and, as supervising Dr. Jeffery Moysey said, "His approach was that I have had this problem, this conviction for abuse of pethidine.

I have undergone treatment. I am now clean. All I can ask you to do is to trust me on that issue and to watch me."

The partners did, observing an apparently dedicated, hardworking doctor who concealed his abusive, sarcastic nature from all whose opinions mattered to him. Acceptance in Hyde seemed simple, with no recurring symptoms of addiction. But patient deaths resumed with his promotion to general practitioner, serving at the clinic and making house calls.

The twenty-seven patients Shipman lost between October 5, 1977 and December 20, 1978 were seniors—ages sixty to eighty-eight—so their passing provoked no surprise. Unlike Fred's time at PGI, from now on patients would expire at home or at "care homes" such as Charnley House on Albert Road.

Of those deaths, fifteen are now deemed natural, including two at separate locations on February 24. Three more presented insufficient evidence for a conclusion. As for the rest, four were later deemed "unlawful" without prosecution: Sarah Marsland (eighty-six), Mary Jordan (seventy-three), Harold Bramwell (seventy-three, killed the same day as a "natural" death), and Annie Campbell (eighty-eight), all dying at their homes. Suspicion of murder attached to five more cases with no charges filed, and again there was a doubling of deaths, with sixty-nine-year-old Thomas Longmate's suspicious passing on the same day as a "natural" case.

That pattern continued into 1979, with four deaths by March 11, three natural and one with insufficient evidence for judgment (falling on the same day as a natural death). Primrose Shipman bore Fred's third child—son David—on March 20. Shipman's fifth patient passed that same afternoon.

From there, the year's death toll increased, twenty-five patients lost between April 14 and December 23. Fifteen died at private homes, nine at residential homes, and one at a local hospital. Sixteen deaths remain listed as natural, two occurring on the same day (August 25), plus two with insufficient evidence for judgment. Two were belatedly deemed unlawful killings but never prosecuted—victims Alice Gorton (seventy-six) and Jack Shelmerdine (seventy-seven), the latter dying at a hospital with Shipman in attendance. Five more rated suspicion of unlawful death.

1980 was another woeful year for Shipman's patients, with ten dying at private homes and eight in residential care facilities. More than two-thirds of those, thirteen, still rate as natural deaths, the rest displaying insufficient evidence for judgment. Ages ranged from sixty-six to ninety-two. For the first time since 1973, none of Shipman's losses gave any cause for suspicion of murder.

The ante was raised in 1981 with twenty-six patients lost under Shipman's care between January 7 and November 10. Of those, fourteen deaths followed house calls and twelve occurred at residential homes. Today, fourteen remain listed as natural deaths, six with insufficient evidence for a conclusion. The year's victims of apparent homicide were May Slater (eighty-four) and Elizabeth Ashworth (eighty-one), killed at their own homes on April 18 and August 26. Suspicion of murder arose in four cases of victims seventy-five to ninety-three years old, but none led to prosecution.

Primrose Shipman was pregnant again by June 1981, and bore son Sam on March 5, 1982. Her condition, and a third child's arrival, had no apparent impact on the pace of life and death in Manchester. Indeed, Sam's birth was bracketed by the deaths of Fred's patients William Baxter (seventy) and Edith Leech (eighty-three), neither fully explained to this day.

Overall, Shipman lost eighteen patients between January 9 and December 15, 1982, with eleven dying at home, the rest in residential care facilities. None was subsequently rated as "unnatural," though suspicion arose in four cases: patients Samuel Harrison (eighty-seven), Alice Holt (seventy-five), Louisa Stocks (eighty), and Wilfred Leigh (seventy-four). Of the remainder, twelve remain logged as natural deaths, two with insufficient evidence for judgment.

Shipman had a relatively quiet year in 1983, certifying only thirteen deaths. For the first time, a majority of eight patients expired at residential homes, the rest following private house calls. Nine cases remain listed as natural today, one with insufficient evidence for judgment. Investigators now name Percy Ward (ninety) and Moira Fox (seventy-seven) as murder victims, though neither case was prosecuted. Suspicion also attached to the death of Charles MacConnell (seventy-two), with the same legal inaction.

In 1983, Shipman was interviewed for Granada television's *World of Action* documentary series. The episode, titled "A Serious Medical Emergency," aired on Halloween, with Shipman ironically discussing how communities should treat the mentally ill.

Death pursued Shipman more energetically in 1984, with thirty patients lost—an average of one every twelve days between January 13 and November 28. Their ages ranged from fifty-one to ninety-seven, with twenty-seven of them aged seventy or older. According to investigators, natural deaths comprised a minority of Fred's cases this year—eleven total—while six present insufficient evidence for conclusions. Unlucky dates were March 26 (three deaths) and April 15 (two).

Nine unlawful deaths were later diagnosed for 1984, including victims Dorothy Tucker (fifty-one), Gladys Roberts (seventy-eight), Joseph Bardsley (eighty-three), Winifred Arrowsmith (seventy), Mary Winterbottom (seventy-six), Ada Ashworth (eighty-seven), Joseph Everall (eighty), Edith Wibberley (seventy-six), and Eileen Cox (seventy-two). Suspicion of homicide lingers in the cases of Doris Bridge (eighty-three), Walter Mansfield (eighty-three), Beatrice Lowe (eighty-eight), and Charles Harris (seventy.)

Shipman suffered a personal loss on January 5, 1985, with his father's death at age seventy, but it hardly seemed to affect him. Harold Sr.'s will split his meager estate between children Pauline and Clive, leaving nothing to his namesake. Fred skipped the funeral, preferring the company of his patients.

And they kept dying, twenty-four in all between January 1 and December 31. Double deaths occurred on January 1, February 1, February 15, and June 26, with only one of those eight judged natural in hindsight.

Overall, natural deaths were a minority in 1985, numbering seven. Two cases revealed insufficient evidence for a conclusion. Considering the rest, authorities deemed eleven deaths unlawful: victims Peter Lewis (forty-one), May Brookes (seventy-four), Ellen Higson (eighty-four), Margaret Conway (sixty-nine), Kathleen McDonald (seventy-three), Thomas Moult (seventy), Mildred Robinson (eighty-four), Frances Turner (eighty-five), Selena Mackenzie (seventy-seven), Vera Bramwell (seventy-nine), and Fred Kellett (seventy-nine). Suspicion of murder lingers in the cases of John Howcroft (seventy-seven), Edwin Foulkes (eighty-eight), and Violet Hadfield (seventy-four), but no prosecutions resulted.

Shipman presided over fewer deaths in 1986, only fifteen between January 4 and December 23, but only four of those are now considered natural. Passing time left one with insufficient evidence for a conclusion. Of the remaining ten, eight are now listed as homicides, though none were prosecuted. Presumed murder victims include Deborah Middleton (eighty-one), Dorothy Fletcher (seventy-four), Thomas Fowden (eighty-one), Mona White (sixty-three), Mary Tomlin (seventy-three), Beatrice Toft (fifty-nine), Lily Broadbent (seventy-five), and James Wood (eighty-two). Suspicion of homicide lingers in the cases of Jozef Iwanina (sixty-three) and Annie Watkins (eighty-one), with Watkins killed the same day as victim Beatrice Toft.

Shipman certified another seventeen deaths between March 7 and December 30, 1987, his deceased patients ranging from age sixty-one to eighty-six. Thirteen died at home, four in care facilities. Six deaths are currently deemed natural, with two occurring on April 17, while two present insufficient evidence for decision. Eight patients adjudged murder victims include Frank Halliday (seventy-six), Albert Cheetham (eighty-five), Alice Thomas (eighty-three), Jane Rostron (seventy-eight), Nancy Brassington (seventy-one), Margaret Townsend (eighty), Nellie Bardsley (sixty-nine), and Elizabeth Rogers (seventy-four). Suspicion remains in the case of Alice Connaughton (seventy-seven), but no cases from 1987 were prosecuted.

In 1988, Shipman's signature appeared on seventeen death certificates between January 5 and December 19. Natural causes claimed five lives, including 100-year-old Alice Rawling, while one case presented insufficient evidence for judgment. Deaths listed as murders include victims Elizabeth Fletcher (ninety), Alice Jones (eighty-three), Dorothea Renwick (ninety), Ann Cooper (ninety-three), Jane Jones (eighty-three), Lavinia Robinson (eighty-four), Rose Adshed (eighty), Alice Prestwich (sixty-nine), Walter Tingle (eighty-five), Harry Stafford (eighty-seven), and Ethel Bennett (eighty). Three victims—Cooper, Jane Jones, and Robinson—were killed in February over a span of two days.

In 1989, there was no respite from death for Shipman's patients, fifteen of whom died between January 31 and November 15. Only three of those cases pass muster today as natural. The rest are all deemed homicides, including victims Mary Hamer (eighty-one), the first victim slain at Fred's surgery on Clarendon Street. According to Fred, Mrs. Hamer—described as "a lively and sociable woman who seems to have enjoyed very good health"—arrived for a scheduled appointment on March 8, displaying symptoms of a heart attack in progress. Fred administered morphine to "ease the pain" and allegedly left her alone to call an ambulance, returning to find her dead. Shipman failed to use resuscitation equipment, fearing Hamer "might have suffered brain damage," and certified the cause of death as coronary thrombosis resulting from hypertension.

The year's other murder victims—all slain at their own homes, no cases prosecuted—include Winfred Chappell (eighty), Beatrice Clee (seventy-eight), Josephine Hall (sixty-nine), Hilda Fitton (seventy-five), Marion Carradice (eighty), Elsie Harrop (eighty-two), Elizabeth Burke (eighty-two), Sarah Williamson (eighty-two), John Charlton (eighty-one), George Vizor (sixty-seven), and Joseph Wilcockson (eighty-five).

Shipman faced the new decade with no fear of apprehension but took a vacation of sorts from murder. Of seven patients lost in 1990, five remain listed as natural, the dead ranging from sixty-eight to eighty-three years old. If authorities are correct, he murdered only two victims that year: Dorothy Rowarth (fifty-six) on September 18, and Mary Dudley (sixty-nine) on December 30. Neither case was prosecuted.

Fred's death rate was low in 1991 as well. Of twelve patient deaths between February 21 and November 17, all but one are still rated natural. The sole exception is Alfred Cheetham (seventy-three), who died at home on March 21; evidence from his case was insufficient for judgment.

Even fewer Shipman patients died in 1992: eight between January 10 and December 20, with six deemed natural.

In September 1992, Shipman left Donneybrook to establish a solo practice in Hyde, called The Surgery. It might as well have been named The Slaughterhouse. His first alleged victim there was Monica Sparkes (seventy-two) on October 7. Suspicion persists for Annie Powers (eighty-nine), but neither case was prosecuted.

Shipman kicked into high gear in 1993, certifying twenty-eight patient deaths between February 12 and December 31. Ten stand today as natural. Sixteen are judged unlawful, although never prosecuted. Victims include Olive Heginbotham (eighty-six), Hilda Couzens (ninety-two), Amy Whitehead (eighty-two), Mary Andrew (eighty-six), Sarah

Ashworth (seventy-four), Fanny Nichols (eighty-four), Marjorie Parker (seventy-four), Nellie Mullen (seventy-seven), Edna Llewllyn (sixty-eight), Emily Morgan (eighty-four), Violet Bird (sixty), Jose Kathleen Richards (seventy-four), Edith Calverly (seventy-seven), Joseph Leigh (seventy-eight), Eileen Robinson (fifty-four), and Charles Brocklehurst (ninety). Heginbotham and Couzens made Fred's first double-header since 1986, both slain on February 24. Suspicion lingers in the cases of Harold Freeman (eighty-three) and David Jones (seventy-three).

Seventeen of Shipman's patients died in 1994, their ages ranging from fifty-three to ninety. Only four cases remain listed as natural today. Eleven now are logged as homicides, with two more under suspicion.

The year's first death occurred on January 4. Friends of victim Joan Harding (eighty-two) described her overall health as "very good," despite bouts of severe depression, and found her "in very good form" at Christmas. That said, she visited Dr. Shipman frequently, for mood swings, anxiety, sinus trouble, arthritis, and "cancer phobia." Recurring pain from a 1992 fracture and recurring nausea brought her to Shipman's office on the day she died, Fred's receptionist describing Joan as looking "washed out and pale." Fred claimed she collapsed in his examination room, apparently from a heart attack. Someone called for an ambulance, then rang again and canceled. Fred certified death from coronary thrombosis and Harding was cremated on January 7.

The year's other murder victims died at home, including Christine Hancock (fifty-three), Elsie Platt (seventy-three), Mary Smith (eighty-four), Ronnie Devenport (fifty-seven), Cicely Sharples (eighty-seven), Alice Kitchen (seventy), Maria Thornton (seventy-eight), Henrietta Walker (eighty-seven), Elizabeth Mellor (seventy-five), and John Molesdale (eighty-one). Prosecutors never pursued their cases.

Shipman lost forty-two patients in 1995, one every nine days. Ages ranged from forty-seven to ninety; eleven cases were cleared as natural deaths, while one revealed insufficient evidence for judgment. Of the remainder, twenty-nine were deemed murders, and one more raised suspicion.

Murder victims in 1995 included Marie West (eighty-one), Alice Kennedy (eighty-eight), Lucy Virgin (seventy), Joseph Shaw (eighty-eight), Netta Ashcroft (seventy-one), Lily Bardsley (eighty-eight), Marie Fernley (fifty-three), John Crompton (eighty-two), Frank Crompton (eighty-six), Vera Brocklehurst (seventy), Angela Tierney (seventy-one), Edith Scott (eighty-five), Clara Hackney (eighty-four), Renate Overton (forty-seven), Kate Sellors (seventy-five), Brenda Ashworth (sixty-three), Ernest Rudol (eighty-two), Ada Hilton (eighty-eight), Irene Aitken (sixty-five), Arthur Henderson (eighty-two), Geoffrey Bogle (seventy-two), Dora Ashton (eighty-seven), Bertha Moss (sixty-eight), Muriel Ward (eighty-seven), Edith Brock (seventy-four), Charles Barlow (eighty-eight), Konrad Ovcar-Remington (seventy-three), Elizabeth Sigley (sixty-seven), and Kenneth Woodhead (seventy-five). Both Sigley and Woodhead were slain on December 14. Suspicion lingers in the May death of Arthur Bent (ninety).

Victims Moss and Ashton were the second and third killed at Shipman's surgery. A patient of Fred's since the late 1970s, Moss complained of "leg trouble" on June 13 but seemed "quite cheerful" to relatives and friends before visiting Fred's office. Moments into her examination, Shipman phoned her daughter to report Moss suffering a heart attack but did not call an ambulance. Moss was dead when her daughter arrived fifteen minutes later. Fred described a "funny do" during her exam, claiming Bertha had suffered "slow heart failure" for years and "there was nothing I could do." He certified her death due to coronary thrombosis caused by hypertension and congestive heart failure. She was cremated on June 15.

Dora Ashton, a patient for eleven years, was considered "fit and healthy for her age" by relatives, despite chronic diabetes and hypertension. She visited the surgery on September 26 for headaches following an ear infection and died fifteen minutes after arriving. Shipman claimed she'd suffered two strokes and collapsed, blaming her death on a cerebral embolism due to atrial fibrillation and ischemic heart disease, whereupon she was cremated.

As 1996 began, Shipman seemed unaware—or didn't care—that murmurs had begun to circulate about his patients' high death rate. Another forty-four died that year, ranging in age from forty-two to ninety-one, with thirteen retrospectively confirmed as natural deaths. Thirty were deemed homicides, while one remains under suspicion.

Designated murder victims in 1996 include Hilda Hibbert (eighty-one), Erla Copeland (seventy-nine), Peter Higginbotham (forty-two), Jane Shelmerdine (eighty), John Greenhalgh (eighty-eight), Minnie Galpin (seventy-one), Marjorie Waller (seventy-nine), John Stone (seventy-seven), Elsie Godfrey (eighty-five), Edith Brady (seventy-two), Valerie Cuthbert (fifty-four), Lilian Cullen (seventy-seven), Renee Lacey (sixty-three), Leah Fogg (eighty-two), Gladys Saunders (eighty-two), Nellie Bennett (eighty-six), Margaret Vickers (eighty-one), Tom Russell (seventy-seven), Irene Turner (sixty-seven), Carrie Leigh (eighty-one), Marion Higham (eighty-four), Elsie Hannible (eighty-five), Elsie Barker (eighty-four), Sidney Smith (seventy-six), Dorothy Andrew (eighty-five), Anne Ralphs (seventy-five), Millicent Garside (seventy-six), Irene Heathcote (seventy-six), Samuel Mills (eighty-nine), Thomas Cheetham (seventy-eight), and Kenneth Smith (seventy-three). Suspicion lingers in the case of Fanny Clarke, age eighty-two.

As in times past, Fred logged two "double" days, pairing one natural death with a murder on April 18 and two homicides on June 25. Another oddity was Fred's killing of patients in clusters. Brothers Kenneth and Sidney Smith lived together until August 30, when Shipman killed Sidney. After neighbor Tom Cheetham died on December 4, Ken Smith began calling Shipman "Doctor Death" and "the angel of death." That stopped with Ken's death on December 17, but Fred wasn't finished, returning to kill Tom's wife Elsie Cheetham in April 1997.

Edith Brady was the fourth victim to die at Shipman's surgery, on May 15, 1996. Investigators described her as a longtime Shipman patient, "very interested" in her health, who "positively enjoyed" clinic visits and held Fred "in high esteem," while Shipman regarded her as "something of a nuisance." He solved that problem with a lethal injection, blaming her death on coronary thrombosis. Brady's remains were cremated on May 17.

Fred escalated his killing pace in 1997, certifying deaths of forty-seven patients between the ages of forty-seven and ninety-five. Only eight cases remain listed as natural today. Another thirty-seven are deemed homicides, while suspicion of foul play remains in two more. Shipman had two "double" days in April, three of the four deaths deemed homicides, the fourth suspicious.

Murder victims in 1997 include Eileen Crompton (seventy-five), David Harrison (forty-seven), Elsie Dean (sixty-nine), Irene Brooder (seventy-six), Charlotte Bennison (eighty-nine), Charles Killan (ninety), Betty Royston (seventy), Joyce Woodhead (seventy-four), Lizzie Adams (seventy-seven), Rose Garlick (seventy-six), May Lowe (eighty-four), Mary Coutts (eighty), Elsie Cheetham (seventy-six), Jean Lilley (fifty-eight), Leah Slater (sixty-eight), Ethel Kellett (seventy-four), Doris Earls (seventy-nine), Ivy Lomas (sixty-three), Vera Whittingslow (sixty-nine), Maureen Jackson (fifty-one), Muriel Grimshaw (seventy-six), John Livesey (sixty-nine), Lily Taylor (eighty-six), Dorothy Hopkins (seventy-two), Nancy Jackson (eighty-one), Mavis Pickup (seventy-nine), Bessie Swann (seventy-nine), Enid Otter (seventy-seven), Florence Lewis (seventy-nine), Mary Walls (seventy-eight), Elizabeth Baddeley (eighty-three), Marie Quinn (sixty-seven), Elizabeth Battersby (seventy), Laura Wagstaff (eighty-one), Bianka Pomfret (forty-nine), Alice Black (seventy-three), and James King (eighty-three). Suspicion lingers over the deaths of Mary Tuff (seventy-six) and Bertha Parr (seventy-seven).

Victim Ivy Lomas was the fifth to die at Shipman's surgery. Her medical history includes frequent respiratory infections and chronic obstructive airways disease limiting her physical activity. Shipman certified her cause of death as coronary thrombosis, but a subsequent autopsy revealed a fatal level of morphine. Following her death, Shipman joked that he should commemorate her many visits with a special plaque in his waiting room reading "Seat reserved permanently for Ivy Lomas."

Gallows humor aside, Shipman must have sensed suspicion closing in by early 1998. He'd silenced Kenneth Smith's remarks concerning "Doctor Death," but other locals were talking. Still, Fred's arrogance propelled him to keep killing in the new year.

Between January 22 and March 24, 1998, Shipman certified nineteen deaths of patients ranging from age fifty-seven to ninety. Four of those remain listed as natural, while the rest are tagged as homicides. A "double header" on February 2 paired one natural death with a murder.

Presumed murder victims during those two months include Mabel Shawcross (seventy-nine), Norah Nuttall (sixty-four), Cissie Davis (seventy-three), Pamela Hillier (sixty-eight), Laura Linn (eighty-three), Irene Berry (seventy-four), Maureen Ward (fifty-seven), Joan Dean (seventy-five), Harold Eddleston (seventy-seven), Margaret Waldron (sixty-five), Irene Chapman (seventy-four), Dorothy Long (eighty-four), Lily Higgins (eighty-three), Ada Warburton (seventy-seven), and Martha Marley (eighty-eight).

The next expression of concern for Shipman's dwindling patient list came on March 24 from Alan Massey, a mortician in Hyde who handled many of Fred's deceased clients, noting both their frequency of sudden deaths and similarity in their appearance when he went to collect them.

"Anybody can die in a chair," Massey explained. "But there's no set pattern, and Dr. Shipman's always seem to be the same, or very similar. Could be set on a chair, could be laid on a settee, but I say 90 percent was always fully clothed. There was never anything in the house that I saw that indicated the person had been ill. It just seems the person, where they were, had died. There was something that didn't quite fit."

That pattern drove Massey to confront Shipman privately. "I asked him if there was any cause for concern and he just said 'No, there isn't.' He showed me his certificate book that he issues death certificates in, and his remarks were 'nothing to worry about, you've nothing to worry about and anybody who wants to inspect his book can do.'"

Massey was briefly satisfied, but his daughter and partner, Debbie Brambroffe, remained uneasy, voicing her concerns to Hyde physician Dr. Susan Booth. British law requires a doctor from an unaffiliated practice to countersign cremation orders issued by a patient's personal physician, with a stipend—dubbed "cash for ash"—paid to the consulting doctor in each case. Dr. Booth recalled that Brambroffe "was concerned about the number of deaths of Dr. Shipman's patients that they'd attended recently. She was also puzzled by the way in which the patients were found. They were mostly female, living on their own, found dead sitting in a chair fully dressed, not in their nightclothes lying ill in bed."

Booth then consulted Donneybrook Medical Center Dr. Linda Reynolds, who informed South Manchester District Coroner John Pollard in March 1998. He spoke to the Greater Manchester Police, who conducted a "virtual covert operation," poring over Shipman's files, then closed the case on finding that recorded treatments and causes of death seemed to match. Detectives didn't realize that Shipman's files had been fabricated, with critical information falsified or otherwise altered on his computer.

Worse, in what some critics call negligence, police failed to uncover Shipman's criminal record or research his background with the General Medical Council. The probe officially concluded on April 17.

Before Fred's September arrest, he would kill three more times.

* * * * *

In fact, Shipman lost *four* patients after police closed their inquiry, but the first to die—ninety-five-year-old Mary Keating—passed from natural causes on April 28 at The Sycamores, a home for senior citizens. When Fred was finally arrested, the conclusion of his killing spree was due to arrogance and simple greed.

Patient Winifred Mellor, age seventy-three, died at home on May 11, slain by a morphine injection after twenty one years as Fred's patient. Joan Melia, also seventy-three, died at home from the same cause on June 12; Shipman blamed her death on pneumonia.

Shipman's final victim, Kathleen Grundy, was a wealthy widow and a former mayor of Hyde, known for her active social life and involvement with various charities, and viewed by all who knew her as being in "remarkably good health" for age eighty-one. On June 23, she visited Shipman's office to have her ears syringed, at which time he persuaded her to give an early-morning blood sample the next day, for a nonexistent study on aging at Manchester University. In fact, what Fred desired was Grundy's signature on a consent form of his own creation.

Shipman went to Grundy's home at 8:30 a.m. on June 24, and she missed an appointment later that morning. Two friends checked on her at noon and found her dead. Shipman blamed cardiac arrest, but postmortem tests revealed a morphine overdose. By then, Shipman had backdated his computer records to cast Grundy as a longtime morphine addict, while forging her signature on a will that left him £386,000 ($497,940 today).

Police initially accepted Fred's diagnosis of death from "old age," but Grundy's daughter—lawyer Angela Woodruff—remained skeptical. Her doubts crystalized when Shipman presented the forged will, contradicting the 1986 original written by Woodruff and kept on file at her law firm. As Woodruff later testified, "My mother was a meticulously tidy person. The thought of her signing a document which is so badly typed didn't make any sense. The signature looked strange. It looked too big.

The concept of Mum signing a document leaving everything to her doctor was unbelievable."

Detective Superintendent Bernard Postles agreed. "You only have to look at it once," Postles said, "and you start thinking it's like something off a John Bull printing press. You don't have to have twenty years as a detective to know it's a fake. Maybe he thought he was being clever—an old lady, nobody around her. Look at it. It's a bit tacky. But everyone knew she was as sharp as a tack. Maybe it was his arrogance."

Postles was convinced he had his man, but now he had a nagging sense that Grundy might not be the doctor's only victim. He launched a new investigation of Shipman, examining fifteen deaths from the year preceding Grundy's death. Six bodies had been cremated, but the coroner's office ordered exhumation of the other nine, with hair and tissue samples dispersed among various forensic laboratories. Grundy's autopsy revealed a morphine overdose within three hours of her death.

Withholding that information from Shipman, Postles obtained a search warrant for Fred's surgery and home. From the clinic, officers retrieved the typewriter used to fabricate Grundy's spurious will. Shipman countered with a transparent lie that his wealthy patient "sometimes borrowed" the machine for use at home.

Next, cyber analysts pored over Shipman's electronic files, amazed to find that Fred—a self-proclaimed "computer expert"—had left clumsy traces of falsification on his hard drive, logging to the second every alteration he had made to patient records over time. Confronted with the evidence, Fred tried to bluff, as indicated by the following exchange regarding victim Winifred Mellor.

> *Detective:* I'll just remind you of the date of this lady's death, 11 May '98. After 3 o'clock that afternoon, you have endorsed the computer with the date of 1 October '97 which is 10 months prior, "chest pains."

Shipman: I have no recollection of me putting that on the machine.

Detective: It's your passcode. It's your name.

Shipman: It doesn't alter the fact I can't remember doing it.

Detective: You attended the house at 3 o'clock. That's when you murdered this lady. You went back to the surgery and immediately started altering this lady's medical records. You tell me why you needed to do that.

Shipman: There's no answer.

On September 7, police charged Shipman with murdering Kathleen Grundy and forging her will. They soon added another fourteen murder counts for victims Marie West, Irene Turner, Lizzie Adams, Jean Lilley, Ivy Lomas, Muriel Grimshaw, Marie Quinn, Laura Wagstaff, Bianka Pomfret, Norah Nuttall, Pamela Hillier, Maureen Ward, Winifred Mellor, and Joan Melia.

Legal maneuvers delayed Shipman's trial until October 5, 1999. The proceedings began on a comic-macabre note, with Primrose Shipman handing out candy to spectators, trying to engage them in friendly small talk, seeming confident that Fred would be acquitted. A post-trial inquiry assessed her pleas of ignorance regarding Fred's murders as being "honest and straightforward."

Jurors and observers at the trial were not so easily deceived.

Preliminaries began with motions from defense counsel Nicola Davies denouncing media coverage of Shipman's crimes as "misleading and inaccurate." Prosecutor Richard Henriques replied that reports had alerted relatives of other likely victims. Next, Davies requested three separate trials, one for Kathleen Grundy, one for other exhumed victims, and another for those cremated. Finally, she moved to exclude "volume eight" of the crown's case, documenting Shipman's stockpiling of morphine. High Court judge Sir John Forbes denied all three motions, scheduling jury selection for October 11.

The crown's parade of witnesses began with Angela Woodruff, followed by pathologist Dr. John Rutherford describing morphine found in patients Shipman falsely certified as dying from natural causes. Detective Sergeant John Ashley ended the week with proof that Fred had altered computer records, backdating diagnoses and fabricating symptoms his victims had never displayed.

Week two presented Shipman's former staff and colleagues, each more damning than the last. Nurse Marion Gilchrist recalled Fred saying "I read thrillers and on the evidence they have, I would have me guilty." Of Kathleen Grundy, he'd complained "The only thing I did wrong was not having her cremated." Another clinic staffer described Shipman falsely claiming he'd called an ambulance for patients stricken at his office, then faking follow-up call to "cancel" the runs. Clinic telephone records proved those calls never occurred.

A sore point with jurors was Fred's callous treatment of his victims' relatives and friends, often teasing them to guess what had happened. A typical exchange involved Winnie Mellor's daughter Kathleen. She testified: "He said, 'Did you realize that your mother has been suffering from chest pains,' and I said, 'No.' He said, 'She called this morning and I came to see her and she refused treatment.' So I says, 'Well I'll be up as soon as I can.' He said, 'No, no there's no need for that.' So I said, 'Has she gone to hospital?' And he said, 'There's no point in sending her to hospital.' And I just went silent then, and he didn't say anything neither. And then I just realized what he was not saying. And I said, 'Do you mean my mother's dead?' He says, 'I see you understand.'"

Since fourteen of the victims named in his indictment died at home, Shipman claimed he couldn't have killed them, as he "never carried morphine" on house calls. Molly Dudley's daughter-in-law countered that lie with a memory of Shipman phoning from Molly's home, saying he'd given the patient a morphine injection and she only had "about half an hour left to live."

On January 31, 2000, jurors convicted Fred of fifteen murders and one forgery charge. Nicola Davies asked Forbes to pass sentence immediately and he obliged, denouncing Shipman's "wicked, wicked crimes." The final sentence: fifteen life prison terms plus four years. Police transported Shipman to prison in Durham. Primrose, a social outcast, moved there to facilitate visits.

Despite Shipman's conviction and imprisonment, his case was far from closed. Police announced the reopening of 175 additional cases, while Secretary of State for Health Alan Milburn ordered a private inquiry.

A survivor's case made news on February 28, when Manchester High Court awarded £225,000 ($290,250) in compensation to Derek Webb, aged forty-seven in November 1989, when Shipman botched

AN ARTIST'S IMPRESSION OF DR. HAROLD SHIPMAN AT PRESTON CROWN COURT. SHIPMAN WAS CONVICTED IN JANUARY OF 2000 OF MURDERING 15 OF HIS FEMALE PATIENTS, MAKING HIM ONE OF ENGLAND'S MOST PROLIFIC SERIAL KILLERS.

his treatment for epilepsy and psychosis. Fred's counsel admitted that Shipman had prescribed twice the proper dose of Epilim, an anti-convulsive drug, leaving Webb with brain damage, subject to "paranoid delusions and fears for his life," confined forever to a nursing home.

As that judgment made headlines, Greater Manchester Police claimed they had evidence supporting twenty-three more murder charges against Shipman, but prosecutor David Calvert-Smith refused to proceed, telling reporters "A fair trial would be impossible."

The first inquiry into Shipman's crimes began on March 10 under Lord Lanning of Tewin, scheduled to report its findings and recommendations in September. Lord Lanning's demand for closed-door hearings angered survivors of Shipman's lost patients. They applied for a High Court review of the secretive plan, and that court disbanded the Lanning Inquiry in July. Secretary Milburn waited two months to announce a new inquiry, finally selecting High Court judge Dame Janet Smith to chair that panel in December 2000.

But government moves slowly. Parliament waited another month to authorize the hearings, and Dame Janet did not reveal its plans or timetable until May 10, 2001. Eight days later, Coroner John Pollard concluded his inquest, listing 188 cases of homicide, 61 more suspicious, and 39 with insufficient evidence for judgment. None of those 288 cases was prosecuted.

Public hearings into Phase 1 of the larger Shipman Inquiry began on June 20, 2001, listing 647 deaths occurring between 1970 and 1998. Of those, 285 were deemed criminal or suspicious, 277 adjudged natural, and 85 lacking sufficient evidence for judgment.

Public hearings on Phase 2 of the inquiry began on May 7, 2002, including four broad topics reviewed in stages: (1) the police investigation of March 1998; (2) certificates of death and cremation; (3) Shipman's handling of controlled drugs; and (4) assorted medical monitoring and disciplinary systems. The panel concluded Stage 1 of

Phase 2 on July 17 and published its first report, reviewing Phase 1, two days later, stating that Shipman killed "at least" 215 victims between 1975 and 1998.

Hearings into Phase 2, Stage 2 convened on October 7, 2002 and concluded on January 27, 2003. Consideration of Phase 2, Stage 3 commenced on May 19, 2003. While that went on, Shipman was transferred to Wakefield Prison in West Yorkshire, nicknamed "The Monster Mansion" for its collection of high-risk murderers and sex offenders. At the time, its notorious inmates included "Gay Slayer" Colin Ireland (d. 2012) and serial child-killer Robert Black (d. 2016).

On July 14, 2002, the panel simultaneously published its second and third reports, detailing evidence collected for Phase 2, Stages 2 and 3. Even so, its timeline of events was not completed until July 18. Meanwhile, hearings on Phase 2, Stage 4 began on July 14, 2002 and continued through December 18, 2003.

Dame Janet's report on the 1998 police investigation found that Greater Manchester detectives were "inexperienced and unfit to handle the case," while retired Chief Superintendent David Sykes was deemed "unable to give effective leadership but did not do anything about it." Detective Inspector David Smith was "out of his depth and made many mistakes but did not ask for help and later lied to cover them up." As a result, police suffered "many missed opportunities to bring Shipman's crimes to light."

Smith also criticized Alan Banks, medical adviser for the West Pennine Health Authority, because "his respect for Shipman closed his mind to the fact that his colleague could have harmed a patient." Worse still, Smith wrote, "If the police and the coroner had moved with reasonable expedition, the lives of Shipman's last three victims would probably have been saved."

Statistician David Spiegelhalter, with the Cambridge Centre for Mathematical Sciences, went further, reporting that proper "statistical monitoring could have led to an alarm being raised at the end of 1996."

Shipman's case took another shocking turn on January 13, 2004—the eve of Fred's fifty-eighth birthday—when guards found him hanged in his cell at 6:20 p.m.

For reasons unknown, death was not pronounced until 8:10 p.m. A report declared that Shipman had hanged himself with bed sheets tied to window bars.

Home Secretary David Blunkett was surprised by the public reaction to Fred's death. He told reporters "You wake up and you receive a call telling you Shipman has topped himself and you think, is it too early to open a bottle? And then you discover that everybody's very upset that he's done it."

Not *everyone*, of course. Some victims' relatives felt cheated by Shipman's death without a detailed confession to all his crimes. London's *Daily Mirror* called Fred a "cold coward" and condemned the Prison Service for permitting his suicide. *The Sun* tabloid disagreed, running the headline "Ship Ship Hooray!"

As with Pakistani child-killer Javed Iqbal (see Chapter 14), opinions vary as to why—or even *if*—Fred killed himself. Some "suicides" in prisons are murders, committed by inmates or guards, but an inquiry completed in 2005 claimed Shipman's death "could not have been predicted or prevented." A prison spokesperson told reporters Fred "was showing no signs whatsoever of pre-suicidal behavior at all"—a claim contradicted by his probation officer. Fellow inmate David Smith told Leeds Crown Court that guards harassed Shipman, suggesting suicide. Smith testified: "An officer told him to go and hang himself and if he didn't know how, he'd be shown."

Assuming Shipman's death *was* suicide, greed may have motivated him. Death before his sixtieth birthday entitled Primrose to a National Health Service lump sum pension payment of £100,000 ($129,000 today) plus £10,000 yearly, versus £5,000 per year if he'd lived until January 14, 2006.

As with Fred's murders, mystery surrounds the disposition of his corpse. On April 2, 2004, the Biography Channel reported conflicting claims that Shipman's family had claimed the body or that it remained at Sheffield's mortuary pending further tests to rule out homicide. A full year after the announcement of Fred's death, *The Guardian* newspaper claimed that his remains were still in custody, while the *Yorkshire Post* alleged that Primrose had taken Fred's body from Wakefield Prison, postponing disposition until the "publicity dies down." According to the *Post*, Fred's widow favored burial, while one of their sons preferred cremation. A *Post* follow-up in April 2005 said Shipman was secretly cremated on March 19.

The Shipman Inquiry continued despite its subject's death. Dame Janet published a fourth report on July 15, 2004, assessing systems for the management and regulation of controlled drugs with suggestions for improvement. A fifth report, released on December 9, 2004, discussed improvements in the process for filing and evaluating complaints against physicians, while suggesting periodic revalidation of doctors.

The panel published its sixth and final report on January 27, 2005, with Dame Janet stating that Shipman had killed three patients— including four-year-old Susan Garfitt—at Pontefract General Infirmary. The report identified 459 patients who died under Shipman's care between 1971 and 1998, concluding with a speculative list of 250 murder victims.

On March 15, 2005, BBC News reported that Fred might have stolen jewelry worth £10,000 ($12,900) from various victims, retrieved by police from his garage. Primrose had requested that the rings, brooches, earrings, bracelets, and necklaces be returned to her, but authorities began mass-mailing inquiries to relatives of former Shipman patients, trying to identify the true owners, requesting sales receipts, photographs, or detailed descriptions. Items left unclaimed, they said, would be returned to Shipman's next of kin under the Police Property Act.

Despite Dame Janet's four-year investigation, confusion lingers today. She claimed the panel "considered" 887 deaths and ascribed 394 to natural causes. The panel's legal team investigated further on 493 cases, concluding that 210 deaths were "certainly or probably" natural; 15 resulted in murder convictions; 200 more were adjudged unlawful; 45 offered "real cause for suspicion" of murder; while 38 had insufficient evidence for judgment.

Even with that authoritative tabulation, media accounts of the panel's findings differ. On August 25, 2005, *The Guardian* cited Dame Janet's estimate of homicides at 250, rather than 215. Author and professor of forensic psychology Dr. Katherine Ramsland writes that the Shipman Inquiry "re-examined 137 patient deaths"—not 887 or 493, as stated in the sixth report—while estimating that Fred had claimed "215 to 260 victims."

After perusing official reports, Dr. Mike Aamodt, professor of psychology at Virginia's Radford University, estimates Shipman's body count "between 200 and 357." Dr. Richard Baker at the University of Leicester says "The real minimum number of Shipman victims was 236." Coroner John Pollard, after criticism from Dame Janet, speculated that "we might be looking at 1,000."

The aftermath of Shipman's killing spree continues to the present day. Fred remains the only British doctor yet convicted of murdering patients—though others were charged and acquitted—and the scope of his crimes sent shockwaves through the medico-legal establishment.

The General Medical Council charged six physicians with misconduct in countersigning cremation forms for Fred's victims, saying each should have noted a pattern between Shipman's house calls and patients dying. Those six were acquitted, but a similar hearing convened in October 2005, targeting Dr. Geraint Brown and Dr. Murtaza Husaini. Both worked at Greater Manchester's Tameside General Hospital in 1994, failing to notice when Shipman deliberately administered a "grossly excessive" dose of morphine to a forty-seven-year-old patient identified only as "Mrs. A." She survived for fourteen months in a persistent vegetative state, until expiring on April 21, 1995—a date matching the hospital death of Shipman victim Renate Overton. On October 26, the GMC convicted Brown and suspended him from practice for twelve months. Dr. Husaini, also convicted of misconduct, escaped with a reprimand.

11.
GREEN RIVER KILLER: GARY RIDGWAY

In October 2015, the *Huffington Post* ranked U.S. states by their frequency of serial murders. Washington placed fifth out of fifty with 277 cases, including the likes of Ted Bundy, Harvey "The Hammer" Carignan, Robert Yates, and Westley Dodd; but none rivaled elusive Gary Ridgway, the "Green River Killer," convicted of forty-nine murders between 1982 and 1998, with twenty-two others confessed. Some investigators think his rampage may have continued until his capture in 2001.

*   *   *   *   *

Gary Leon Ridgway is a Utah native, born in Salt Lake City on February 18, 1949. The second of three sons born to Thomas and Mary Ridgway, Gary endured violent parental arguments and maternal domination as a child. He was a bed-wetter until age thirteen; after each episode, his mother soaped his genitals, producing mixed feelings of sexual attraction and fantasies of matricide in her son. His dyslexia contributed to his failing one year in high school.

When Gary was sixteen years old, he stabbed a six-year-old boy. His victim survived, despite a lacerated liver. IQ tests that year scored Ridgway in the "low eighties," ranked as "below average intelligence." Despite his fits of rage, classmates and relatives considered Gary "friendly but strange."

After graduating from high school at age twenty, Ridgway married nineteen-year-old Claudia Barrows in August 1970, then joined the Navy, serving aboard a supply ship and witnessing combat in the Vietnam War. While overseas, he frequently patronized brothels; and because he refused to use condoms, he contracted gonorrhea. At home, Claudia also played the field; mutual infidelity prompted their divorce in January 1972.

Ridgway married Marcia Brown in December 1973, and they had a son, Matthew, in 1975. Their home life was contentious, Marcia complaining that Gary once placed her in a chokehold. At the same time, Ridgway allegedly embraced religion, proselytizing door-to-door, reading the Bible aloud at work and at home, weeping during sermons at church, and insisting that Marcia follow the strict teachings of their conservative pastor.

In sharp contrast to those principles, he pressured Marcia to have sex in public places and at rural sites (where some of his victims' corpses were later discovered). All Gary's wives remarked upon his hypersexual behavior: he demanded intercourse several times daily, and police learned that he kept on patronizing streetwalkers throughout his marriages. The strain became too much for Marcia, and she and Gary divorced in May 1981.

By then, authorities assert that Ridgway had crossed the line from cheating on his wives and buying sex to rape and murder. Most of his victims were sex workers or runaways found along Pacific Highway South— the "Sea-Tac Strip" between Seattle and Tacoma, Washington. He strangled most, then dumped their bodies in or near the Green River, often in clusters, and sometimes with pyramidal stones inserted into their vaginas. On occasion, he drove bodies into Oregon, hoping to confuse investigating authorities.

Ridgway usually showed a photo of his son to his victims to gain their trust, then drove to a secluded area to rape and strangle his subjects from behind. He switched from manual choking to garrotes over time when women fighting for their lives bruised and scratched his arms. He killed some at his home, others at his workplace, but most in his pickup or in woods surrounding the Green River. He sometimes returned to his body dump sites to engage in necrophilia with his deceased victims. Later, in custody, he denied taking pleasure from sex with corpses, explaining it as a "convenience" to forestall hunting fresh prey and risking arrest.

In August 1982, after the discovery of Ridgway's first two victims, King County Sheriff Barney Winckoski assigned Detectives Robert Keppel and Dave Reichert to the case, beginning the largest and longest hunt for a serial killer in U.S. history. Others soon joined the team, but they and Reichert returned to normal duties in November 1982, leaving Keppel alone. As the murders continued, new sheriff Vernon Thomas added more investigators during 1983 and formally created the Green River Task Force in January 1984, including members of seven other agencies. FBI profiler John Douglas visited Seattle and suffered a near-fatal brain infection while there.

Police arrested Ridgway for soliciting prostitutes in 1982 and added his name to the Green River suspect list a year later, but he reportedly passed a polygraph test in 1984. By 1985, he was dating Judith Mawson, who became his third wife in June 1988.

Before their wedding, in April 1987, officers took hair and saliva samples from Gary, planning tests for the relatively new procedure of DNA analysis, but the process moved slowly. The samples reached various labs in 1988, but primitive testing methods reduced them in size. Three more years elapsed before a match was reported, and Ridgway kept killing in the meantime.

Judith Mawson recalled speaking to detectives in 1987 but denied any knowledge of the case, reporting that her husband watched no TV news. In later interviews, after divorcing Ridgway in September 2002, Judith remembered that his home had no carpets when she moved in (because Gary allegedly used them to wrap bodies for transport). Gary told reporters that his murders slacked off after marrying Mawson, who he "truly loved." In retrospect, Judith said, "I feel I have saved lives by being his wife and making him happy."

Perhaps—although he killed at least four more, in 1990, 1991, and 1998, while logging another arrest for soliciting prostitution on November 16, 2001.

Every marriage has its secrets.

By 1998, the task force's victims list included fifty-four names. In order, they included:

- "Jane Doe B-17," white female, fourteen to eighteen, killed between 1980 and 1984; found January 2, 1986
- Wendy Coffield, sixteen, disappeared on July 8, 1982; found July 18
- Gisele Lovvorn, seventeen, missing July 17, 1982; found September 25
- Debra Bonner, twenty-three, vanished July 25, 1982; found August 12
- Marcia Chapman, thirty-one, disappeared August 1, 1982; located August 15
- Cynthia Hinds, seventeen, missing August 11, 1982; found August 15

- Opal Mills, sixteen, vanished August 12, 1982; located with Chapman on August 15

- Terry Milligan, sixteen, missing August 29, 1982; found April 1, 1984

- Mary Meehan, eighteen, lost September 15, 1982; located November 13, 1983

- Debra Estes, fifteen, missing September 20, 1982; found May 30, 1988

- Linda Rule, sixteen, vanished September 26, 1982; discovered January 31, 1983

- Denise Bush, twenty-three, missing October 8, 1982; found June 12, 1985

- Shawanda Summers, disappeared October 9, 1982; located August 11, 1983

- Shirley Sherrill, eighteen, last seen October 20–22, 1982; found June 14, 1985

- Kristi Vorak, thirteen, missing since October 31, 1982; still undiscovered

- Rebecca Marrero, twenty, vanished December 3, 1982; still missing

- Colleen Brockman, fifteen, vanished December 24, 1982; found May 26, 1984

- Sandra Major, twenty, also missing December 24, 1982; found December 30, 1985

- Alma Smith, eighteen, disappeared March 3, 1983; located April 2, 1984

- Delores Williams, seventeen, disappeared between March 8 and 14, 1983; found March 31, 1984

- Gail Matthews, twenty-three, vanished April 10, 1983; located September 18, 1983

- Andrea Childers, nineteen, lost April 14, 1983; located October 11, 1989

- "Jane Doe B-10," white female, twelve to eighteen, killed before May 1983; found March 21, 1984

- Sandra Gabbert, seventeen, missing April 17, 1983; located April 1, 1984

- Kimi-Kai Pistor, fifteen, also lost April 17, 1983; found December 15, 1983

- Marie Malvar, eighteen, missing April 30, 1983; located September 26, 2003

- Carol Christensen, twenty-one, vanished May 3, 1983; discovered May 8

- Martina Authorlee, eighteen, missing May 22, 1983; found November 14, 1984

- Cheryl Wims, eighteen, vanished May 23, 1983; found March 22, 1984

- Yvonne Antosh, nineteen, missing May 31, 1983; located October 15

- Carrie Rois, fifteen, last seen between May 31 and June 13, 1983; found March 10, 1985

- Constance Naon, nineteen, missing June 8, 1983; discovered October 27

- Kelly Ware, twenty-two, vanished July 18, 1983; found October 29th

- Tina Thompson, twenty-one, lost July 25, 1983; located April 20, 1984

- Patricia Leblanc, fifteen, missing August 12, 1983; never found

- April Buttram, sixteen, missing August 18, 1983; still undiscovered

- Debbie Abernathy, twenty-six, lost September 5, 1983; found March 31, 1984

- Tracy Winston, nineteen, missing September 12, 1983; located March 27, 1986

- Maureen Feeney, nineteen, lost September 28, 1983; found May 2, 1986

- Mary Bello, twenty-five, disappeared October 11, 1983; found October 12

- Pammy Avent, fifteen, vanished October 26, 1983; still missing

- Delise Plager, twenty-two, missing October 30, 1983; found February 14, 1984

- Kimberly Nelson, twenty-one, vanished November 1, 1983; located June 14, 1986

- Lisa Yates, nineteen, disappeared December 23, 1983; discovered March 13, 1984

- Mary West, sixteen, lost February 6, 1984; found September 8, 1985

- Cindy Smith, seventeen, missing March 21, 1984; found June 27, 1987

- Patricia Barczak, nineteen, vanished October 17, 1986; located February 3, 1993

- Roberta Hayes, twenty-one, lost February 7, 1987; found September 11, 1991

- Rose Kurran, sixteen, missing August 26, 1987; located August 31

- Marta Reeves, thirty-six, lost March 5, 1990; found September 20

- Darcy Warde, sixteen, missing April 24, 1990; so far undiscovered
- Cora McGuirk, twenty-two, disappeared July 12, 1991; still missing
- Patricia Yellowrobe, thirty-eight, missing January 1998; found August 6

Dave Reichert won election as sheriff in 1997. In April 2001, he organized an evidence review team to rejuvenate the Green River investigation. Before its dissolution, the revived task force reviewed some 400,000 pages of documents, 15,000 photographs, 500 audiotapes, and 170 videotapes. September finally brought word of a DNA match between Ridgway and one of the Green River victims.

On November 30, 2001, armed with that DNA match, police arrested Ridgway at the Kenworth truck factory where he worked as a spray-painter. Initial charges filed on December 5 accused him of aggravated murder in the cases of victims Chapman, Mills, Hinds, and Christensen. Ridgway pleaded not guilty at arraignment on December 18.

An amended round of charges, filed on March 27, 2003, accused Gary of murdering victims Coffield, Bonner, and Estes after forensic scientists matched microscopic paint flecks from their corpses to the Kenworth plant. Ridgway pleaded not guilty to those counts on April 3.

Ridgway initially was held in maximum security at the King County jail, then moved to an Airway Heights Minimum-Medium Security Level Tank in August 2003. Meanwhile attorneys, led by Anthony Savage, negotiated a plea bargain on June 13, sparing Ridgway from execution in return for his confession to forty-eight murders from the task force roster, with directions to some undiscovered graves. Gary formally pleaded guilty on November 5. Six weeks later, on December 18, he received forty-eight consecutive life prison terms, effectively barring parole.

Deputy prosecutor Jerry Baird explained the bargain as a kindness for the relatives of "41 victims who would not be the subject of *State v. Ridgway* if it were not for the plea agreement." Lead prosecutor Norman Maleng told reporters: "We could have gone forward with seven counts, but that is all we could have ever hoped to solve. At the end of that trial, whatever the outcome, there would have been lingering doubts about the rest of these crimes. This agreement was the avenue to the truth. And in the end, the search for the truth is still why we have a criminal justice system. Gary Ridgway does not deserve our mercy. He does not deserve to live. The mercy provided by today's resolution is directed not at Ridgway, but toward the families who have suffered so much."

Jailers in Walla Walla consigned Ridgway to solitary confinement at the Washington State Penitentiary in January 2004. On February 9, prosecutors began releasing videotapes of Gary's confessions to murdering seventy-one victims, calling murder his "career" and saying he buried later victims to preclude further acts of necrophilia.

And the case still would not die.

On November 20, 2005, a hiker found victim Tracy Winston's skull near Tiger Mountain, southeast of Seattle, twenty-four miles northeast of where the rest of her headless skeleton had surfaced in March 1986.

On December 21, 2010, more hikers found Rebecca Marrero's skull outside Auburn, Washington, near the site where Ridgway had directed officers to Marie Malvar's remains in 2003. Prosecutors charged Gary with Marrero's murder on February 11, 2011, and he pleaded guilty on the 18th, receiving a forty-ninth life prison term. Further DNA testing finally identified Sandra Major's remains in June 2012.

On May 14, 2015, based on his notoriety and persistent death threats, authorities transferred Ridgway to United States Penitentiary, Florence High—a "supermax" lockup east of Cañon City, Colorado, opened in 1993 to house high-risk inmates. Other occupants of Florence High have included terrorists Eljvir Duka and Walli Mujahidh, Mexican Gulf Cartel drug lord Osiel Cárdenas Guillén, and Internet "Silk Road" black-market website founder Ross Ulbricht.

Ridgway's admissions still leave some Green River cases unresolved. He denied killing listed task force victim Amina Agisheff in July 1982, whose remains surfaced in April 1984. Her age (thirty-five) and stable employment make her an unlikely target for Gary in his quest for sex workers and teenage runaways.

Gary *did* confess to killing sixteen-year-old Kassee Lee (née Woods) in August 1982 and dumping her corpse at a drive-in theater off the Sea-Tac Strip, but searchers found no body there and Lee's case remains officially unresolved.

Another question mark hovers over Kelly McGinnis, missing since June 1983. She had been questioned by police while "dating" Ridgway for cash near the Sea-Tac Strip. Her remains have not been found, and Gary omitted her from his confessions.

Ridgway is suspected of killing Tammie Lyles and Angela Girdner in separate attacks on June 9, 1983, their corpses found within a mile of confessed victims Bush and Shirell in 1998 and 2009, respectively; neither made the list of his confirmed victims.

Patricia Osborn, nineteen, vanished on October 20, 1983 and remains missing, another woman excluded from Ridgway's admissions.

Finally, while Gary was long suspected of murdering drug-addicted streetwalker Rose Kurran in August 1987, he was formally excluded as her killer in August 2016.

While Ridgway's guilt remains unclear in certain cases, women still alive pointed police toward an alternate suspect in August 1982. Working girls Susan Widmark (twenty-one) and Debra Estes (fifteen), reported that the driver of a blue-and-white pickup truck solicited sex, then assaulted them at gunpoint in separate incidents.

After raping Widmark, the gunman allowed her to dress, then drove on, commenting on recent Green River murders, before she escaped at a stoplight, memorizing a partial license plate number. Estes told a similar story of forced fellatio, after which the man handcuffed her, then inexplicably released her in a wooded area.

In September 1982, police stopped professional butcher Charles Clinton Clark in a pickup matching the suspect vehicle's description. A background check revealed that Clark owned two pistols, and both victims identified him from a driver's license photograph. In custody, his firearms confiscated, Clark confessed to the two attacks, then presented iron-clad alibis for several dates when missing Green River victims had disappeared. Another victim, Mary Meehan, vanished at the very time when officers were booking Clark into jail. His subsequent indictment for sexual assault left the killer at large.

Another suspect, targeted by Detective Reichert, was a forty-four-year-old unemployed taxi driver and volunteer searcher for Green River victims who seemed to fit John Douglas's profile. Detained for "vigorous interviews," the cabbie was later absolved of any guilt.

In December 1988, yet another suspect surfaced, when several viewers of a "Crime Stoppers" TV program reported sighting prison escapee William J. Stevens, at large since 1986 after skipping out on a burglary sentence. When arrested, Stevens was enrolled at the University of Washington, studying pharmacology. A search of his home revealed numerous guns, multiple driver's licenses, credit cards under various names, and explicit nude photos of known sex workers. As with Charles Clark, however, the fugitive's documented movements cleared him from involvement in the slayings.

Murders of high-risk victims continue in Washington, throughout the nation, and worldwide today. Predators go wherever they can find compliant prey.

12.

PIGGY PALACE: ROBERT PICKTON

Vancouver's Downtown Eastside is the poorest neighborhood in British Columbia—in all of Canada, for that matter. No other slum or ghetto in the country matches the squalor of this ten-block urban wasteland, with its rundown hotels and pawnshops, stained and fractured sidewalks, gutters and alleyways strewn with garbage, used condoms, and discarded hypodermic needles. Downtown Eastside has another name as well, used commonly by residents and the police who clean up after them.

They call the district "Low Track," and it fits.

Low Track is Vancouver's Skid Row. Its cold heart is the intersection of Main and Hastings, nicknamed "Pain and Wastings" by the denizens who know it best. Low Track is the heart of British Columbia's rock-bottom drug scene, estimates of its junkie population ranging from five to ten thousand at any given moment. The drugs of choice are heroin and crack cocaine, supplied by motorcycle gangs or Triad and Yakuza cartels that stake out choice blocks for themselves and defend their turf with brute force. (Travel writers call Vancouver the "most-Asian city" outside the Far East.)

Most of Low Track's female addicts support their habits via prostitution, trolling the streets night and day, haunted creatures rendered skeletal by what one *Seattle Times* reporter has dubbed "the Jenny Crack diet." Safe sex is an illusion in this neighborhood, which boasts the highest HIV infection rate in North America.

Low Track's recent history is a tale of unrelenting failure. Vancouver lured affluent tourists by the hundreds of thousands to Expo '86, but the prospect of easy money brought a corresponding influx of the poor and hopeless, most of them gravitating to Downtown Eastside. Around the same time, competition among drug cartels flooded the district with cheap narcotics, breeding a new generation of addicts. Surrounding districts passed new laws to purge their streets of sex workers, driving the women out of Burnaby and North Vancouver, into Downtown Eastside. In 1994, federal cutbacks left welfare recipients short of cash, while mental hospitals disgorged patients onto the streets. By 1997, careless sex and shared needles had taken their toll in Low Track, with a quarter of the neighborhood's residents testing HIV-positive. So far, government needle-exchange programs have failed to stem the plague, despite provision of some 2.8 million needles in Low Track each year.

Downtown Eastside is infamous for its "kiddy stroll," featuring prostitutes as young as eleven. Some work the streets, while others are secured by their pimps in special trick pads. New prospects arrive every day, runaways and adventure-seekers dubbed "twinkies" by those already trapped in The Life. A 1995 survey of Low Track's working girls revealed that seventy-three percent of them entered the sex trade as children; the same percent were unwed mothers, with an average of three children each. Of those, ninety percent had lost children to the state; fewer than half knew where their children were. Nearly three-quarters of Low Track's prostitutes were Aboriginals. More than eighty percent were born and raised outside Vancouver. In 1998 they averaged one death per day from drug overdoses, the highest rate in Canadian history.

But there were other dangers on the street as well, including predators hunting for more than bargain-basement sex.

Streetwalkers are by nature an elusive breed. Many begin as adolescent runaways and never lose the habit of evasion, changing names and addresses so often that investigators have no realistic hope of tracking a specific individual. When hookers vanish—as opposed to being slain and left in garbage dumpsters, motel rooms, canals, or vacant lots—no one can say with any certainty whether they have disappeared by choice or through foul play.

Too often, no one cares.

No pattern was discernible when women started vanishing from Low Track in 1978. Lillian O'Dare, age thirty-four, was first on September 12, rather surprisingly reported missing the same day. Wendy Allen was next; she vanished in March 1979, but broke the pattern when authorities found her alive, living under an assumed name in Ontario, in July 2006.

The war of nerves began on June 25, 1983, when Rebecca Funo disappeared, logged as missing on June 28. In December, Yvonne Abigosis, twenty-five, disappeared; she had phoned her sister in Calgary, announcing plans to visit soon, but never arrived. Police stalled until 2002 before seeking her DNA samples.

Sherry Rail, forty-three, dropped from sight on January 30, 1984, but nearly three years elapsed before she was reported missing on January 8, 1987. Linda Grant, mother of three, vanished in October.

Sheryl Donahue traveled from Grand Prairie to Vancouver for a job interview in May 1985, then seemingly vanished; she was reported missing on August 31. Before police logged that report, on August 1, Laura Mah vanished from Low Track. Her missing-person report reached authorities in 1999.

In 1986, Elaine Allenbach, thirty-three, told friends she was moving to Seattle on March 13, but she never made it. They reported her missing in mid-April.

No disappearances were recorded for 1987.

Teressa Williams, twenty-six, was last seen alive on July 21, 1988, but not reported missing until March 17, 1999.

Two more women vanished in 1989. Ingrid Soet, a forty-year-old mental patient, disappeared on August 28, 1989, and was listed as missing on October 1, 1990. No one seems sure when Elaine Dumba was last seen, but she finally was reported lost on April 9, 1998.

Low Track's hunter(s) took another break in 1990, then returned to claim two victims in 1991. Sex worker Nancy Clark, twenty-five, stopped making her normal rounds on August 22, reported missing one day later. Mary Lands, twenty-eight, vanished without leaving a ripple sometime before year's end and was reported missing thirteen years later, in 2004.

Vancouver's first recorded black victim, thirty-nine-year-old Kathleen Wattley, went missing for eleven days before friends reported her disappearance on June 29, 1992. Elsie Sebastien, forty, vanished on October 16, officially noted as missing on May 16, 2001.

The tally doubled in 1993. Gloria Fedyshyn, twenty-seven, disappeared in January, but her absence went unnoticed until July 2002. Friends reported Teresa Triff, twenty-four, missing on April 15 but could not recall when they had last seen her. Likewise, no one remembered when they'd stopped seeing Sherry Baker, twenty-five, and while they all agreed it was sometime in 1993, they waited eleven years to tell police. The disappearance of drug addict Leigh Miner on December 14 was ignored by detectives even when they finally acknowledged that a serial killer was at large.

Angela Arseneault was 1994's lone victim, last seen on August 19, reported missing ten days later. The pace ramped up again in 1995, starting with forty-seven-year-old Catherine Gonzales in March, logged as missing in February 1996. Catherine Knight, thirty-two, who disappeared in April 1995, was reported missing to authorities on November 11. Dorothy Spence, thirty-six, was last seen living on August 30 and reported the day before Halloween. Diana Melnick, twenty-seven, vanished two days after Christmas; police were alerted on December 29.

Frances Young, thirty-eight, was the first to vanish in 1996. Reportedly suffering from depression when she left her West Side home for a stroll on April 6, she was reported missing three days later. Tanya Holyk, twenty, mother of one, disappeared on October 29 and was logged as missing on November 3. The year ended with Olivia Williams disappearing on December 6, noted by police on July 4, 1997.

Maria Laliberte went missing on New Year's Day 1997 and was belatedly reported missing on March 8, 2002. Reports of what happened to new mother Stephanie Lane, twenty, are oddly confused. Some accounts claim she disappeared on January 10, others that she was hospitalized for an episode of drug psychosis on March 10 and vanished the next day, upon release from the hospital. Sharon Ward disappeared from New Westminster on St. Valentine's Day. Andrea Borhaven, twenty-six, "never had an address" and "just bounced off the walls" according to Low Track acquaintances, who noted her absence in March 1997 but delayed telling police until May 18, 1999. Sherry Irving, twenty-four, dropped from sight in April, reported missing on March 21, 1998.

The district's sole known transgender victim, twenty-eight-year-old Kellie Little (born Richard), disappeared on April 23, 1997, abandoning her beloved cat and trailing a dismal record of foster homes, jail terms, and drug abuse. Victim Cara Ellis, twenty-six, was known to friends as "Nicky Trimble." None could say exactly when they had seen her last, sometime between New Year's and summer 1997. Memories of Janet Henry were more precise, perhaps because she'd survived a near-miss with serial child-killer Clifford Olson in the early 1980s. Last seen alive on June 25, 1997, Henry was reported missing on the 28th.

And the grim year's toll continued. Jacqueline Murdock, a mother of four, vanished on August 13 or 14 and was reported missing on October 30, 1998. Marnie Frey, twenty-five, also disappeared in August and was logged as missing on September 4, 1998. Helen Hallmark, twenty-one, was the month's third victim, reported missing nineteen days after Marnie Frey. Cindy Beck, thirty-three, dropped from sight in September and was reported missing months before the August victims, on April 30, 1998. On November 26, 1997—sixteen days before her forty-eighth birthday—Cindy Feliks became the bloody year's last victim.

The official search for Vancouver's missing women began in September 1998, after an Aboriginal group sent police a list of victims allegedly murdered in Downtown Eastside, with a demand for a thorough investigation. Authorities examined the list and pronounced it flawed. Some of the "victims" had died from disease or drug overdoses, others had left Vancouver and had been found alive; but Detective Dave Dickson was intrigued by the complaint and launched his own inquiry, drawing up a list of Low Track women who had simply disappeared without a trace. There were enough names on that second list to worry Dickson and inspire his superiors to create an investigative task force.

The four-year search for answers had begun.

Vancouver police launched their review with forty unsolved disappearances of local women, dating back to 1971. The lost came from all walks of life and all parts of Vancouver, but the search for a pattern narrowed the roster to sixteen Low Track prostitutes reported missing since 1995. By the time detectives made their first arrest in the case, that list would grow to include fifty-four women who had vanished between 1983 and 2001. Headquarters assigned eighty-five investigators to the case; but in the early stages of their search, police were busy trying to decide if they had a serial killer at large in Vancouver.

One who thought so was Inspector Kim Rossmo, creator of a "geographic profiling" technique designed to map unsolved crimes and highlight any pattern or criminal "signature" overlooked by detectives assigned to individual cases. In May 1999, Rossmo reported an unusual concentration of disappearances from Low Track, but his superiors dismissed the notion in their public statements, insisting that the vanished women might have left Vancouver voluntarily, in search of greener streets. Inspector Gary Greer advised the press that "We're in no way saying there is a serial murderer out there. We're in no way saying that all these people missing are dead. We're not saying any of that."

Rossmo, meanwhile, stood by his theory and resigned from the force after receiving a punitive demotion. A judge dismissed his subsequent lawsuit against the Vancouver P.D. in 2001.

Internal dissension was not the only problem faced by police in their search for Low Track's vanished women. Canada's Violent Crime Linkage System did not track missing persons without some evidence of foul play, and task force investigators approached it empty-handed. In the absence of a corpse or crime scene, or even a specific date for most of the disappearances, forensic evidence was nonexistent. Pimps and prostitutes were naturally reluctant to cooperate with the same officers who might throw them in jail. (At one point, detectives identified a man who had serially assaulted five streetwalkers in two months, but none of the victims would file a complaint.) Resources were perpetually limited, despite increasing media attention to the case.

Still, the detectives forged ahead as best they could. In June 1999, they met with relatives of several missing women, seeking information and DNA samples for prospective identification of remains. Police and coroners' databases were reviewed throughout Canada and the United States, as were various drug rehabilitation facilities, witness-protection programs, hospitals, mental institutions, and AIDS hospices. Burial records at Glenhaven Cemetery were examined, going back to 1978.

Grim news came from Edmonton, Alberta, where police had logged twelve unsolved prostitute murders between 1986 and 1993. Closer to home, four sex workers had been killed and dumped around Agassiz, B.C., about 60 miles east of Vancouver, in 1995 and '96, but none of them was from the Low Track missing list.

The search went on, each new day reminding officers that they were literally clueless, chasing shadows in the dark.

And women kept on disappearing.

Kerry Koski, a thirty-nine-year-old mother of three, vanished on January 7, 1998, and was reported missing on the 29th. Inga Hall, forty-six or forty-seven and a mother and grandmother, disappeared on February 26, and was logged as missing on March 3. Sandra DeVries, twenty-nine, who went missing on April 14, was reported by friends on the same day. She left behind a journal reading, in part, "I think my hate is going to be my destination, my executioner."

So 1998 wore on. Shelia Egan, twenty—a sex worker since fifteen—vanished on July 11 and was reported missing on August 5. Street-walker Julie Young, thirty-one, disappeared in October. Angela Jardine, twenty-seven, dropped from sight on November 10 or 20 (accounts differ). Michele Gurney, twenty-nine, a sex worker diagnosed schizophrenic in 1986, disappeared on December 11, and was logged missing on the 22nd. Two days after Christmas, Marcelle Creison joined the missing list, reported on January 11, 1999. Two other victims claimed in 1998 passed unnoticed at first: Ruby Hardy, thirty-nine, last saw her family before year's end, but no one can recall precisely when; and Terry Peterson, likewise, vanished without notice and was only reported missing in 2004.

A grim New Year saw Jacqueline McDonnell, twenty-three and a mother of one, disappear on January 16, 1999. Brenda Wolfe, thirty, a mental patient, mother, and self-styled "street enforcer" who protected weaker Low Track residents for pay, disappeared herself on February 1, and was reported missing on April 25, 2000. Georgine Papin, thirty-four, vanished on March 2 and was reported lost in March 2001.

The murders then went on hiatus from March until November 27, 1999, when forty-three-year-old Wendy Crawford disappeared; she was reported missing on December 14. Two days past Christmas, Jennifer Furminger, twenty-eight, left her son and cocaine habit forever. Four days later, Tiffany Drew disappeared and was reported missing on February 8, 2002.

Late in 1998, task force detectives got their best lead yet from thirty-seven-year-old Bill Hiscox. Widowed two years earlier, Hiscox had turned to drugs and alcohol after his wife died, but was rescued from the downhill slide when his foster sister found him a job at P&B Salvage in Surrey, southeast of Vancouver. The proprietors were Robert William "Willie" Pickton and his brother David, of Port Coquitlam. Hiscox's helpful relative was Robert Pickton's "off-and-on" girlfriend in 1997, and Hiscox picked up his paychecks at the brothers' Port Coquitlam pig farm, described by Hiscox as "a creepy-looking place" patrolled by a vicious 600-pound boar. "I never saw a pig like that, who would chase you and bite at you," he told police. "It was running out with the dogs around the property."

Hiscox had grown concerned about the Picktons after reading newspaper reports on Vancouver's missing women. He said Robert Pickton was "a pretty quiet guy, hard to strike up a conversation with, but I don't think he had much use for men." Pickton drove a converted bus with deeply tinted windows, Hiscox told authorities. "It was Willie's pride and joy," he said, "and he wouldn't part with it for anything. Willie used it a lot." The brothers also ran a supposed charity, the Piggy Palace Good Times Society, registered with the Canadian government in 1996 as a non-profit society intended to "organize, co-ordinate, manage and operate special events, functions, dances, shows and exhibitions on behalf of service organizations, sports organizations and other worthy groups." According to Hiscox, the "special events" that convened at Piggy Palace—a converted building at the hog farm—were drunken raves that featured "entertainment" by an ever-changing cast of Downtown Eastside prostitutes.

Police were already familiar with the Pickton brothers. David Francis Pickton had been convicted of sexual assault in 1992, fined $1,000, and given 30 days' probation. His victim in that case told police Pickton had attacked her in his trailer at the pig farm, but she managed to escape when a third party came in and distracted him. Port Coquitlam authorities sought an order to destroy one of David's dogs in April 1998, under the Livestock Protection Act, but the proceedings were later dismissed without explanation. Pickton had also been sued three times for damages resulting from traffic accidents in 1988 and 1991, settling all three claims out of court.

Soon after Piggy Palace opened, the Pickton brothers and their sister, Linda Louise Wright, found themselves in court again, sued by Port Coquitlam officials for allegedly violating city zoning ordinances. According to the complaint, their property was zoned for agricultural use, but they had "altered a large farm building on the land for the purpose of holding dances, concerts and other recreations" that sometimes drew as many as 1,800 persons. Following a New Year's Eve party on December 31, 1998, the Picktons were slapped with an injunction banning future parties, the court order noting that police were henceforth "authorized to arrest and remove any person" attending public events at the farm. The "society" finally lost its nonprofit status in January 2000, for failure to provide mandatory financial statements.

Other charges filed against Robert Pickton were more serious. In March 1997, he was charged with the attempted murder of a drug-addicted prostitute, Wendy Lynn Eistetter, whom he stabbed several times in a wild melee at the pig farm. Eistetter told police that Pickton had handcuffed and attacked her on March 23, and that she had escaped after disarming him and stabbing him with his own knife. A motorist found Eistetter beside the highway at 1:45 a.m. and took her to the nearest emergency room, while Pickton sought treatment for a single stab wound at Eagle Ridge Hospital. He was released on $2,000 bond, but the charge was later dismissed without explanation in January 1998.

The stabbing had crystallized Bill Hiscox's suspicion about Robert Pickton, whom he called "quite a strange character." Aside from the assault, Hiscox told police, there were "all the girls that are going missing, and all the purses and IDs that are out there in his trailer and stuff." Pickton, Hiscox told detectives, "frequents the downtown area all the time, for girls."

Police recorded Hiscox's statement and a detective accompanied him to the pig farm, afterward vowing "to push the higher-ups, all the way to the top, to investigate." Subsequent press reports indicate that the farm was searched three times, apparently without result. The brothers would remain on file, "persons of interest" to the inquiry, but no surveillance would be mounted on the farm.

Back in Vancouver, meanwhile, the list of missing women grew longer, with no end in sight.

* * * * *

Not every woman on the missing list was gone forever. Between September 1999 and March 2002, five of the lost were found, dead or alive, and thus were deleted from the roster of presumed kidnap victims.

The first to vanish had been Patricia Gay Perkins, twenty-two years old when she abandoned Low Track and a one-year-old son in a bid to save her own life. An incredible eighteen years elapsed before she was reported missing to police, in 1996. Another three years passed before she saw her name on a published list of Vancouver's missing women, on December 15, 1999, and telephoned from Ontario to tell police she was alive, drug-free, and living well.

Another survivor, also discovered in December 1999, was fifty-year-old Rose Ann Jensen. She had dropped out of sight in October 1991 and was reported missing a short time later, added to the official "missing" roster when Vancouver's task force organized in 1998. Police found her alive in Toronto while scanning a national health-care database. Vancouver Constable Anne Drennan told reporters that Jensen had left Downtown Eastside "for personal reasons. It doesn't appear she knew she was being looked for."

Relatives of Linda Jean Coombes twice reported her missing, in August 1994 and again in April 1999. Unknown to her family or police, Linda had died of a heroin overdose on February 15, 1994, her body delivered to Vancouver's morgue without identification. Her mother viewed a photo of the "Jane Doe" corpse in 1995 but could not recognize her own child, wasted by narcotics, malnutrition, and disease. Identification was finally made in September 1999, via comparison of DNA material submitted by the family, and another name was removed from the official victims list.

A similar solution removed Karen Anne Smith from the roster. Reported missing on April 27, 1999, she had in fact died on February 13, at the University of Alberta Hospital in Edmonton. The cause of death was listed as heart failure related to hepatitis C. Once again, DNA contributed to the belated identification.

Another Low Track prostitute, twenty-four-year-old Anne Wolsey, was reported missing by her mother on January 1, 1997, though the actual date of her disappearance was anyone's guess. Five years later, in March 2002, Wolsey's father called from Montreal to tell police that his daughter was alive and well. Estranged from his ex-wife by a bitter divorce, Wolsey's father—like Anne herself—had been unaware of the police report filed in Vancouver until a suspect's arrest renewed media interest in the case.

Five out of fifty-four were deleted from the list of vanished women, but their slots never remained empty for long. There were always new victims, it seemed. But where had they gone?

Police are never entirely without suspects when sex workers are victimized. In fact, a more common problem is *too many* suspects, with streetwalkers often unwilling to file charges or testify at trial. So it was in Vancouver, as the task force began logging names and descriptions of potential predators.

One who the detectives considered was thirty-six-year-old Michael Leopold, arrested in 1996 for assaulting a Low Track streetwalker, beating her and trying to force a rubber ball down her throat. A passerby heard the girl's screams and frightened Leopold away, but he surrendered to police three days later. Granted, he had been in custody since then, held in lieu of bond while he awaited trial; but with disappearances dating back to the mid-1980s, any sadist with a propensity for attacking women rated a closer look. Leopold regaled a court-appointed psychiatrist with his fantasies of kidnapping, raping, and murdering prostitutes, but he insisted that the 1996 assault had been his only foray into real-life action. Task force investigators ultimately absolved Leopold of any involvement in the disappearances, but he had a rude surprise in store at his trial, in August 2000. Convicted of aggravated assault, Leopold received a fourteen-year prison sentence, with credit for the four years served before the trial.

Another suspect in the case was forty-three-year-old Alberta native Barry Thomas Neidermier. Convicted in 1990 of pimping a fourteen-year-old girl, Neidermier apparently left prison with a misguided grudge against streetwalkers. In 1995, police jailed him again, this time for selling contraband cigarettes from his Vancouver tobacco shop, driven out of business by a heavy fine. In April 2000, Vancouver police charged Neidermier with violent attacks on seven Low Track sex workers, the charges against him including battery, kidnapping, sexual assault, robbery, unlawful confinement, and administering a noxious substance. None of Neidermier's alleged victims were drawn from the Vancouver missing list, and Constable Anne Drennan told reporters "It's impossible to say at this point whether or not Neidermier may be related to those cases. Certainly he is a person of interest, and he will continue to be a person of interest."

More frustrating still were the suspects described to police without names or addresses. On August 10, 2001, Vancouver police announced their search for an unidentified rapist who had attacked a thirty-eight-year-old victim outside her Low Track hotel a week earlier. "During the attack," police spokesmen said, "the man claimed responsibility for sexually assaulting and killing other women in the Downtown Eastside." The victim had escaped by leaping from her rapist's car, and while she offered a description to authorities, the boastful predator remains at large.

And there are countless more, besides. The Downtown Eastside Youth Activities Society maintains a daily "bad date" file, page after page of reports from local prostitutes who have been threatened or injured by nameless "tricks." Their tales run the gamut from verbal abuse to beatings and stabbings, presented as a warning for those who support themselves and their habits on the streets.

All in vain.

As a new millennium dawned in Vancouver, the task force investigation had expanded to include more than three times the number of missing women initially listed in 1998. Some of the new presumed victims had been missing since the mid-1980s, their disappearance recognized only now, while others continued to vanish from Low Track with the search still in progress. Warnings and surveillance went for nothing, it seemed, as more women dropped out of sight.

Victims from 2000 included Tiffany Drew, twenty-five, mother of three, last seen alive in March. No date of disappearance is available for Sharon Abraham. Dawn Crey, forty-two, mother of one son, vanished on November 1, reported missing on December 11. Debra Jones capped the year, vanishing on December 21, reported to police on Christmas Day.

Eight disappearances were recorded in 2001. Patricia Johnson, twenty-five, went missing first, on February 23, and was reported to police on May 31. Yvonne Boen, thirty-three, vanished on March 16, as was reported five days later. Heather Chinnock, thirty, a mother of two from Colorado, disappeared on April 1, and was logged missing on June 19. Heather Bottomley vanished on April 17. Angela Joesberry, twenty-two and a mother of one, disappeared on June 6, as was reported two days later. Sereena Abbotsway, a victim of fetal alcohol syndrome, was nineteen days shy of her thirtieth birthday when she vanished on August 1; her disappearance was reported three weeks later. Diane Rock, thirty-four and a mother of five, vanished on October 19. The killer's last known victim, Mona Wilson, was a twenty-six-year-old mother of one when she dropped from sight on November 23 and was reported missing one week later.

It was over, but no one knew that yet.

Because the Downtown Eastside disappearances spanned so many years, Vancouver police had to consider the possibility that some sexual predator identified with other crimes might be responsible for some of the earlier cases. Unfortunately, in British Columbia and the Pacific Northwest generally, there was no shortage of monsters competing for attention.

First among equals in that respect was Seattle's elusive "Green River Killer" (see Chapter 11), ultimately blamed for the death or disappearance of at least forty-nine girls and women during the 1980s and 1990s. The "River Man" was also suspected of forty-plus slayings in neighboring Snohomish County, but his murder spree had ended with a whimper, leaving police and FBI profilers wringing their hands in frustration.

Another long-shot candidate was Dayton Leroy Rogers, a sadistic foot fetishist dubbed the "Molalla Forest Killer," who began stalking prostitutes around Portland, Oregon in January 1987. By August of that year he had claimed eight lives and injured twenty-seven other victims, identified after he carelessly performed his last killing before multiple witnesses. Incarcerated since August 7, 1987, Rogers was examined and finally rejected as a possible suspect in the Vancouver abductions listed before that date.

Keith Hunter Jesperson was a British Columbia native, born in 1956, who washed out of training for the Royal Canadian Mounted Police after an injury left him unfit for active duty. Instead, he hit the road as a long-haul trucker, traveling widely across North America—and murdering various women in the process. Nicknamed the "Happy Face Killer" for the smiling cartoon signature on taunting letters he sent to police, Jesperson was jailed for a Washington murder in March 1995. At one point, he claimed 160 slayings, describing his female victims as "piles of garbage" dumped on the roadside, and while he later recanted those statements, convictions in Washington and Wyoming removed him permanently from circulation. Once again, no link could be found between "Happy Face" and the vanished Low Track women.

Other prospects were considered and rejected in their turn. George Waterfield Russell, sentenced to life imprisonment for the murders of three Bellevue, Washington women in 1990, was discounted because he enjoyed posing his mutilated victims, putting them on display after he slaughtered them in their own homes. Robert Yates, convicted in October

2000 of killing thirteen prostitutes around Spokane, Washington, was suspected of two more murders in a neighboring county but could not be placed in Vancouver for any of the local disappearances. John Eric Armstrong, a U.S. Navy veteran arrested in April 2000, confessed to slaying thirty women around the world, but his statements excluded Vancouver and no evidence was found to contradict him.

In Vancouver itself, police cast an eye on twice-convicted rapist Ronald Richard McCauley. Sentenced to seventeen years in prison on his first conviction, in 1982, McCauley was paroled on September 14, 1994. A year later, in September 1995, he was charged with another assault, convicted, and returned to prison in 1996. While never formally charged with murder, he is described by police as their prime suspect in the slayings of four Low Track prostitutes killed in 1995 and early 1996. Three of the victims were dumped between Agassiz and Mission, B.C., about 35 miles southeast of Vancouver, where McCauley resided; the fourth was found on Mt. Seymour, in North Vancouver. Besides those cases, in July 1997, Vancouver police declared McCauley a suspect in the 1995 disappearances of Catherine Gonzales, Catherine Knight, and Dorothy Spence. No charges were forthcoming, however, and McCauley was forgotten four years later, as the spotlight focused on another suspect.

Vancouver residents were unprepared for the announcement when it came, on February 7, 2002. That morning, Vancouver Constable Catherine Galliford told reporters that searchers were scouring the Pickton pig farm and adjacent property in Port Coquitlam, first examined back in 1997. "I can tell you a search is being conducted on that property and the search is being executed by the missing-women task force," she reported.

Robert Pickton was already in custody, jailed on a charge of possessing illegal firearms.

A LOOK AT THE OUTBUILDING AT THE PIG FARM OF ROBERT WILLIAM PICKTON, CANADA'S MOST PROLIFIC SERIAL KILLER. HE WAS CHARGED WITH MURDERING MORE THAN 20 VANCOUVER WOMEN.

Bailed out on that charge, he was arrested once more on February 22, and this time faced two counts of first-degree murder. On February 25, authorities identified the victims as Sereena Abotsway and Mona Wilson.

Pickton professed to be "shocked" by the charges, but relatives of the victims were equally agitated, noting that both women had vanished three years after the Piggy Palace was identified as a potential murder scene. On March 8, investigators declared that DNA recovered from the farm had been conclusively identified as Abotsway's. On April 2 Pickton was charged with three more counts of murder, naming victims Jacqueline McDonnell, Heather Bottomley, and Diane Rock. A sixth murder charge, for Angela Josebury, was filed against Pickton one week later. As in the first two cases, all four victims had been slain since Bill Hiscox had fingered Pickton as a suspect in the Low Track disappearances. On May 22, a seventh first-degree murder charge was filed against Pickton when the remains of Brenda Wolfe were found on his farm.

DNA tests continued, but with disappointing results for victims' families. Between June 25 and August 8, genetic traces of Helen Hallmark,

Patricia Johnson, Cindy Beck, and Sarah DeVries were found at the farm, but in insufficient quantities to support further charges. Despite that official announcement, Hallmark and Johnson *were* included, with victims Papin and Furminger, when prosecutors filed new murder counts on September 20.

If Pickton was the Low Track slayer, critics asked, why had the searches of his property in 1997 and '98 failed to uncover any evidence? More to the point, how could he abduct and murder additional victims between 1999 and 2001, when he should have been under police surveillance?

Worse yet, some said, in 1999, police received a tip that Pickton had a freezer filled with human flesh which he sometimes sold or gave away. Officers interviewed Pickton again and obtained his consent for another search of his farm, but never conducted one.

Proclaiming his innocence on all charges, Pickton was scheduled for trial in November 2002, but detectives were not finished with their search at Piggy Palace. The full operation, they announced on March 21, 2002, might drag on for a year or more. As for other victims and any further charges, they refused to speculate.

On February 13, 2002, before Pickton was slapped with his first murder charges, spokesmen for Prostitution Alternatives Counseling Education claimed that 110 streetwalkers from British Columbia's Lower Mainland had been slain or kidnapped in the past two decades. Computer data generated by the Royal Canadian Mounted Police placed the number even higher: 144 sex workers murdered or missing with foul play suspected throughout the province at large.

It may be comforting to think one human monster is responsible for all those crimes, at least within Vancouver, but is it a realistic hope? Before Pickton's indictment, detectives favored other theories. Some believed a long-haul trucker was disposing of Vancouver's prostitutes, while others thought the missing women had been lured aboard foreign cargo ships, gang-raped and murdered by crewmen, then buried at sea. Still others rejected the serial-killer hypothesis until the very day of Pickton's arrest. The only thing certain about Vancouver's mystery, by then, was its bitter divisiveness.

Victoria attorney Denis Bernsten announced on April 17, 2002, that he would file a multimillion-dollar class-action suit against Robert Pickton, the Vancouver Police Department, and the Royal Canadian Mounted Police, seeking damages for relatives of the missing and murdered women. Bernsten accused police of "willful negligent action" in the case, telling reporters "Deaths may have been prevented. All of these women were somebody's child. Someone loved them."

Among surviving relatives, meanwhile, there was dissension over calls for a public inquiry into police handling of the protracted investigation. Lynn Frey, stepmother of missing Marnie Frey, told the press "Everyone's fighting about lawyers, inquiries, or fundraising, yet none of that is going to bring our loved ones back." Several Aboriginal families complained of "interference" by the Vancouver Police Department's Native Liaison Unit, with officers allegedly telling them not to speak with journalists. Victim Helen Hallmark's mother defied the ban, declaring "We need to meet among ourselves, and I'm tired of the Native Liaison Unit telling us what to do." In response to the perceived whitewash, Kathleen Hallmark announced plans to retain a partner of famed attorney Johnny Cochrane and pursue her legal remedies in court.

In the midst of that tumult, Canadian musicians declared their intent to release a special song, "A Buried Heart," with proceeds from its sale directed toward construction of a drug treatment and recovery center in Downtown Eastside. Artists signed on for the project included headliners Sarah McLachlan and Nellie Furtado, Colin James, Gord Downey, and John Wozniak. In a parallel effort, Val Hughes—sister of missing Kerry Koski—told reporters that a Missing Women's Trust Fund had been established at the Bank of Montreal, accepting donations for construction of a "rapid opiate detoxification center in Downtown Eastside."

Beyond hope for the future, there was anger. Val Hughes supports the ongoing task force investigation, but she told *The Province* "Like all family members, I feel molten rage when it comes to the Vancouver city police. Their view was that it didn't matter if a serial killer was at work, as long as it was confined to one geographical area where the women were expendable people no one cared about. They told us our loved ones were just out partying. We want a full public inquiry, not to interfere with the criminal prosecution but to get answers."

Robert Pickton's trial began in New Westminster on January 30, 2006. He pleaded not guilty to twenty-seven counts of first-degree murder, then settled back for legal arguments involving the admissibility of evidence.

Justice James Williams dismissed one count, involving a "Jane Doe" victim still unidentified today, then stayed prosecution in the cases of victims Borhaven, Bottomley, Chinnock, Crawford, DeVries, Drew, Ellis, Feliks, Furminger, Hall, Hallmark, Holyk, Irving, Jardine, Johnson, Jones, Koski, McDonnell, Melnick, and Rock. That left six deaths for jurors to consider, victims Abotsway, Joesbury, Frey, Papin, Wilson, and Wolfe.

On December 9, 2007, jurors acquitted Pickton of the first-degree murder charges, convicting him on lesser counts of second-degree murder that bars life imprisonment without parole, permitting a judge to set the deadline on parole hearings between ten and twenty-five years. Justice Williams imposed the twenty-five-year maximum on December 11.

Both the prosecution and Pickton's defenders appealed, the former objecting to various evidentiary rulings and severance of twenty cases from the total number of slayings charged. Pickton's lawyers sought a new trial on the six counts for which he stood convicted. On June 25, 2009, a three-judge Court of Appeal upheld the prosecution's claims of judicial error, then stayed that decision to avoid dismissal of Pickton's conviction. The panel rejected Pickton's appeal by a vote of two to one. Defense attorneys took their case to the Supreme Court of Canada, which unanimously crushed Pickton's last hope on July 30.

On August 4, 2010, Judge Williams ordered Pickton's transfer from British Columbia's provincial prison at Kent to a federal lockup at Port Cartier in Québec. There he remains today, theoretically eligible for release on parole in late 2032, at age 83.

13.
"GOOFY": LUIS GARAVITO

Colombia's worst "official" serial killer was known by many names before his final capture and identification. Over a five-year period, some frightened residents called him *El Loco* ("The Crazy"), "The Monster of Génova," or *La Bestia* ("The Beast"), for his rape, torture, and mutilation of boys. Others dubbed him *El Cura* ("The Priest"), for one of his common disguises. He even had a comical nickname: *Tribilín*, the Spanish name for Walt Disney's cartoon character Goofy.

But there was nothing comical about Luis Alfredo Garavito Cubillos, a savage pedophile and sadist convicted of at least 139 murders (some reports say 189) in Colombia and neighboring Ecuador. Today, the very mention of his name still sparks disgust and outrage, coupled with calls for resumption of capital punishment, abandoned by constitutional reform in 1910, after a year-long moratorium on executions.

Colombia's Constitution of 1991 declares, "The right to life is inviolable. There will be no death penalty." But relatives and friends of Garavito's victims tend to disagree.

Luis Garavito was born on January 25, 1957, at Génova, in Colombia's western coffee-growing region of Quindío. He was the oldest of seven sons born to brutal father Manuel Antonio Garavito, raised in a violent home where he and his siblings suffered frequent beatings and emotional abuse. In later statements, Garavito also described being sodomized repeatedly by two male neighbors during childhood, a trauma which, if true, undoubtedly skewed his concept of sexuality while filling him with rage.

Garavito quit school after five years and left home at sixteen, supporting himself as a store clerk, and later as a street vendor of prayer cards and religious icons. He consumed large quantities of alcohol and displayed aggressive, erratic behavior that dictated a drifter's lifestyle, wandering from one town to the next as locals turned against him. German forensic biologist Mark Benecke, researching Garavito's case in 2005, documented an early suicide attempt and reported that Garavito spent five years in psychiatric care as a young man.

Apparently, it did no good.

Dr. Benecke, in an article for the European journal *Minerva Medica*, wrote of Garavito:

> Another observation that might speak against regular
> intelligence is that Garavito cannot restrict his train of
> thoughts. He will jump from one topic to the other, and

even if he starts a conversation on a topic that he feels is interesting (plane crash, etc.), he will switch to a different topic only seconds, or minutes later. Because of the complete absence of any psychological treatment, he is not used to talking about personal matters, even if it would aid his cause. For example, one of the first things he talked to us about was an article from a popular science magazine that he found very interesting; he had written down notes next to the article. The article was dealing with children abused by their parents. When we asked why this caused his attention, he would absolutely not comment on this issue and switched the topic as if he had not heard the question. This is remarkable because it is the opinion of the police that Garavito was maltreated as a child.

One thing he had no difficulty focusing upon was homicide.

Most serial killers begin to murder in their late teens or early twenties, a handful much younger, but Luis Garavito was a relative "late bloomer," claiming his first confirmed victim in 1992. Given the scope and detail of his subsequent confessions, coupled with the wide range of police investigation after he was captured, it appears that he restrained himself—from murder, at least, if not molesting children—until age thirty-five.

But once he started, Garavito made up for his late start with a vengeance.

Between 1992 and early 1999, Garavito roamed throughout Colombia and into Ecuador, brutally raping and torturing scores of boys between the ages of six and thirteen, finally killing each in turn with a knife or screwdriver. His oldest victim—age sixteen, killed in March 1994—was small for his age and physically handicapped.

Typically, Garavito would befriend his chosen victims and escort them on long walks to isolated areas, then overpower and sodomize them. After the initial rape, Garavito frequently bound his captives to trees with nylon rope, subjecting them to other forms of torture before cutting their throats or beheading them. Like Pedro López (see chapter 8), he concealed their remains, often returning to one site repeatedly until the place ran out of space for fresh corpses.

Most of Garavito's victims were impoverished street children, common in cities throughout Latin America. Colombia, particularly, has suffered successive waves of crime and mayhem in the years since World War Two, beginning with *La Violencia* of 1948–58, continuing through rampant guerrilla warfare and widespread narco-terrorism to the present day, uprooting families and whole communities, sending their hungry children to the streets, where they survive by theft, shining shoes, peddling newspapers or chewing gum, and prostitution.

Preying on the smallest and weakest outcasts of society, Garavito evaded detection for years, although he usually lived, worked, and killed around sizable cities. Street children, in a sense, were already missing and forgotten, many of them orphaned, and police simply regarded them as one more problem on an endless list of urban maladies. Garavito, proud of his success, regarded himself as a "superior being," but in fact Colombian society was his accomplice.

As with the selection of children he slaughtered, Garavito's transient lifestyle raised no questions in Colombia or Ecuador. Until his drinking and obstreperous behavior turned neighbors against him, he seemed "normal," both to casual acquaintances and a string of single mothers who invited him to share their homes. He seems to have formed real attachments to those women, some of them older than he was, and appeared to dote on their children. Dr. Benecke writes that "Garavito seemed to be a caring social father, since his girlfriends never complained about him or stated any form of abuse concerning themselves or their children. They even mentioned that he enjoyed friendly play with his social children. In at least one case, Garavito continuously sent money back to one of his girlfriends during his travels. The investigators believe that Garavito may have lived together with these women on a platonic basis."

His sex drive, after all, led him down other, darker avenues.

Within a chosen city, Garavito was invisible, peddling fruit or other items from a pushcart like thousands of other street vendors. He kept no trophies from his victims, other than photos clipped from their I.D. cards, and concealed their bodies well enough that none were found before he had moved on to some new killing ground. Later, from prison, Garavito claimed that he felt sympathy for certain victims who complained of their abusive parents, but his feelings never stopped Luis from raping, torturing, and killing them. Most estimates place his final body count at 200 or higher.

The first hint of a maniac at large came from western Colombia's Valle del Cauca Department, where police found four boys slaughtered during 1995. Two of the dead were cousins, all four described by relatives and friends as youths from lax or broken homes, children of low intelligence. In each case, they had last been seen alive shortly before the noon hour. Their bodies were found together, discarded in tall shrubbery atop a hill on the outskirts of Santiago de Cali.

Police had no leads in that case, and they were distracted by other duties, pursuing—or collaborating with—the Cali Cartel, a multibillion-dollar cocaine syndicate led by the Rodríguez Orejuela brothers and a cohort, José Santacruz-Londoño. Corrupt police are seldom known for their efficiency at fighting crime, and Cali's murder rate defied even the best detectives' efforts to keep up with homicides as they occurred.

Garavito surfaced next in Puerto Boyacá, on the Magdalena River in the Boyacá Department, in June 1996. There, on June 8, he bought candy for a group of boys, persuading one of them to follow him off from the shop at a distance, riding a bicycle. Searchers found the boy five days later, decapitated, with his severed penis placed inside his mouth. Police questioned the victim's friends and soon identified Garavito as the stranger who had treated them to sweets, but Luis stayed cool under interrogation and the other boys confirmed that he had left the candy store alone, before their playmate vanished.

Disturbed, perhaps, by his encounter with authorities, Garavito moved on to Pereira, in the Risaralda Department, where he killed a thirteen-year-old boy on or about June 17, 1996. At his victim's final resting place, as in so many other cases, homicide investigators found a bottle of the cheapest schnapps available for sale in the vicinity.

In November 1997, police discovered a mass grave in a ravine near Pereira, a coffee-growing region in the foothills of the Andes Mountains. At least twenty-five boys were buried together (some reports say thirty-six), a fact that initially led detectives to discount a lone offender. Speculation on an organ-trading ring collapsed when autopsies revealed that most victims had been stabbed repeatedly but were subjected to no surgery. Next, theorists blamed a satanic cult, but the gravesite revealed no signs of occult rituals.

The grim discovery prompted communication with police in other areas, revealing that young boys had been murdered in eleven of Colombia's thirty-two departments. In Armenia, capital of the Quindío Department in western Colombia, officers began searching for similar homicides nationwide. Creation of a national task force followed, revealing more cases with young victims raped, bound, tortured, and mutilated, and death resulting from stab wounds and slashed throats. The victims were boys plucked from the streets or municipal parks where they worked or played unattended by adults. Investigators recognized a pattern now, but still had no clue to the killer's identity or whereabouts.

In February 1998, hikers found the nude corpses of two boys lying together on a hillside near Génova, Garavito's hometown. Searchers discovered a third victim the following day, only yards from the first two. All three had their hands bound and bore clear evidence of anal penetration, bite marks, and genital mutilation. A knife was also found at the scene, and while fluid samples were collected, budgetary restrictions barred any scientific testing. Likewise, the local law could not afford a profiler to help them with the case.

Simple investigation proved that the latest victims had been local boys, ages eleven and thirteen, who worked as street vendors in Génova to augment their families' meager income. All had last been seen alive around 10 a.m. on different days, and one victim's mother recalled her son coming home on the day he vanished, telling her that he'd been hired to help a man transport some cattle. No one else had seen the man, however, and again the trail went cold.

Garavito struck next at 6:00 a.m. on the morning after Halloween, known in Colombia as *Dia de los Niños*, "Day of the Children." He found a boy roaming the streets, searching for candy lost the night before, and offered to help find the missing treats. Instead, the trusting child was trussed up, tormented, and slain.

Investigation of the older killings slogged along, meanwhile, but made no visible progress. Hundreds of cases were examined, many of them with the victims unidentified or never reported missing. (Street children in "Third World"

FORENSIC INVESTIGATORS CARRY THE REMAINS OF AS MANY AS 36 BOYS FOUND IN MASS GRAVES FOUND IN PEREIRA, COLUMBIA IN NOVEMBER OF 1998.

nations rate the same official disregard as street*walkers* worldwide.) Forensic anthropologists at Bogotá's Institute for Legal Medicine reconstructed faces for some of the skulls recovered, but established techniques such as dental examination failed in most cases, since the victims either had never seen a dentist in their short lives, or their records had been lost in the earthquake of June 23, 1998. At least twenty-seven of Garavito's victims remain unidentified today.

Luis was finally captured by chance. On April 22, 1999, a homeless resident of Villavicencio, capital of the Meta Department, interrupted Garavito's assault on his latest victim, a twelve-year-old boy. Police broadcast a description of the would-be rapist, and a taxi driver spotted Garavito on the street a short time later, calling patrolmen to arrest him. Garavito identified himself as "Bonifacio Morera Lizcano," telling police that he had lost his identity papers. Investigators soon discovered that their suspect had no fingerprints on file.

Jailed on suspicion of attempted sodomy, Garavito found himself under the spotlight of intense investigation. Telephone numbers found in his pocket led detectives to his relatives, one of whom produced a box Garavito had left with her for safekeeping. Inside it, police found photos clipped from the I.D. cards of multiple victims, plus a calendar with cryptic notes that proved to be a timeline of murder. Further investigation turned up hotel registration records placing Garavito in several towns on dates when known murders had occurred. Searching the homes of friends where he had lived, police found newspaper clippings about the killings.

All that took time, while Garavito sat in jail awaiting trial. Officers finally confronted him with knowledge of his birth name on October 28, and Garavito launched into a long, detailed confession of the murders he had perpetrated, spanning seven years and two countries. He described trolling for victims, choosing them by personality or skin tone (soft, and not too dark) and posing as a priest, transient, or prospective employer with offers of menial jobs. Some wily street kids had refused offers of cash; others, young addicts, had been lured with promises of drugs. Whenever possible, he cautioned victims not to tell their parents that they had found a job or met an adult benefactor.

The first round of confessions cleared 140 slayings in fifty-four cities. Garavito directed police to undiscovered gravesites, adding further victims to the list. On October 30, Attorney General Alfonso Gomez Mendez told reporters "We have so far found 114 skeletons and we're still investigating the disappearance of other children. This tale of serial killing has shocked Colombians." So much so, in fact, that General Rosso Jose Serrano, commander of Colombia's National Police, urged that Garavito receive a special exemption from the country's ban on capital punishment.

That did not happen, but The Beast still faced a string of murder trials. In the first case tried—at Tunja, capital of Central Boyacá Province—he received the maximum permissible sentence of thirty years on May 27, 2000, for the June 1996 slaying of fourteen-year-old Silvino Rodriguez. Also included in that verdict was the attempted rape charge for his final attack, but the judge struck 7½ years from the sentence in exchange for Garavito's guilty plea and cooperation in finding more graves.

Other trials followed, with the last concluded on November 3, 2001. Reports of the accumulated verdicts contradict each other: some say Garavito received sentences totaling 1,853 years and nine days for 139 murders; others claim he was sentenced to 835 years for 189 slayings. Yet another story reports a cumulative sentence of 2,600 years. It matters little, in any case, since Colombian law prescribes a maximum prison term of thirty years for any inmate—reduced in Garavito's case to 22½ years. Further time may yet be deducted for "good behavior" in prison.

Throughout his trials, Garavito never appeared in a courtroom. Colombia's penal code streamlines judicial procedures where suspects confess, corroborated by forensic evidence, and neither side wished for open trials to increase public fury. Even so, the prospect that The Beast might be at large again by 2022, albeit at age sixty-five, provoked a storm of controversy.

On June 11, 2006, Bogotá's Radio Cadena Nacional television network broadcast an interview with Garavito on its "Special Pirry" program, hosted by journalist Guillermo "Pirry" Prieto La Rotta. In their prison conversation, Garavito sought to minimize his crimes, seemed optimistic regarding early release, and expressed hopes of pursuing a political career to "help" abused children. Prieto closed the segment by announcing that with time off for good behavior, Garavito could be eligible for parole in 2009.

In reaction to that announcement, a judicial review of Garavito's confessions determined that further trials were still possible, in murder cases omitted from his confessions. Conviction for one or more of those crimes could extend Garavito's sentence, and if trials were timed strategically, that procedure might keep him confined for life. Social media weighed in on the subject, with two Facebook pages opposing Garavito's release, and Colombia's Congress has increased the maximum prison term in future trials from thirty to sixty years.

Soon after his RCN interview, Garavito reportedly tried to commit suicide by repeatedly banging his head against the steel bars of his cell at Valledupar prison, located in the capital of northern Colombia's César Department. Built to house a maximum of 256 inmates, the Valledupar lockup held 954 in 2014, an overcrowding rate of 273 percent. Ranked as one of Colombia's worst prisons—a sad distinction of sorts in itself—Valledupar had a decrepit, frequently broken-down plumbing system which left some of its cellblocks flooded while granting an average ten minutes per day of access to running water. At last report, 300 writs of protection remained on file from various Valledupar prisoners, claiming that their jailers routinely denied petitions for medical care.

Still, things might have been worse for "Goofy." Kept in a solitary cell for his own protection from other inmates, Garavito allegedly has access to a telephone for six hours per day.

In 2013, Colombian author Mauricio Aranguren Molina published the only full-length book released to date on Garavito's case, titled *El gran fracaso de la fiscalía: 192 Niños asesinados. Captura y confesión de Garavito: "La bestia"* (*The Great Failure of the Prosecutor: 192 Children Killed. Capture and Confession of the Beast*). At present, the book is available only in Spanish.

14.

ACID TEST: JAVED IQBAL

On December 2, 1999, police in Lahore, Pakistan, received a parcel by mail. Inside, they found a notebook and a letter signed by one Javed Iqbal—no relation to the Islamic philosopher/jurist of the same name who spent three years in the 1980s as senior justice of Pakistan's Supreme Court. The letter gave its author's home address, stating, "I have sexually assaulted 100 children before killing them, and have disposed of their bodies in barrels of acid."

Officers believed the missive was a joke and threw it in the trash.

Across town, at the same time, a similar parcel arrived at the offices of *Daily Jang*, an Urdu language newspaper. Inside it, another confessional letter was clipped to a notebook detailing the slaughter of 100 children. Instead of discarding the package, reporters grabbed their cameras and rushed to Iqbal's dingy three-room house on Ravi Road. What they discovered there forced homicide investigators to retrieve their letter from the wastebasket and make a beeline for the crime scene.

At the house, reporters were already photographing bags filled with children's clothing, eighty-six pairs of shoes, and two vats containing hydrochloric acid with remains of two dissolving skeletons. Bloodstains, including handprints, marked the walls. A placard tacked to one wall read: "All details of the murders are contained in the diary and the thirty-two-page notebook that have been placed in the room and had also been sent to the authorities. This is my confessional statement."

A second sign, nearby, announced: "I am going to jump into the River Ravi to commit suicide." A third proclaimed: "The bodies in the house have deliberately not been disposed of so that the authorities will find them after my suicide."

Other evidence included plastic bags containing photographs of boys, ranging in age from six to sixteen years, described in Iqbal's diary as victims he strangled before dismembering their corpses, dissolving them, and dumping any remnants in the River Ravi. Iqbal detailed his method of hunting victims, luring them away from local tourist spots and markets to his home, where he sodomized and killed them. In explanation of his crimes, Iqbal called himself a victim of the "police system, irregularities in [the] jail system in Pakistan and injustice in other sections of society."

The murders, he wrote, had spanned six months, just long enough to reach his goal of killing 100 children. "In terms of expense," he wrote, "including the acid, it cost me 120 rupees [78¢] to erase each victim." A police spokesman told reporters what they already knew: "The recovery of human remains suggested that some killings occurred, but we still have to verify the exact number of victims."

To answer that question, officers displayed some of the evidence retrieved from Iqbal's home at their Ravi Road headquarters, inviting parents of missing children to view the items. By December 11, parents of 72 victims had identified photos and clothing, some coming from as far away as Faisalabad, Jhang, Mardan, Peshwar, Sargodha, and Toba Tek Singh.

Clearly, Iqbal had not exaggerated in his letter to authorities.

Meanwhile, detectives launched Pakistan's largest-ever manhunt, detaining Javed Iqbal's brothers and various friends for interrogation. Four of those arrested—teenagers Sajid Ahmad, Mamad Nadeem, and Mamad Sabir, with Muhammad Ishaq, an adult accused of selling acid to Iqbal—were charged as accomplices. Police claimed Ishaq had breakfast with Iqbal a few hours prior to surrendering for interrogation.

On December 7, Ishaq fell from an upper-floor window at police headquarters during questioning, dying on impact. Police called it a suicide, while journalist Irfan Husain wrote "This is such a common occurrence that by now one would imagine the police could have thought of a better cover-up for death in custody." Three officers were arrested, with two of their commanders transferred to another precinct. Husain observed that the transfers were "a bit like shutting the stable door after the horse has bolted."

And throughout Lahore, the manhunt continued.

Javed Iqbal Mughal was born in Lahore—capital of Punjab, Pakistan's most populous province—on October 8, 1956, the sixth child and fourth son of affluent merchant Mohammad Ali Mughal, proud owner of two villas on Railway Road. Javed graduated from Lahore's Islamia High School and started his first business enterprise, a steel recasting business, operating from one of his father's villas, while still a student at nearby Islamia College. He also occupied the office/factory, joined by an ever-changing group of younger boys.

Psychologists later described Iqbal as a pampered child who developed "bad habits"—sodomy performed on younger males—early in life. As a teen, he cruised popular hangouts on a shiny new motorcycle, inviting prospective partners back to his home/office, and met many more by soliciting pen pals through various children's magazines. After receiving photographs from correspondents, Iqbal drew up a list of the most attractive and showered them with gifts worth thousands of rupees, including coins, cologne, and concert tickets. Relatives noted his fawning entourage, but Iqbal fended off their criticism with denials of any impropriety.

In 1983, Iqbal surprised his family with news of his impending marriage. The bride-to-be, coincidentally, was the older sister of a favorite playmate. One Mughal family member opined, "The purpose was to stop the boy from deserting him." At the same time, Iqbal persuaded his youngest sister to marry another boyfriend, Muhammad Iqbal (again, no relation). Javed's marriage was short-lived, but he was never short of partners in the bedroom.

Iqbal's lifestyle grew increasingly erratic as he moved into his thirties. After assaulting a respected resident of Lahore's Shad Bagh commercial district, Javed was hauled before a *panchayat* (council of elders) and confessed his crime, signing an affidavit vowing to refrain from future violence. The *panchayat* distributed copies of Iqbal's confession around Shad Bagh and ordered him to visit 100 shops, delivering his personal apology to the proprietors.

There is no record of Iqbal assaulting any more adults, but he was still preoccupied with minors. Late in 1990, a man accused Iqbal of sodomizing his son. Police missed Javed but arrested his father and two brothers, holding them in hopes that Javed might surrender. The three sat in jail for a week, until officers nabbed one of Javed's boyfriends and locked him up as well. Within hours, Iqbal surrendered and received a six-month jail term for one count of sodomy.

Mohammad Ali Mughal died in 1993, leaving Javed 3.5 million rupees ($22,575). With his father's influence removed, Iqbal was no longer protected from the consequences of his dalliance with boys in Shad Bagh. On the next occasion when he was discovered with a child, his neighbors thrashed him and drove him from the neighborhood.

He settled next in Rana Town, another district of Lahore that featured a large bazaar and a workers' welfare boarding school. He built a large home there in 1995, with a backyard swimming pool and a "pond" in the basement. He also assembled a small fleet of cars, including a Lancer, a Toyota, a Suzuki FX, and a Mitsubishi Pajero SUV. The latter vehicle was his favorite, with space for a half-dozen boys to join Iqbal as he toured the neighborhood, constantly searching for more.

Later, when Iqbal moved from Rana Town to Fatehgarh, he lured more youths with a shop selling video games. Parents soon caught wind of his predilection and ordered their sons to shun the store. Undaunted, Iqbal closed the shop and opened an aquarium, then a gymnasium, next a discount store, and finally his own air-conditioned Sunny Side School (closed when no one enrolled). Trying to curry favor with police, he launched a monthly magazine detailing their "heroics," publishing interviews with lawmen singled out for special praise.

None of it helped in February 1998 when Iqbal faced charges of sodomizing two teenagers at gunpoint, near Lahore's Data Darbar complex, one of the oldest Muslim shrines in South Asia. According to the charge, Iqbal paid his two victims 113 rupees (73¢) after raping both in turn, then asked them to meet him again at the same spot the following week. Instead, their father turned up with police, and Iqbal was arrested.

Lahore's High Court granted bail to Iqbal on April 6 and passed the case to a judicial magistrate on June 15. Records indicate the case was dropped when no witness appeared against Iqbal in court, but his neighbors were not so forgiving. That September, one of Iqbal's employees joined a local masseur in beating Javed and another employee, named Arbab. Iqbal spent twenty-two days in Lahore General Hospital, recovering from head injuries, and while police initially treated the case as a robbery, saying the attackers stole 8,000 rupees ($52) from Iqbal, they soon received a complaint from beating victim Arbab's parents, charging Iqbal with sodomy. Arrested as he left the hospital, Iqbal once again posted bail and went free.

Recovery from the September beating was slow and painful. Cut off financially by relatives, Iqbal sold his house, cars, and business to pay for rehabilitative therapy—and he began to plot revenge. In conversations with his brothers, Iqbal said he had obtained a chemical that would reduce a human corpse to bare bones within minutes. According to his diaries, Iqbal began to kill in May 1999, later declaring "I did it to avenge an attempt on my life by my boys, the death of my mother, and injustice in society."

A BBC reporter asked police how 100 boys could vanish into acid vats unnoticed, but the answer was obvious to many of Lahore's 7.1 million residents. Most of those lost were the city's poorest denizens, some of them beggars, others drawn from the legion of waifs who work the streets, selling cheap goods or themselves while living hand to mouth. Despite Pakistan's outwardly strict religious code, many street children fall prey to sexual predators.

While the Koran forbids homosexuality and Sharia law makes it a capital crime, some older Muslim men pursue boys without regard to age. A 1997 survey conducted by Pakistan's National Coalition for Child Rights found such relationships common in Lahore and in the country's Northwest frontier provinces, where having one or more young male lovers was deemed "a matter of pride," or "a symbol of social status."

And there is no shortage of prospects for predatory pedophiles around Lahore. In a nation where forty-eight percent of all children suffer from malnutrition, an estimated ten thousand run away from home each year. Thousands more are shipped to richer Middle Eastern countries as under-age camel jockeys, risking their lives for the amusement of wealthy gamblers. Despite laws restricting child labor, some 3.3 million worked at filthy, dangerous jobs in 2000 alone. Of those, 100,000 were bonded laborers—slaves, in effect—who spent their days stoking brick kilns. Amidst all that, Pakistan's Human Rights Commission found, "the physical and sexual abuse of children was believed to be rampant."

Soon after Javed Iqbal mailed his confessions and fled underground, reporter Irfan Husain wrote: "The whole macabre case underlines the terrible sexual frustration and perversion that lie just below the surface of our hypocritical society. The abuse of young boys is an unspoken but rampant aspect of everyday life here, and sodomy is the dark—but all too common—side of sexuality here. What happened on such a staggering magnitude in Lahore recently occurs daily on a smaller scale elsewhere without editorials being written or inquiry committees being formed."

And the police were no help.

As Husain wrote, "The sad fact is that despite endless talk of police reforms, our police force remains as mired in inefficiency and corruption as ever. The reason so many parents did not report their sons as missing is that they were afraid of having anything to do with the police. Indeed, the experience of the vast majority who are forced to come into contact with our cops is anything but salutary; nine times out of ten, they are shaken down even when reporting a crime." In December 1999, the mother of one identified Iqbal victim told *Time* magazine: "It never even occurred to me to go to the police for help."

A typical victim of Javed Iqbal—his ninety-seventh—was a youth named Ijaz, who supported himself by offering massages to men in Iqbal

Park, surrounding Lahore's Minar-e-Pakistan, a monument celebrating passage of a 1947 resolution separating Pakistan from India. Ijaz charged strangers 20 rupees (13¢) for rubdowns. In early November 1999, when Iqbal and two young companions offered Ijaz 50 rupees (32¢) for a massage to ease Iqbal's alleged paralysis, Ijaz leaped at the chance and took his brother Riaz along to Javed Iqbal's home. Riaz soon grew bored, later telling police "I left Ijaz at the house and went home. Ijaz did not return home in the night and when I went to the Ravi Road house in the morning I was told that he left shortly afterwards."

In fact, he was dissolving in an acid bath one of the two bodies recovered on December 2, 1999.

Javed Iqbal eluded capture until December 30, 1999, when he walked into the offices of *Daily Jang* and surrendered. By then, some reporters were calling him "Kukri" ("cucumber" in Urdu) for reasons unclear. He chose the newspaper's office, Iqbal said, because he feared police would kill him on sight. Before contacting the authorities, editor Jameel Chishti and crime reporter Asad Sahi videotaped Iqbal's latest confession, repeating claims that he had been brutalized by police in 1998, after complaining of the beating by an ex-employee and his masseur accomplice. Soon after that incident, Iqbal said, his mother had died from grief, prompting Iqbal's crusade for revenge.

Police arrived to collect Iqbal after he finished taping his confession. Jameel Chishti published Iqbal's words in the *Daily Jang* on December 31 but withheld the tape from police for another two weeks. Meanwhile, officers collected samples of Iqbal's handwriting, and an analyst matched them to letters and notebooks mailed to police and the newspaper. On January 13, 2000, Iqbal repeated his confession to police magistrate Mian Ghulam Husain, despite warnings that the statement could be used against him at trial. Iqbal's three young cohorts also confessed in open court, denying any torture by police in custody.

Formally indicted for murder on February 17, all four defendants pleaded not guilty before Additional Sessions Judge Allah Bakhsh Ranjha and a courtroom packed with spectators. Hedging on his previous confessions, Iqbal testified "Whatever I wanted to say has been distorted. I have seen the children being killed. I am an eyewitness to that. I was considered an insane person. But I beg that my point of view must also be heard. I considered myself as a culprit because I have been made a culprit by police."

In particular, he blamed one officer, Inspector Karamat Bhatti, who allegedly despised Iqbal for planning to expose Bhatti's corruption.

Pakistani trials are often closed to the public, but that of Iqbal and his codefendants became a media circus. Spectators thronged the courtroom and plaza outside, while armed guards surrounded the courthouse. Sajid Ahmad, Mamad Nadeem, and Mamad Sabir seemed to enjoy the attention, giggling among themselves as if they had no concept of potential consequences. Iqbal joined them to a point, smiling for media

JAVED IQBAL (SECOND FROM LEFT) LISTENING TO HIS SENTENCE TO DEATH FOR MURDERING ONE HUNDRED CHILDREN IN PAKISTAN'S WORST SERIAL KILLING.

photographers, but was intent on undermining the confessions he had issued previously.

Now, facing the gallows, Iqbal swore that he had killed no one. In fact, he claimed, some of those his early statements named as victims "were living with different people and were surely compulsive homosexuals." Others had returned home to their families, he said, "but their parents are silent about it." The vats recovered from his home, Iqbal averred, held only oil and bits of beef included to deceive police.

Prosecutors countered those assertions with Iqbal's confessions and testimony from 105 witnesses, including 73 parents of missing children. Witness Shafiq, owner of a Lahore photo shop, testified that he had developed thirty-one of the victim photographs recovered by police from Iqbal's home. Power failures in the courthouse stalled the trial erratically, as it continued for two months, including complaints from Iqbal's court-appointed attorney, Najib Faisal, saying authorities had threatened to withhold his fee of 30,000 rupees ($194) if he cross-examined prosecution witnesses.

The court watched Iqbal's *Daily Jang* confession six times on March 2, interspersed with testimony from editor Chishti and crime reporter Sahi. Under cross-examination by Najib Faisal and Abdul Baqi, attorney for Iqbal's codefendants, Sahi admitted that a longer tape existed and had been locked away by Chishti but denied that it was "being withheld dishonestly."

In his summation, prosecutor Asghar Rokari placed equal weight on Iqbal's original confessions and the circumstantial evidence recovered from his home on Ravi Road, noting that a charge of "carnal intercourse with young boys" still awaited Iqbal from the case filed in 1998. Rokari's aide, Burhan Muazzam Malik, addressed the court briefly, asserting that while minor defendants could not be sentenced to death under Pakistani law, attainment of puberty qualified Iqbal's codefendants as adults.

The court convicted all four defendants on March 15. Javed Iqbal and Sajid Ahmad, just turned twenty, were sentenced to death, while Mamad Nadeem received a 182-year prison term (fourteen years for each of thirteen victims), and Mamad Sabir was sentenced to sixty-three years.

Hanging is Pakistan's only legal form of execution. While the court deemed hanging sufficient for Ahmad, Judge Allah Baksh Ranja imposed a unique sentence on Javed Iqbal, adopting the Sharia concept of *Qisas* ("an eye for an eye"). Ranja ordered that Iqbal be taken to the park bearing his name, where he had trolled for victims, and be strangled there with the same chain found in his home that he had used to throttle his victims. Afterward, Ranja declared, "Your body will then be cut into a hundred pieces and put in acid, the same way you killed the children."

While parents of the victims celebrated that sentence, other voices rose in protest. On the day of sentencing, Moinudeen Haider, Pakistan's Interior Minister, told reporters "We are signatories to the Human Rights Commission. Such punishments are not allowed." Defense counsel Najid Faisal announced an immediate appeal, saying "This sentence is not inevitable. There is no law which allows a person to be hanged publicly, to cut up pieces of the body. It is against the constitution of Pakistan." Asma Jahangir, United Nations special rapporteur on extrajudicial, summary, and arbitrary executions, told the Associated Press "You don't answer back a sick man in a sick way by the state. This is judicial anger and emotionalism. It is barbaric and arouses the fascistic instincts in a society."

On appeal, Lahore's High Court declined to issue a decision on Iqbal's sentence, passing the problem off to a local Sha'aria (religious court). On March 25, Pakistan's Council of Islamic Ideology released a statement opposing the verdict, on grounds that dismemberment and acid baths violate the Koran's injunction against desecrating human remains.

In fact, Javed Iqbal would never face the gallows. At 5:00 a.m. on October 8, 2001, guards reportedly found Iqbal and condemned accomplice Sajid Ahmad hanged with bedsheets in their adjacent cells at Lahore's Central Jail, in the city's Kot Lakhpat industrial district. Jail superintendent Mian Farooq told reporters "We are investigating the matter, and nothing has so far been ascertained."

One of Farooq's subordinates, Abdussattar Ajiz, told a different story, claiming Iqbal and Ahmad had committed suicide sometime between 10:00 p.m. and 2:00 a.m., while a guard named Iftikhar Husain stood watch outside their cells. Husain, for his part, told journalists "I was asleep when the incident took place." Ajiz added another twist, saying that Husain woke to find both prisoners dead, untied the bedsheets and posed them as if sleeping, then left work at 2:00 a.m. without informing his superiors.

Police and journalists remained suspicious. After rushed postmortems at the city morgue, the newspaper *Dawn* reported:

> Strangulation marks were found around the blood splashed necks of the two prisoners, doctors in the mortuary said. They said hands, feet and nails of the deceased had gone blue. They were bleeding from mouth and nostrils and the tongue of one of them had a cut mark, the doctors said. An injury mark was also found around Sajid's neck, they said, adding that countless healed wounds inflicted with a blunt weapon were also found on all over the body of Javed Iqbal.

Fearing accusations of murder, officials announced that Iqbal had attempted suicide more than a dozen times in custody. Besides that, an unnamed guard declared, "His behavior was strange. Javed would start demanding milk at midnight. Sometimes, he would demand fruit which was not available in market. He used to keep the jail staff engaged."

Enough to get him killed from spite, perhaps?

Iqbal had appealed his death sentence, voicing fears that officers would kill him before his case was reviewed. Coincidentally or otherwise, the double "suicide" occurred just four days after Pakistan's highest Islamic Court agreed to hear appeals from both Iqbal and Ahmad. Six Central Jail officials were suspended, but prosecutors filed no charges against them. A *Dawn* editorial summed up the feeling of most observers, saying "Had the two wished a death by hanging, they needed only to withdraw their appeals."

That said, *Dawn* proclaimed, "Javed was one of the most hated people alive, particularly after his surrender and his 'confession' before a magistrate. It may be argued however that this was less because most people found his guilt had been established beyond reasonable doubt and more because he held a mirror of sorts to society. Had he not shown that the grieving parents and guardians had been negligent, that society was a jungle and there was no shelter for lost boys, that nobody was even keeping a count, that the state could not care less? He had practically accused all those speaking in the name of his victims of having, in fact, been his accomplices and dared them to prosecute him."

15.

"THE WEREWOLF": MIKHAIL POPKOV

For three quarters of a century, from 1917 to 1991, Soviet officials denied the existence of serial killers in Russia. Such "decadent" crimes, they proclaimed, were limited to Western capitalist nations. In support of that fiction, police often ignored—or actively concealed—murders committed by practitioners such as Nikolai Shestakov (twelve victims), Vladimir Storozhenko (thirteen), Philipp Tyurin (twenty-nine), Vasili Komaroff (thirty-three), Gennady Mikhasevich (thirty-three), and Andrei Chikatilo (fifty-six).

Since the Soviet Union's demise, we know that Russia ranks fifth among Earth's top-ten worst nations for the total number of serial slayers. At least four still-unidentified killers, with forty-eight victims among them, have been hunted by Russian detectives since 1997.

No continent except Antarctica is safe.

Serial killers frequently display a fascination for police work. Many follow the investigations of their own crimes and inject themselves into the case, falsely posing as a witness or joining in searches for missing victims. Others taunt authorities with letters, phone calls, and the like. Some try to become police officers and, having failed, settle for jobs in private security. A few, like Gerard Schaefer (see Chapter 7) and the last of our extreme killers, make the cut to wear a badge that becomes their hunting license, preying on the persons they have sworn to serve and protect.

Meet "The Werewolf," a sadistic lawman who allegedly set out to "cleanse the streets of prostitutes" in Angarsk, the administrative center of Angarsky District in Irkutsk Oblast, located on the Kitoy River in southeastern Siberia.

Mikhail Viktorovich Popkov was born in Angarsk on March 7, 1964. By his own later account, his mother—an abusive alcoholic—set him on the course that would consume his life and seal the fates of women whose appearance or behavior brought those ugly memories to mind. Final estimates of Popkov's body count, correlated with his escalating confessions, range as high as eighty-four victims. All but one of them were women, the lone male a fellow policeman Popkov murdered on a whim, while driving near Irkutsk.

After joining the Angarsk police department, Popkov met and married another officer, two years his junior, named Elena. Their only child, daughter Ekaterina or "Katya," was born in 1987, five years before Popkov reportedly claimed his first victim. Detectives, unaware that they were hunting one of their own, initially dubbed their unknown subject

"The Wednesday Murderer," after the weekday when several of his victims were found, left nude in woodlands or on roadsides. On multiple occasions, wife Elena furnished Popkov with an alibi for specific crime dates, which investigators failed to question. Even after he began confessing from a prison cell, authorities absolved Elena and Ekaterina of involvement in the crimes and cover-up.

Popkov agreed that both women were innocent, telling authorities "I had a double life. In one life I was an ordinary person. I was in the service in the police, having positive feedback on my work. I had a family. My wife and daughter considered me a good husband and father, which corresponded to reality. In my other life I committed murders, which I carefully concealed from everyone, realizing that this was a criminal offense. My wife and daughter never knew about the crimes I committed and did not even suspect this."

As for his choice of prey, Popkov portrayed it as random. "The victims were those who, unaccompanied by men, at night, without a certain purpose, were on the streets," he said, "behaving carelessly, who were not afraid to enter into conversation with me, get into my car, and then go for a drive in search of adventures for the sake of entertainment, ready to drink alcohol and have sexual intercourse with me. They abandoned their husbands and went out to party as if it was the last day on Earth. Not all women became victims, but those of a certain negative behavior, I had a desire to teach and punish. Others did not behave in such a way; they were afraid. The exception was the murder of Elena Dorogova, who was hurrying to the [railway] station to meet her mother. On this occasion, the woman was sober."

Investigators later noted that most of Mikhail's victims were full-figured and of below average height—perhaps another echo of the mother Popkov despised.

Another victim who broke the usual pattern was a teacher at his daughter's music school. Popkov later said, "Her corpse was found in the forest along with the body of another woman. My daughter asked me to give her money, as the school was collecting to organize funerals, and I gave it to her."

In short, Popkov took victims as they came, often luring the tipsy ones into his "safe" patrol car for nighttime lifts home, then driving to remote locations, where he raped and murdered them. His first killing happened "spontaneously," Popkov said, adding "I just felt I wanted to kill a woman I was giving a lift to in my car." Likewise, he claimed, "The choice of weapons for killing was always casual. I never prepared beforehand to commit a murder. I could use any object that was in the car—a knife, an axe, a bat. I never used rope for strangulation, and I did not have a firearm either." Some weapons, seized from criminals, he stole from the police station. "I had the opportunity to take them," he explained. "Then I threw them away either at the crime scene or nearby, wiping them with something to remove my fingerprints."

Such a casual approach to murder sometimes breeds mistakes, of course. On one occasion, after assaulting two women together and leaving them for dead, Popkov realized that he had lost his police token— equivalent to a badge—during his struggle with the victims. Rushing back to the scene, Popkov said "I found the token right away, but saw that one of the women was still breathing. I was again shocked by the fact that she was still alive. I finished her with a shovel."

At least two other intended victims survived his attacks, and while one identified his picture from a police photo lineup, investigators chose to believe the alibi furnished by Popkov's wife. Elena and their daughter stood by Popkov after his arrest, apparently sincere in their conviction of his innocence.

"We have been married for 28 years," Elena told reporters. "If I suspected something wrong, of course I would divorce him. I support him. I believe him. If he were to be released right now, I would not say a word and we would continue to live together."

MIKHAI POPKOV LISTENING TO THE VERDICT IN HIS MURDER TRIAL AT THE IRKUTSK REGIONAL COURT IN RUSSIA IN JANUARY 2015. IT IS BELIEVED HE MURDERED AS MANY AS 84 PEOPLE.

Daughter Katya initially shared that opinion, saying "I do not believe any of this. I always felt myself to be 'Daddy's girl.' For twenty-five years we were together, hand in hand. We walked, rode bikes, went to the shops, and he met me from school. We both collect model cars, so we have the same hobby. I wanted to be a criminologist, so I read a book with tips of how investigators catch serial killers and there were also basic classifications [of killers]. Daddy doesn't fit any of these classifications. He doesn't look like some maniac."

Later, as Popkov began to confess, both women—Katya now married, a teacher and mother—left Angarsk to begin new lives in other cities, their illusions shattered.

Popkov rarely quibbled over details of his slayings, granting that he beheaded one woman, but he staunchly denied removing another's heart, insisting "I did not cut out the hearts of the victims." Or perhaps he just forgot, as numbers multiplied. He *did* admit, however, that he sometimes performed necrophilia, raping his victims after death.

Another risk of raping strangers was disease. As Popkov told the tale, he stopped committing murders in 2000 after he contracted syphilis from one victim, whereupon he "became impotent." Around the same time, he left the police department to work as a security guard, first for Angarsk Oil and Chemical Company, and later for a private agency.

By 2012, detectives grudgingly realized that they must consider the possibility of a killer cop at large. Some 3,500 past and present policemen—including Popkov—were asked to provide DNA samples, and all complied. Only Popkov's sample matched forensic evidence from multiple crime scenes, and officers arrested him on June 23, 2012, when he went to buy a new car in Vladivostok, some 4,000 miles east of Angarsk, near Russia's borders with China and North Korea.

At the time, he was suspected of slaying twenty-nine victims, ranging in age from nineteen to forty years old. After brief denials, Popkov confessed to those crimes and was formally charged on October 31 with twenty-nine counts of murder, plus two attempted murders of victims who survived their injuries.

One living victim who agreed to testify at Popkov's trial was "Svetlana M.," attacked on January 29, 1998, when she was fifteen "but looked older." She described how a policeman stopped to offer her a lift, then drove her to a forest near the village of Baikalsk, in the Slyudyansky District of Irkutsk Oblast, where he forced her to disrobe and bashed her head against a tree. She woke in a hospital bed the next day, having survived the night naked, in sub-freezing weather. Despite Svetlana's description of the officer, Elena Popkov gave her husband an alibi, and police spent years erroneously searching for a metalworker, professional driver, railway employee, heating station engineer, or cemetery worker.

Even after Popkov's confession to twenty-nine slayings, Nikolai Kitaev, an ex-police investigator critical of the manhunt's handling, suspected that official files might contain "at least a dozen more" of Popkov's victims. In 2013, Mikhail Zavorin—a member of the original task force—said, of Popkov, "He is charming and sociable. Women like him but he is a beast inside, and it is always hard to fight a werewolf."

At trial, in January 2015, Popkov told the Irkutsk Oblast Court, "I admit my guilt in full. Committing the murders, I was guided by my inner convictions." Russia's moratorium on capital punishment spared him from execution, resulting in a life prison sentence, but prosecutors were not finished with him yet. By October 2015, speculation flourished that he might have killed another twenty women scattered over Siberia and the Russian Far East, while some newspapers went further still, guessing at sixty-one murders in all.

By March 2017, Popkov himself had raised the total to eighty-two victims, still marveling at his ability to dupe police psychiatrists while he remained on active duty. "I never thought of myself as mentally unhealthy," he told the *Siberian Times*. "During my police service, I regularly passed medical commissions and was recognized as fit." Popkov called the tally of eighty-two murders his "final" figure—far eclipsing that of "Rostov Ripper" Andrei Chikatilo—while still insisting that throughout the slayings "I was a good husband and father."

On January 10, 2018, a second trial convicted Popkov of murdering an additional fifty-six women, bringing his official tally to seventy-eight. Authorities believed his confessions of eighty-two slayings but were unable to prove the last four, with victims unidentified and undiscovered. Some detectives suspect that The Werewolf may have hedged on his admissions, placing the true death toll at eighty-four.

From his Siberian prison cell, Popkov blames technology for his capture and convictions. "I was born in another century," he says. "Now there are such modern technologies, methods, but not earlier. If we had not got to that level of genetic examination, then I would not be sitting in front of you."

And his victims might still be dying.

SOURCES

1. "BLUEBEARD": GILLES DE RAIS

Bataille, George. *The Trial of Gilles de Rais*. Paris: Jean-Jaques Pauvert, 1965.

Benedetti, Jean. *The Real Bluebeard*. New York: Stein & Day, 1972.

Winwar, Frances. *The Saint and the Devil*. New York: Harper & Brothers, 1948.

Wolf, Leonard. *The Life and Crimes of Gilles de Rais*. New York: Clarkson N. Potter, 1980.

2. "THE BLOOD COUNTESS": ERZSÉBET BÁTHORY

McNally, Raymond. *Dracula Was a Woman*. New York: McGraw-Hill Book Co., 1983.

Penrose, Valentine. *The Bloody Countess: The Atrocities of Erzsébet Báthory*. London: Calder & Boyars, 1970.

3. AXE MEN

Davis, Miriam. *The Axeman of New Orleans: The True Story*. Chicago: Chicago Review Press, 2017.

Hair, William. "Inquisition for Blood." *Louisiana Studies* 11 (Winter 1972): 274–282.

James, Bill, and Rachel McCarthy James. *The Man from the Train: Discovering America's Most Elusive Serial Killer*. New York: Scribner, 2017.

Klingensmith, Beth. "The 1910s Ax Murders." Dissertation, Emporia State University, 2006.

Marshall, Roy. *Villisca: The True Account of a Mass Murder*. Chula Vista, CA: Aventine Press, 2003.

4. "ANGEL MAKERS"

Unknown Gender History, https://unknownmisandry.blogspot.com/

5. HANDS OF DEATH: HENRY LUCAS AND OTTIS TOOLE

Cox, Mike. *The Confessions of Henry Lee Lucas*. New York: Pocket Books, 1991.

Gilmore, Tim. *Stalking Ottis Toole: A Southern Gothic*. CreateSpace, 2013.

London, Sondra. *True Vampires: Blood-Sucking Killers Past and Present*. Los Angeles: Feral House, 2003.

Norris, Joel. *Henry Lee Lucas: The Shocking True Story of America's Most Notorious Serial Killer*. New York: Zebra, 1991.

6. "SERIOUS MURDERS": DONALD GASKINS

Gaskins, Donald, and Wilton Earle, *Final Truth: Autobiography of a Serial Killer*. New York: Pinnacle, 1993.

Hall, Frances Swain. *Slaughter in Carolina*. Florence, SC: Hummingbird Publishers, 1990.

7. "DOING DOUBLES": GERARD SCHAEFER

Schaefer, G. J., and Sondra London. *Killer Fiction: Stories That Convicted the Ex-Cop of Murder*. Los Angeles: Feral House, 1997.

8. "MONSTER OF THE ANDES": PEDRO LÓPEZ

Green, Ryan. *Colombian Killers: The True Stories of the Three Most Prolific Serial Killers.* CreateSpace, 2016.

9. "MAD DADDY": SAMUEL LITTLE

"Confessions of a Killer," FBI, https://www.fbi.gov/news/stories/samuel-little-most-prolific-serial-killer-in-us-history-100619

10. "DOCTOR DEATH": HAROLD SHIPMAN

Clarkson, Wensley. *The Good Doctor: Portrait of a Serial Killer.* London: John Blake, 2001.

Sitford, Mikaela. *Addicted to Murder: The True Story of Dr. Harold Shipman.* London: Virgin Books, 2000.

Whittle, Brian, and Jean Ritchie. *Prescription for Murder: The True Story of Dr. Harold Frederick Shipton.* New York: Warner Books, 2000.

11. GREEN RIVER KILLER: GARY RIDGWAY

Keppel, Robert. *The Riverman: Ted Bundy and I Hunt for the Green River Killer.* London: Constable & Co., 1995.

Reichert, David. *Chasing the Devil: My Twenty Year Quest to Capture the Green River Killer.* New York: Little, Brown and Co., 2004.

Rule, Ann. *Green River, Running Red: The Real Story of the Green River Killer—America's Deadliest Serial Murderer.* New York: Free Press, 2004.

12. PIGGY PALACE: ROBERT PICKTON

Cameron, Stevie. *On the Farm: Robert William Pickton and the Tragic Story of Vancouver's Missing Women.* New York: Knopf, 2010.

Shenher, Lorimer. *That Lonely Section of Hell: The Botched Investigation of a Serial Killer Who Almost Got Away.* Vancouver, Canada: Greystone, 2015.

13. "GOOFY": LUIS GARAVITO

Armstrong, Frances. *Luis Garavito: Hunting the Beast: The Story of a Colombian Serial Killer.* Independently published, 2017.

Green, Ryan. *Colombian Killers: The True Stories of the Three Most Prolific Serial Killers.* CreateSpace, 2016.

15. "THE WEREWOLF": MIKHAIL POPKOV

Swinney, C. L. *Werewolf Killer: The True Story of a Russian Cop Turned Serial Killer.* RJ Parker Publishing, 2017.

INDEX

IMAGE CREDITS

Alamy: Archive PL: 73 right;
British News Service: 158;
Keith Corrigan: 16; Historic
Collection:188; The History
Collection: 6; Russian Look Ltd.:
244; Science History Images: x

AP Photo: 73 left; 96, 220, 226;
Khalid Mehmood Chaudary: 239;
K.M. Choudary: 231; Andy
Hickman/Orlando Sentinel Star:
137; Mary Louise Miller: 117;

Julia Quenzler/PA: 181; Dan
Sheehan/Florida Times Union:
91; Pat Sullivan: 92

FBI: 150, 154, 157

Getty Images: 198; Bettmann:
118; Keystone-France: 71;
iStock/Getty Images Plus: Marek
Trawczynski (fingerprint): cover,
ii; Yakovliev (skull): cover, viii

Library of Congress: 47

Shutterstock: 215; Dmitry
Dmitriyev/EPA: 248

**courtesy of Wikimedia
Commons:** xi, 1, 68, 143

ABOUT THE AUTHOR

Michael Newton has been a freelance author since 1977, publishing 339 novels and nonfiction books as of 2020, with five more awaiting release. His history of the Florida Ku Klux Klan, *The Invisible Empire,* won the Florida Historical Society's Rembert Patrick Award as "Best Book in Florida History" for 2002. In 2006, the American Library Association honored his *Encyclopedia of Cryptozoology* as one of the year's twelve Outstanding Reference Works. Writing as "Lyle Brandt," Newton won the Western Fictioneers' first Peacemaker Award for Best Western Novel of 2010, for *Manhunt.* Another "Brandt" novel, *Avenging Angels,* was also a Peacemaker Best Novel finalist in 2011, as well as being a Best Paperback Original finalist for the Western Writers of America's Spur Award in 2011. His novel *West of the Big River: The Avenging Angel,* was nominated as a Peacemaker Best Novel in 2014. Newton's published books on multiple murder, preceding *Extreme Killers,* include *Mass Murder* (1988), *Hunting Humans* (1990), *Serial Slaughter* (1992; updated as *Century of Slaughter* in 2000 and 2007), *Raising Hell* (1993), *Bad Girls Do It!* (1993), *Silent Rage* (1994), *Daddy Was the Black Dahlia Killer* (1995), *Still at Large* (1998), *Waste Land* (1998), *Rope* (1998), *Stolen Away* (2000), *The Encyclopedia of Serial Killers* (2000; 2nd edition 2005), *A Encyclopédia de Serial Killers* (Brazil, 2005), *Serial Killers* (2008), *Die große Enzyklopädie der Serienmörder* (Germany, 2009), *The Texarkana Moonlight Murders* (2013), *The World's Worst Serial Killers* (2014), *The Dark Strangler* (2015), *Hangman* (2016), *Iron Curtain Killers* (2017), *Hearts of Darkness* (2018), and *Doctor Death* (2019).